JAPAN, THE HUNGRY GUEST

(Japanese Business Ethics vs. Those of the U.S.)

by

Jack Seward

and

Howard Van Zandt

LOTUS PRESS
Tokyo, Japan

Published by Lotus Press Ltd.
Chofu P.O. Box 15, Chofu-shi, Tokyo, 182-91 Japan
Copyright in Japan 1985 by
Jack Seward and Howard Van Zandt
ISBN: 4-89788-018-1
Cover design by Akira Tsuchiya

Printed in Japan by Komiyama Printing Co.

Contents

Foreword   5

Chapter One   Ethics in Japan and America   15
Chapter Two   Japanese Ethics: A Background   23
Chapter Three   Morality in Today's America   45
Chapter Four   Business Ethics and Codes   53
Chapter Five   The Influence of Religion on
                   Japanese Business Ethics   83
Chapter Six   The Work Ethic in Both
                   Countries   95
Chapter Seven   Foreign Trade   127
Chapter Eight   Corporations   163
Chapter Nine   Government: The Ethics of
                   Their Elected and Non-
                   Elected Officials   209
Chapter Ten   The Ethics of Legal Action   221
Chapter Eleven   Negotiations, Conferences, and
                   Contracts   247
Chapter Twelve   Ethics in Advertising   259
Chapter Thirteen   Corruption, Bribery, Scandals,
                   and Sex Tours   271

Afterword   289

Foreword

As the 21st century approaches, the world finds itself confronting shortages of food, natural resources, and space that will bring about changes in society, economies, and cultures that cannot help but transform man's destiny.

As part of this world and its problems, the U.S. and Japan account for almost half of all its production outside the Communist bloc of nations as well as the largest overseas trade in history. The Japanese, our partners in this trade, have enjoyed—or suffered from—varying images, and like the little boy in the fable, when they are seen to be bad, they are very, very bad indeed. These days, because of the trade imbalance, their businessmen are increasingly regarded as hungry guests at the world dining table or, in the words of George Murakami, "Dr. Fu Manchus with briefcases:" work-happy collectivists who live and conspire in computerized termites' nests—or rabbit hutches.

Comparing their living space to rabbit hutches, an analogy with some validity (witness the "hole-in-the wall" hotel rooms now becoming popular in Japan), has links with their description as being a "Society of Hares" and with their 'sudare' (bamboo screen) mentality.

In the former, the behavior of Japan has been likened to that of the rabbit, whose long, twitching ears reflect an ardent willingness and need to catch sounds, e. g., information, quickly, but because the rabbit's vocal chords are not developed, it cannot effectively communicate its needs, rebuttals, or vindications. As it hops about hither and yon, it gives observers the impression of being a completelly illogical and unpredictable creature, motivated by first one haphazard emotion and next another. And no matter how mild and unobtrusive it may appear to be, it has the disconcerting habit of sneaking into the vegetable gardens of neighbors and ravishing their crops.

Whatever the merits of comparing Japan's societal structure and ethnocentricism with those of a hutch of hares, it would seem that Americans do tend to associate the Japanese with several other creatures of unsavory habits. According to a study commissioned by Japan's Asahi TV in May, 1981, many Americans see a connection between the Japanese and alligators, lizards, cobras, and chameleons and with such traits as being sneaky, deadly, and cunning, this *Asahi* survey being based on in-depth inquiries more sophisticated than the usual straightforward questionnaire techniques.

The *sudare* is a Japanese bamboo screen or curtain that permits those behind it to see out without being seen. If we imagine a *sudare* screen hanging over the entrance to this rabbit hutch, we can envision what is called the *sudare* mentality of the Japanese people: always studiously watching the outside world, ever on guard against the raptor, while never revealing the intricacies of their dark world inside the hutch.

The *sudare* mentality description suggests that many Japanese feel that they risk more in trying to teach foreigners to understand their culture than they gain. Some of them do strive for such understanding, however, but their rabbit-like lack of communicative skills and their cast of mind militate against their success, an example being their occasional preference for silence. ("If everything is expressed, what then is left?") Nor do they like logic in human or national relationships and, to paraphrase H.L. Mencken, "no one ever went broke underestimating the dominance of feeling over logic in the Japanese mentality." This failure in competent communication abroad is suggested in what Clyde Prestowitz, Deputy Assistant Secretary of Commerce, has said about Japanese diplomats: "(they) make the mistake of believing if they can explain their policy often or well enough, the U.S. will ultimately agree with it," reflecting a very fundamental Japanese belief: when confronted with foreign failure to comprehend, the Japanese position is always correct. The Japanese verb meaning 'to understand' also means to 'agree with,' and "If you understand what we're saying, how is it possible for you *not* to agree with us?" is the Japanese position.

Given Japan as the culturally homogeneous unit that it is and their relativistic or, as some would say, opportunistic—view of right and wrong, it should surprise no one that their ethical views should come into conflict with ours as they cross the Pacific. On one side is an America where the basic civic principles are freedom and equality. On the other is a Japan where theirs are the primacy of the group, the acknowledgement of the *hombun* or one's place in the vertical hierarchy, and the concept of *on*—what one owes to parents, teachers, ancestors, coworkers, employers, and the Emperor—all of which constitute an unspoken social contract that is as effective as it is mysterious to Western minds.

Also mysterious to the West is the Japanese reticence to view themselves as an economic superpower. Having just moved from the House of Want to the House of Have, they do not yet really feel at home in their new circumstances, however affluent they may appear to be with their huge trade surpluses. Having lived on their "Pacific Ring of Fire" archipelago for centuries, almost unarmed, bereft of most significant natural resources, and largely dependent on the outside world for gas and oil, they feel a profound sense of vulnerability and have trouble understanding how anyone could perceive them to be a threat. For almost the first time in their long history, the Japanese have not had to seriously concern themselves with the threat of poverty, but still they are not adjusting easily to the new role as a prosperous consumer society assigned them by the West. As one Japanese diplomatist has said, "All we have ever really wanted to import for the past 1,500 years were books."

On the subject of books, three kinds that have much appeal to the Japanese these days are 1) those, like the *Fragile Blossom*, by Zbigniew Brzezinski that illustrate how vulnerable and tenuous is Japan's position in the world today, 2) those, like *Japan as Number One*, by Ezra Vogel, that pull out all stops in a litany of praise to the Japanese way of doing things, and 3) oddly perhaps, serious works that are sharply critical of the Japanese, for whatever else one may say about them, they are, first and always, the zealous student-nation, and no matter how much they may yearn for praise, the necessities of learning how to cope with the West (and to understand what they may be doing wrong) override even the need for self-esteem, just as potent obligation outweighs even formidable powers of reticence on the Japanese scale.

While the Japanese are avidly reading such books, Americans are beginning to take more note of Japan and while most of us, according to a Gallup poll of several years back, still do not read even one book a year, those who do buy books for purposes other than living room decoration are being offered a spectrum of works about Japan that range from the excellent (Jared Taylor's *Shadows of the Rising Sun* and Frank Gibney's *Miracle by Design*) to the trivial. Then there was a freshet of books (*Theory Z*,

The Art of Japanese Management, *The Book of Rings*, and *Zen and Creative Management*) that readers rushed to buy thinking to get a 'quick fix' on what was troubling our economy and advice on what it was the Japanese were apparently doing right.

In the post-war world of fiction about Japan by foreign authors, nothing worthwhile has been offered for national distribution in this country, and even the massively successful *Shōgun*, although it did serve to raise the level of our interest in Japan perceptibly (Chicago bars ran out of *sake* and for a week or so after the TV series the trendy among us said "*Hai*" and "*Wakarimashita*" with diligence), did not give us a very accurate picture of the Japanese at the beginning of the Tokugawa Era, although, to be sure, few of us were interested in such history, whether warped or true. (Author Clavell, who spent only a few weeks in Japan doing the research for his book, would have his readers believe that the samurai of those days would say "*Kinjiru. Gomen nasai*" to a Western 'barbarian.' That, at least, gave the knowledgeable reader a moment or two of knee-slapping mirth.)

Together with their sense of vulnerability is the social sentiment that they have become scapegoats and vents for those American frustrations and irritations arising from the stultification of the American dream of democracy and the good life for all the world's peoples. Probably the greatest shock ever suffered by the people of Japan was their defeat in the Pacific War, for it irrefutably disemboweled a value system in which they had believed with soul and heart. While some of the blame for the defeat was assigned to the leaders who led them into this debacle, the serious economic planners of the early postwar era identified productivity differential as the major cause of the defeat, with a result that productivity buttressed by investment leading to productivity is ever uppermost in

Japanese minds, so they easily conclude that this same factor is the cause of the present American economic malaise, together with the decline of the Protestant ethic: "Hard work and readiness to postpone consumption by saving and investing." This they judge to have been replaced by the hype slogans of today's marketplace: "Buy it now. You only go around once. You deserve the best. Why wait? Fly now, pay next year." In short, "Borrow. Spend. Buy. Waste. Want."

The Japanese find themselves in full agreement with Brookings Institution Economist Lawrence Krause's diagnosis: "The damage that the Japanese do to the U.S. is trivial compared to what we do to ourselves—through bad management and bad planning."

While resenting what they perceive as our blaming others for our own troubles, the Japanese still tend to regard the U.S. as the forever-forgiving parent who should understand, in the spirit of noblesse oblige, that the U.S. has a special responsibility, as seen in the Japanese *amae* syndrome, to look after and defend Japan and to allow Japan its perennial trade surplus as a buffer against its inherent economic weakness and in compensation for its inferior position, openly and willingly acknowledged, in the guardian-protege relationship between the two countries.

As the trade imbalance grows in Japan's favor and as American perceptions of the lack of corrective action on Japan's part increase, a kind of restive snarling mounts across our land, particularly in those groups whose oxen are being gored and from those still nursing hatreds of the past. (The city of Chicago just rejected a needed $260 million loan from Japan's Mitsubishi Bank, at a rate considerably lower than competing banks, because of memories of Pearl Harbor, World War II, and alleged "Japanese destruction of our steel mills, our auto factories, and our whole electronics industry.")

The danger to Japan is that Sherwin Goldman's "pain principle" in American politics will come into play, whereby the "passionate protests of the minorities whose interests are being damaged will, more often than not, prevail in the political arena over the opposed but less strongly held opinions of a majority with less vital personal interests at stake."

However vital or trivial the personal interests at stake are, however, a conviction that the Japanese are not playing the game of trade fairly, that many of their commercial actions are unethical is taking hold in the minds of Americans, so that there arises a need to examine questions of ethics in both Japan and America in the hope that some light of understanding can be shed in those dark corners where unjustified allegations are born as well as on those actions that truly are unethical in the minds of civilized men, with the expectation that they may be corrected.

Instead of focussing narrowly on specific codes of business ethics, the authors have assumed a broader mandate and have addressed themselves to the provenance of business ethics: the morality, traditions, and even the history of the circumambient societies. Even as broad as their brush has been, however, it has not been sufficiently broad to cover all aspect of ethics. Many nagging questions remain untouched. For instance, is Japanese copying ethical or is it what any other sane nation would have done in the same circumstances? Is our indifference to the fate of Amerasians—those by-products of our momentary passions" and "mementoes of our condescending miscegenation"—in Japan and the Far East ethical? Are we indifferent because we do not wish to be reminded of our sins and because we are willing to let the "sins of the fathers" come to rest on their sons? Is the Japanese belief that all happiness is a form of truancy really ethical in today's free world that is striving to raise the level of legitimate individual aspirations and fulfillment?

In Japan the pursuit of happiness has been sacrificed for social order and closely-knit efficient economic organizations, which is a fundamental reason why the Japanese way of doing things could never be imported en masse into the U.S. In Japan happiness is not respected as a legitimate goal in life, and the Japanese will seldom admit their own good fortune or easy circumstances. In a column about marriage, a Japanese social commentator recently wrote, "Marriage is just a part of our life and responsibilities. It is not something that is meant for enjoyment, just as the purpose of life itself is not the attainment of happiness." There you have it.

It is this very willingness to set aside happiness and personal fulfillment as legitimate life-goals that has enabled the Japanese to accomplish their noteworthy economic feats. They have accepted generally lower standards of personal comfort than any other people in the industrialized world while working longer, more carefully and with less interruption than any others. And, of course, they had our aid, for—after helping to put them back on their feet after the war in the Pacific—we bought much of what they made, tolerated dumping, paid for their defense umbrella, allowed them to keep our products out of their markets until their own gained in competitive prowess, naively believed their promises that they would dismantle this or that trade barrier "soon," and generally did nothing while their export surplus grew to $34 billion a year.

Aside from the problem of an ever-growing trade imbalance, which can be corrected only by resolute unilateral action on the part of the U.S., another danger lies waiting down the road, one tied to the adamant cultural pride of the Japanese and their attitude of "humble superiority." As the Japanese—the hungry guests—continue to pour forth their flood of merchandise and capture an increasing share of world markets, so will grow their tendency to attribute their economic success to their culture, to the "Japanese Way." Already we are seeing this theme promoted in articles and lectures: "Japanese Culture: The Foundation of Japanese Technology and Success" being a recent example. It was a similar belief in the superiority of their culture and of the *Yamato-damashii* (the Japanese Spirit) over the materialism of the West that betrayed Japan into its reckless nationalistic actions of the Thirties.

Japan also faces the problem of growing competition from other Asian nations that stand today about where Japan stood 10 or 15 years ago and the dilemma that her industry must grow by some six percent yearly in order to maintain her competitive strength, although such a growth rate in the traditional industries is hardly substainable on the basis of predicted available manpower and present retirement policies. This means that Japan must not only go on being successful but, as the hungry guest, must also be *increasingly* successful, which will be difficult indeed with other more voracious guests like Korea, Taiwan, Singapore, *inter alia*, crowding up to the same finite world trade dining table.

The world trade dining table and the shares on the plates of each of the diners are sure to change greatly by the end of this century, and it is to be hoped that the table manners or ethics of the guests will play a role in fending off the bitterness, chaos, arrogance, and even bellicosity that could easily arise from changing shares of the pot.

Chapter One

Ethics in Japan and America

Those persons the Japanese call *ryōmin* would be referred to by Americans as decent men and women of good intentions, but those so praised in America might well differ, to varying degrees, from their Japanese counterparts, while neither group would be exactly like respectable persons of sound moral fiber in, say, Saudi Arabia. All would depend on the definition of decency in any given culture and what those within that culture were taught as children about such values as truthfulness, fairness, kindness, honor, trustworthiness, et al.

How effective such values are in making the culture a safe, orderly, and just place in which to live varies with the society—and the observer, but what is of concern here is what happens when such values from differing cultures conflow and confront each other in the international arena, for a "moral" Japanese might well be shocked by the words and actions of a "moral" American—and vice versa.

After visiting a public bath, a member of Commodore Perry's 1854 expedition to Japan noted in his diary that he "turned away with a hearty curse" from the "lewdness" of the men and women bathing nude in the same tub with each other, while in 1868, after some years of increasing Western presence in Japan, an official of that country wrote that his countrymen should "give up their ignorant opinion that foreigners (meaning Westerners) are wild bar-

barians, dogs, and sheep. We must arrange to show they are to be considered on the same level as the Chinese.'' (Despite their massive cultural contributions to Japan, the Chinese were nonetheless viewed as being several rungs down the ladder from the people of Japan, so the above official was only promoting us from the seventh or eighth level to the third or fourth.)

Nor should such views be particularly surprising, since cultures in confrontation are fond of giving unpleasantness a foreign provenance while embracing as native-born that of which they approve. Witness how what is called the French Disease in England is called the English Disease in France.

The whole question of morality (aside from sexual morality, which will be taken up later herein) is one in which the difference between Japanese and American views and practices can be discouragingly wide and will continue to contribute to dissension between the two Pacific allies as much any other factor.

Western ethics—or the science of moral duty—can be broadly divided into three theories: one in which happiness is considered to be the *summum bonum* or greatest good, a second concerned with perfectionism or self-realization, and a third dealing with the relation of man to divine law or the universe.

Of these three only the third would be given house room in Japan—and even then only in the attic or cellar. The Japanese do not accept happiness as a legitimate goal to be seriously pursued by sober men and women. This is not to say they would rather be unhappy than happy or that they are not inwardly pleased when happiness—or an ''absence of pain,'' if you prefer—comes their way, but they avoid publicly announcing it as one of their main abjectives in life and do not polish it frequently and hold it up in admiration for themselves and others to aspire to.

Nor would they ascribe to the second theory, since "self-realization" focuses too much attention on the individual, whereas in Japan a person's objectives in life, his motivations, and loyalty are oriented to one or more of the groups of which he is a member. In the U.S. success is tied to and gauged by the efforts and aspirations of the individual. We see ourselves as free individuals with specifiable inalienable rights living in a democracy whose role it is to preserve those rights for us.

A Japanese, in contrast, looks upon himself as a member of a national family to whom he has certain obligations and duties and considers it to be the role of this national family or state to preserve and enhance a benevolent social order that is immutably Japanese. In fact, before the coming of the Western nations and their freight of political thought, the Japanese did not use such a word as 'rights' but concerned themselves more with justice and righteousness for and by all.

The third ethical theory—the one about the relation of man to the universe or to divine law—can be countenanced to a degree by the Japanese because a fundamental principle of Japanese ethics could be expressed in the phrase, "One in manyness, many in oneness," that sees the universe as a great, closely-knit mass in which each microscopic human being is a very nearly indistinguishable speck of not-so-important matter: in any event, a microcosm in importance in relation to the macrocosm of the mass itself. And while a religious basis exists for Japanese ethics (to be examined later on), it is not a clear-cut, pervasive, sacrosanct genesis like that of the Ten Commandments, from which all moral rivers flow, in the Christian world.

To the Japanese, morals are more fluid than static or absolute. This so-called situational ethic is based on continuing human experience rather than on a body of dogma.

Flexibility and conformability to prevailing circumstances could be said to be the watchwords in Japanese morality. The two distinct concepts of what is good and what is bad, as seen in unilateral determinism, do not please the Japanese ethical sensibility, for these two concepts should relate to social circumstances, whose very complexity may not be within the limits of a court's understanding. This is illustrated by such expressions as "Even the position of a criminal may be thirty percent correct" and by the fact that the demons and ogres in Japan's fairy tales and other stories for children are often a mixture of bad and good.

Our courts of law find an accused person guilty or innocent—one or the other, with no middle ground—although there may occasionally be 'mitigative circumstances' to lighten a penalty. In contrast, the Japanese often take the position that both parties are somewhat responsible for the dispute, although, needless to say, this thinking does not extend to certain arrant, straightforward crimes. In many civil matters, however, such as breach of marital or commercial contract, the Japanese pursue the ideal of compromise and mutual apology, with most ruffled feathers soothed and patted down before the matter becomes a cause for public embarrassment.

One of the coauthors (JS) recalls the occasion when he was driving past Shinagawa Station en route to the airdrome in Haneda. It was about nine o'clock in the evening; the street and sidewalks were crowded but well-lighted. A traffic light being immediately ahead of him, JS had slowed down to less than ten mph: about six or seven, in fact. As he passed the pedestrian island where a dozen or so persons were waiting for a streetcar (this was in the early Fifties), a drunken man suddenly collapsed and fell off the island directly into the path of JS's car, and no more than two feet from it. There was no way the author could have stopped in time. His right front tire ran over the inebriate's head. (However, evidently God takes care of drunkards as well as little children and the United States of America, for the man was not killed. In fact, he was not even seriously injured and walked out of the emergency hospital, albeit swaying on the unsteady feet the Japanese call *chidori-ashi*, a short while later.)

A police box stood catty-cornered across the intersection, so three policemen were on the scene of the accident within a few seconds. A lengthy interrogation followed in which JS repeatedly emphasized while he was most concerned about the condition of the drunkard and sympathetic to his plight, he had done nothing wrong. He had been perfectly sober, he had observed all traffic regulations, his car was barely crawling along and certainly well within the speed limit, and he had been alert and had seen the drunkard fall off the island, but he, the drunkard, had been so close to the right front fender of the car that there had not been the slightest possibility of the car being stopped, even at its crawling pace, in time to avoid hitting the man.

Nonetheless, the police continued to insist that JS submit an apology. Apologize for what? he asked over and over. (Actually, he feared that by apologizing, he would be indirectly admitting his guilt and thereby making himself vulnerable to a subsequent suit for damages by the injured man, the extent of whose injuries was not then known.) Later, at midnight, he left the police station with the matter unresolved and the following day discussed the situation with an international lawyer, whose advice was, "Sign the apology," which he did. End of matter—but here we see the Japanese view that both parties are partly responsible and apologies will go far toward the realization of an amicable solution. (Perhaps JS should also have demanded that the inebriate apologize to him for getting falling down drunk and causing him much inconvenience and loss of time.)

The Christian strives for moral impeccability, though seldom attained. We attempt to internalize, to imbed firmly a universal ethic—an abstract, absolute moral philosophy—and to deal sternly, in accordance with precisely prescribed punishments, with the sinners who have broken these commandments. The Japanese, on the contrary, start from the premise that man is a weak vessel requiring tolerance and compassion vouchsafed in recognition of the circumstances and have little enthusiasm for setting up and cementing eternal moral codes independent of ad hoc circumambient social circumstances.

The recent trend in the American administration of justice has also been toward this same compassion and tolerance—excessively so in the belief of many—but in our case it seems only to have engendered more crime, so there must obviously be other factors active in the social milieu in Japan that discourage malefactors.

If the Watergate scandal had taken place in Japan, it is likely the Japanese would have dealt more tolerantly with Richard Nixon, a man not entirely bereft of competence, but had he been Japanese, he would have quickly resigned, probably after making a nation-wide apology on television. What is interesting about the recent Kakuei Tanaka case is the ex-premier's refusal to apologize or resign even after being found guilty in court. (This is being written just after the first verdict that Tanaka has stated he will appeal and will fight even if "it takes a decade.") Seemingly Tanaka's intransigence would indicate a shift in Japan's ethical traditions, but a more probable explanation is an innate arrogance of power on the part of the not-well-educated ex-premier—and still Member of the Diet—and many in the Liberal-Democratic Party.

The Japanese avoid judging acts as bad or good per se

but consider the circumstances giving rise to them. They recognize human frailty and exercise compassion in judging acts. We too recognize frailty—and human baseness—and wonder if these might not enter also into the motivations of the human beings judging the acts.

Better, we would say, to establish codes not easily manipulated by such changeable human frailties, to which one supposes the Japanese could reply, "Might not those responsible for such codes be fallible, too?"

Walter Lippman's definition of ethics was "an authoritative code of morals (that) has force and effect when it expresses the settled customs of a stable society." Once established, this code supposedly exists independently as an inner conviction in the minds of decent men and women. As the individual goes through life, he will—like a voyager in a small boat on a mighty river—find before him islands or forces of good and evil, to be welcomed or avoided as suits his philosophy. But such concentrations of good and evil, so typical of both Western and Chinese thought, are alien to the Japanese ethical sense, which prefers the social relativism of the situational ethic as propounded by the philospher Tetsuro Watsuji in his classic book on ethics:

> "The problem of ethics is not in the conscious mind of each individual but rather in the *relationships bet-ween individuals*. It is not possible to comprehend how a good action differs from a bad action, or the true meaning of duty, responsibility, or virtue unless they are considered from the viewpoint of the relationship between one man and another."

Having learned that the Japanese have no immutable code of ethics, the Westerner is tempted to move forward to the assumption that the Japanese are shifty, unreliable, and impossible to understand or predict, but a saving grace is that once the bonds, relationships, and obligations in the weft and warp of society have been accepted and fixed in place, the Japanese can cleave to them with amazing tenacity. (Witness the case of Sergeant Shoichi Yokoi, who hid out in the Guamanian bush for twenty-eight years in obedience to his superior officer's last command not to surrender.) *Shinyō* or trustworthiness is a central operative word in many Japanese social interactions, and the very frequency of its use attests to the importance the Japanese attach to steadfastness in observance of obligations and maintenance of social ties.

And whether the Japanese are predictable or not depends, at least to some extent, on how well the observer can read the signs, and surely there is little that they themselves fear more than unpredictability. An "unpredictable future" worries them as much as the "insecurity of livelihood" they fret about so much.

Chapter Two

Japanese Ethics: A Background

Such distinguished scholars as Dr. Kazutaka Watanabe and Professor Chie Nakane, along with a host of others, have commented on the comparative absence of principles from the makeup of the Japanese, and since principles are more to be found in absolute than in situational ethics, this should not be surprising.

Even so, codes of moral behaviour *have* flourished and taken root in Japan, some imported and adapted, and indeed modern Japan probably functions—and functions well, it would seem—under the precepts of Neo-Confucian ethics, molded to fit more snugly the land to which they were transplanted.

Before the advent of Buddhism in the sixth century, the religion of Japan was a poorly-defined body of native rituals and animistic beliefs without even a name, which later came to be called *Shintō* or the Way of the Gods to distinguish it from *Butsudō*: the Way of Buddhism. Its gods were kind and amiable and even its "bad" gods (*akugami*) were depicted as merely mischievous and playful instead of wicked. Indeed, there is little evidence of a satanic spirit of evil in *Shintō*, where sins were called *tsumi*, a word whose etymology suggests something concealed, such as an act frowned on socially but not really wrong morally. The *tsumi* were acts or conditions that gave rise to feelings of shame but not those of guilt. The Japanese, in that stage of their social development, were like the children speaking in the quotation:

> ". . . we knew not the doctrine of ill-doing, no, nor dreamed that any did."

As in parts of the Mosaic Code, such admonitions as were recorded after the acquisition of a written language addressed themselves to defilement and ritual purity, an early stage in the evolution of ethical ideas. Throughout, to depict good actions and thoughts, the admonitions made use of such adjectives as clean, bright, and pure, somewhat reminiscent of the symbolic descriptions of the clear rivers and white mountains of northern Italy used by Hemingway in *A Farewell to Arms* for the same purpose.

In the words of renowned authority on Eastern religions Hajime Nakamura, "one of the outstanding characteristics of the Japanese way of thinking is the affirmation (acceptance) of the world as it is." What surrounded them in their daily lives was the sure, the absolute, not what might exist far off in heavenly realms.

When Buddhism came to Japan, they altered it to a religion that focused its concerns on the present workaday world. In Buddhism as it was practiced in India, the believer was expected to suppress all emotions, but the Japanese could not accept this. They felt as Priest Nichiren did when he said, "I shed tears when I'm happy; I shed tears when I'm sad."

Nor did the Japanese Buddhists insist on a strict adherence to the precepts against drinking liquor, the consumpion of meat, or sexual activities. In fact, one famous priest, Onkō (1718–1804), taught that "Morality consists in obeying one's natural impulses."

Reticence to recognize evil is at the core of an understanding of the situational ethic in Japan, an oft-quoted saying being *"Honshin ni oite wa akunin wa inai"* or "No one is evil at heart." Misdeeds were reguarded not as manifestations of pure meanness but as temporary venial falterings from the path of correct (pure, clean) behavior. Although the Japanese later devised and practised punishments that would have made monsters like Dominican friars Torquemada and Robert le Bourge of the Papal Inquisition seem gentle (such as the execution of robber Goemon Ishikawa and his tiny son by standing them in a large pot of oil and boiling them to death), there were many centuries in Japan's early history when it seemed that the Japanese could not bring themselves to truly abhor criminals. Crucifixion did not appear until the *Sengoku Jidai* (Era of the Warring Provinces: circa 1467–1568), and even then it may have been a Christian import. There was only one burning at the stake in those early years, and during the entire four hundred years or so of the Heian Period (794–1185), the penalty of death was not invoked even once.

Even today in Japan this attitude underlies the treatment of criminals. In *Parade* magazine of January 15, 1984, the warden of the Yokosuka Prison, Kaoru Kayaba, is quoted as saying, "All human beings are 98 percent good and 2 percent bad. The men who end up in prison are not more evil than others in our society. They are weaker. . . . " To be sure, the treatment of prisoners in these prisons is fearsome indeed, including unheated cells, denial of most reading materials, censorship of mail, among others, but some Americans who have done time there state that they prefer Japanese prisons to ours, because their guards were "fair and trustworthy."

Whatever the treatment of the prisoners by the guards is, it must have a remarkable effect on the Japanese prisoners as well, for when the walls of one prison crumbled and fell during the great Kanto earthquake, not one of them took advantage of the opportunity to leave the area.

The penal code itself played but a minor role in legalistic Japan during the long years it was under the influence of T'ang China because it was seen that the punishing of a wrong-doer in no way rectified the disturbance already done to the social order.

Our Christian God punishes unrighteousness and from our acceptance of the fitness of such punishment derives our abstract idea of justice. An eye for an eye and a tooth for a tooth, saith the Old Testment, but to the Japanese, now or then, the loss of an eye did not always justify the loss of another eye. They insisted—and still insist—on viewing the matter in several lights, considering all circumstances, before taking unerasable steps.

In any event, at the core of *Shintō* shone no exalted Code of Behavioral Commandments such as in Christianity. Certainly the lack of a written language up until about A.D. 400 and its rather slow development and diffusion thereafter was a contributory cause, but another explanation sometimes heard is the absence of invasions with their accompanying social upheavels in early Japanese history. Essentially this is the same explanation given for the dearth of public eloquence and for reticent communicativeness on the part of the Japanese. One's skills at communication were honed prior to acts of aggression—or resistance to aggression—in order to justify his hostility toward his foes and to motivate his supporters. In like ways one supposedly made statements about the rightness of his own acts and the wickedness of those of the people who opposed him, before an act of war. Such statements would constitute the core of a system of values that could be polished and shaped into ethical codes.

It is a neat explanation, and possibly true, but there *was* considerable civil warfare in Japan in the early centuries of our Christian era: According to ancient Chinese records civil war preceded the ascension of Queen Himeko to the throne and then another broke out when a king succeeded her. And if the theory is said to work only in the event of foreign wars, the conquest of Paekche (now part of Korea) by the Empress Jingo in about A.D. 200 comes to mind, as well as the two attempted Mongol invasions of Japan of the thirteenth century. True, the priest Nichiren did storm through Japan noisily predicting—accurately— one of the Mongol invasions, thereby kindling considerable religious fervor, but considering Nichiren's flagellation of other religious sects—"Zen is a religion of devils, Shingon means national ruin, and the Risshu congregation is a pack of traitors"—he could hardly be thought of as a beacon for ethical words and acts and certainly left no code worthy of the name.

Jun Dazai, the Chinese scholar, held there was no ethical code in early Japan when he wrote in his *Bendōsho*: "originally in Japan there was nothing that might be called a 'Way.' Proof of this is the fact that there are no native Japanese words for humanity, righteous conduct, decorum, filial piety, or fraternal love."

Dazai's position is refuted in an interesting way by the renowned scholar Atsutane Hirata (pp. 96–97, Vol. I, *Hirata Atsutane Zenshū*). First, however, Hirata admits that Dazai was not alone in that stance: ". . . the majority of Confucian pedants and other scholars partial to Chinese learning . . . state that in old Japan there were no moral teachings like those of China."

Hirata then counters Dazai and the "other scholars" by saying that "the Japanese of those times all practiced— constantly and properly—those virtues the Chinese called humanity, righteous conduct, the five cardinal virtues, and so forth without feeling any need to give them names or even to teach them to others. . . . Essentially this is the Japanese quality of Japan . . . a magnificent example of Japan's superiority to the rest of the countries in the world.

. . . the very fact that in olden Japan there was no 'Way' is the most laudable thing about this country . . . to have to invent a Way for the guidance of its people should be a confession of shame for any country.''

Hirata thereby implies that all Japanese behaved correctly all the time, which is difficult to accept. A more likely explanation is that the Japanese then were no less reticent than they are today about setting down specific behavioral expectations and forming contracts (and what are ethical codes if not social contracts?) and defined desirable values as ''what is best at a given time, under certain circumstances.''

Perhaps also operative was the religious outlook of the Japanese of all ages: that there is no clear line of division between the divine and the human and that now and then these are identified as being one and the same. Therefore, if we are divine—or more precisely, if we are superior beings or *kami*—why presume to teach us how to behave?

Actually, despite all the above discussion, the lack of of ethical codes and the reasons for that lack in early Japan can be confirmed and the reason identified: Neither Shinto nor Buddhism was notable for providing ethical principles to guide the conduct of man. Rather, these religions addressed themselves more to the problem of allaying man's anxieties about the problems of everyday life than to his social conduct or his reformation of society on the basis of his religious beliefs. As pointed out by Shinran (1173–1262), ''If a righteous man can be saved, why not a sinner?'' In other words, either can rise to the Elysian fields of Takamagahara so why bother with codes of conduct? Man is naturally good so why not let him live according to his instincts, guided when need be by the keenly felt but not necessarily openly expressed pressures of circumambient society?

The march of time, however, brought difficult domestic

problems to Japan as the clans multipied and the society became more complex. The Mongol invasion of 1281 greatly strained the economy, and the administration of the Hojos, which had been just and fair in most respects, debilitated and was overthrown.

The Hojos were followed by the Ashikaga Shoguns, the first of whom was Takauji. He and his kin and close supporters were men of vaulting ambition, merciless, greedy, and without a scruple. They ruled Japan from 1336 to 1573, a period of almost two and a half centuries characterized by incessant civil warfare and a general decline in moral standards. The Ashikaga Shogunate fell in 1573, but it was not until 1615, with the fall of Osaka Castle and the suicide of Hideyori Toyotomi, that Ieyasu Tokugawa set the stage for the unification of Japan and brought about an end to internal strife. To accomplish this Ieyasu had basely broken oath after oath, as if only by exceeding the immoralities of those preceding him could he bring to an end this Age of Amorality.

Ieyasu died the following year, 1616, but the regime he founded, the House of Tokugawa, lasted for some 250 years, brought peace and stability to the islands of Japan, and—most important to our discussion—adopted Neo-Confucianist principles as the ethical code of the country.

Chinese Confucianism held the following five relationships to be the foundation of the social order: father and son, superior and inferior, elder brother and younger brother, husband and wife, and friend and friend. It stressed the virtues of harmony, loyalty, duty, obedience, propriety, courtesy, reverence, the proper performance of rites and ceremonies, and correct behavior. Filial piety was held up as the "root of moral power in a man."

Whereas in China filial piety or obedience to and respect for parents was taught as the primary human duty, the Neo-Confucianist scholars of Tokugawa Japan laid more emphasis on homage and fealty to a superior, and this distinction has been made clear in countless tales, true and fancied, in which the hero sacrifices a member of his family for the sake of his liege lord. Witness Yoshio Oishi, leader of the Forty-Seven *Rōnin*, who cast aside his faithful wife to take up with a loose woman in order that he might thereby strenghten the illusion that he was sunk in depravity and had abandoned any thoughts of taking vengeance on Lord Kira.

In the ethical system inculcated on commoner and samurai alike, loyalty to one's clan chief was at the peak of the system of values, a fortunate circumstance that made it easier for the Meiji planners to transfer loyalty from the lords of the *han* (fiefs) to the Emperor Meiji just restored to his throne in Tokyo.

Following hard on the Meiji Restoration came the tidal wave of Western knowledge, some of which was adapted judiciously and some swallowed whole. When Fujimaro Tanaka was named Vice-Minister of Education in 1873, he invited David Murray of Rutgers University to act as his advisor and together they had several American and European textbooks, including some on morals, translated into Japanese for use in Tanaka's school system. Other influences were at work as well, so that, until about 1880 when a reaction began to set in, the Western influence was dominant in morals education during that brief but important period.

On 30 October, 1880, however, the famous Imperial Rescript on Education, whose majestic words were as familiar to pre-1945 school children in Japan as the Pledge of Allegiance to the Flag is to their counterparts in the U.S., was promulgated and said in part:

> "Ye, Our Subjects, be filial to your parents, affec-
> tionate to your brothers and sisters; as husbands and

wives be harmonious, as friends, true—pursue learning and cultivate arts, and thereby develop intellectual faculties and perfect moral powers; furthermore, advance public good and promote common interests; always respect the Constitution and observe the laws; should emergencies arise, offer yourselves courageously to the State. . . ."

Such a rescript should not seem entirely unfamiliar to American eyes for it bears certain points of similarity to the so-called "American's Creed," which it preceded and which was printed in the frontispiece of many of our standard textbooks on Civics or American Government.

"I believe in the United States of America as a government . . . established on the principles of freedom, equality, justice, and humanity. . . . I therefore believe it is my duty to my country to love it, to support its Constitution, to obey its laws, to respect its flag, and to defend it against all enemies."

Previously in his Charter Oath of Five Articles, the Emperor Meiji had already instructed his people to "Seek knowledge throughout the world and greatly add to the life of the foundation of the Imperial regime," so with his Imperial Rescript on Education he was only driving the point home.

It should be small wonder that the Japanese of today revere education, its benefits having been stressed to them in so many ways, including the maxims to be found in *Jitsugo-kyō* (Teachings of the Young). Although these maxims were attributed to Buddhist monks of the ninth century, they were assiduously studied in Japan for many centuries thereafter, three examples of them being:

"Though thou shouldst heap up a thousand pieces of gold, they should not be so precious as one day of study." "The body, with its passions, is not pure: and

ye should swiftly search for intelligence." "Treasures
that are laid up in a corner decay; treasures that are
laid up in the mind decay not."

By contrast, some American texts of the nineteenth century seemed at times to display a distrust of the intellect
and discussed at length the differences between Americans
and Europeans. One of the failings of the latter, such texts
taught, was an "excess of learning." One such moral
story told about a little girl who liked to read books more
than play with her friends and concluded that "she reads
and thinks too much." Another proposed that "Manliness
is superior to a knowledge of Greek, and self-reliance is
better than a knowledge of Latin," probably reflecting the
requirements of a nation still hard at the work of pushing
its frontier west.

Perhaps because of such American texts of the nineteenth century and because of Buddhist teachings dating
from the ninth century and the Emperor Meiji's orders to
pursue and acquire knowledge, we have today an America
where the football star is more respected than the student
who earns all A's and a tiny island nation like Japan that
has risen Phoenix-like from rubble and ashes to give mighty
America a hard run for its money in many fields of
endeavor.

Be that as it may, the inculcation of loyalty to the state
as personified by the Emperor and a Neo-Confucianist
code of ethics slightly adjusted to suit the climate of Japan
were the overriding purposes of the educational system
from the date of the Imperial Rescript on Education until
the coming of the U.S. forces of occupation in 1945. The
core of traditional Confucianist ethics—filial piety—was
deftly sublimated from *kō* to *chū*: e.g., from obligation
to parents to loyalty to the Emperor. The words quoted
by Herbert Passin in his fine book *Education and Society*

in Modern Japan—"Precious are my parents that gave me birth so that I might serve His Majesty"—encapsulate the doctrine neatly.

A major instrument used to achieve the goal of moral training, which was given first priority by the Elementary School Regulations of 1890, was the ethical course called *shūshin*, whose textbooks taught largely in parables reminiscent of the sermons of Jesus Christ.

For instance, one such parable called the "Pursuit of Knowledge" relates the story of a boy named Noboru whose natural artistic talent was such that he was urged by many to study under a qualified teacher. He encountered difficulties, but he persevered because "he wanted to set his parents' minds at ease." He rose early in the morning to cook his own rice and study by the light of the fire. When at last he began to sell some of his paintings, he turned all his earnings over to his parents. The parable ends with the proverb, "Hardships build character."

Other parables concerned such subjects as teachers, education, study, planning, scientific attitudes, serving the Emperor in the army or navy, sacrificing one's life to "put the Emperor's mind at ease," and so forth.

Doubtless the school courses in *shūshin* did much to enhance moral consciousness, and beginning in the 1930's, increasing emphasis was laid on the nationalistic content of these courses, concomitant with the growth of aggressive imperialistic intent on the part of Japan's *gumbatsu* (military clique). The Educational Reform of February, 28, 1941 (Imperial Ordinance No. 148) extended compulsory schooling from six years through the "end of the academic year of the (child's) fourteenth birthday" and stated such expectations as that in Article 3: "Morals, which are to be based on the Imperial Rescript on Educa-

tion, should guide pupils in practicing national morality. . . ."

This Ordinance is spotted with other 'expectations' that
make clear the direction Japan was taking: "make pupils
understand the trends in the Far East and the rest of the
world . . ." ". . . lead them to realize the actual situation
and the responsibilities of our Empire. . . ." ". . . pupils
will be taught to be happy they were born in our Empire. . . ." ". . . will make them understand the features
of our history and land that have brought forth a superior
national character. . . ."

The failure of this intensive education in morals to prevent the atrocities of the Japanese soldiery in China and
Manchuria in the 1930's and in the Pacific from 1941 until August, 1945—together with the thought of a so-called
yellow race humbling white men from Singapore to Pearl
Harbor—was what shocked most of the Western world to
the roots of their teeth, and for which more than a few
still have not forgiven the Japanese. Needless to say, excesses were also committed by the Allied Forces opposing
the Japanese as the war wore on, and many have pointed
to the atomic bombings of Hiroshima and Nagasaki as
"crimes against humanity" heinous enough to balance the
scales.

It is not the purpose of this chapter, however, to enter
into this debate, but point out, as has been done often
enough before, that there has always been a serious question of whether Japanese ethics extended to non-Japanese
(about which more later) and that situational ethics functioned poorly if at all away from Japan. The Japanese proverb "*Tabi no haji wa kakizute* (When on a journey, one
not need not feel any shame—or, more loosely, a traveller
can get away with anything) points precisely to this situation, for shame brought on by the disapproval of others
more than guilt occasioned by inner convictions and the

absolute ethic is what restrains the Japanese from acts frowned on by society. (Ruth Benedict characterized Japan as more a shame than a guilt culture, although she did write, on page 222 of her classic *The Chrysanthemum and the Sword*, ". . . Japanese sometimes react as strongly as any Puritan to a private accumulation of guilt." Her emphasis on shame has been questioned as perhaps excessive and debated by such eminent scholars as George De Vos, Takie Sugimura Lebra, and Takeo Doi, who has stated that "feelings of guilt are a function of human relationships" in Japan. A different view from all these was proposed by the late Herman Kahn in an interview quoted in an April, 1971 issue of the *Asahi Evening News*: "Japan is neither a shame society nor a guilt society.")

Be that as it may, shame does without doubt exert some restraining influence, and the absence of forces which could arouse shame must have been at least a part of the explanation of the cruelties of the Japanese soldiery. The average Japanese, then and today, can be likened to a fly caught in a spider's web, whose sticky gossamer threads partially or wholly restrain the movement of his otherwise free will. If he breaks free from one thread, he may then be caught in another so that finally he abandons the struggle and is held firmly in one place—the place of his *hombun*, the role assigned to him by society.

In December, 1945, a few months after the close of the war in the Pacific, the Tokyo office of the Supreme Commander for the Allied Powers issued a directive to the Japanese government ordering the "suspension of the teaching of morals, Japanese history, and geography." SCAP's first intention had been only to remove from existing schoolbooks matter of an ultranationalistic nature, but upon close examination it found such matter to be so thoroughly and deeply imbedded that it would be better to withdraw those books from use entirely and substitute new ones. "All courses in Morals (*Shūshin*) in all educational institutions, shall be suspended immediately...." read the directive.

Attempts were made to substitute Western ethical principles for the pre-1945 "national morality" with various degrees of success, depending on the observer. Judging from recent crime statistics, Japan would now appear to be a highly moral nation, but the younger generations display a syndrome that worries the establishment. In February, 1983, for example, the Minister of Education Mitsuo Setoyama blamed the current increase in juvenile delinquency in Japan on imported ideas: "I think the most deep-rooted cause of the problem may be the influence of American policy during the postwar occupation." The minister went on to say that the American occupation policy had been aimed at destroying the Confucian morality that had prevailed in Japan until 1945. He praised the pre-war education system which emphasized filial piety without which, Setoyama averred, "there is no place for education."

Prime Minister Yasuhiro Nakasone himself has often called for a revival of the "old ethics," and it appears to be his personal ambition to restore the Emperor to his pre-war glory and to stress loyalty and duty to the nation at the expense of individual rights.

Shūshin, now called sociological ethics to distinguish it from political ethics, has gradually been making a comeback, however. In 1974 then-Prime Minister Kakuei Tanaka proposed that *Kimigayo*, the Japanese national anthem, be sung daily in schools and that all pupils be made to witness a flag-rasing ceremony. Both proposals created a furor, especially when it was found that most of the pupils did not know the words to the national anthem. These sobering reports caused much reflection on the situation, which was attributed by many to the fact that courses in *shūshin* were no longer taught. From then on increasing efforts were made to re-insert *shūshin* into the curricula so that in 1982, for instance, 170,000 high school graduates chose to take sociological ethics from among six optional subjects in the social studies category in their university pre-entrance examinations, a leap of 40,000 over the previous year. It should be pointed out, however, that, according to the *Yoroku* column in the 9 February, 1983 edition of the *Mainichi Daily News*, the popularity of this choice does not reflect a growing interest in ethics on the part of Japan's youth so much as it is a testimony to the ease with which they can earn good grades on this section of the test, its questions mostly being answerable with ordinary common sense and not the askew kind often featured in political and economic exams.

Having been grounded so thoroughly in pre-1945 *shūshin* courses which taught that Japan's "Way" was not only superior but also uniquely correct, the Japanese were shocked by the defeat of 1945 into the most intense re-examination of basic values undertaken by any nation in modern history. Into the resultant vacuum came almost willy-nilly Western ethical values, to be rejected or adopted in part or in whole. As might have been expected, the passage of nearly forty years since the defeat and the coming to influence of a generation not even born on that day when the surrender documents were signed aboard the *USS Missouri* in Tokyo Bay have given rise to further reflection about which values Japan should emphasize in its future policies, domestic and international.

As Ikuo Oyama stressed in his book *Japan's Future Course*, there is a need in Japan today for a more international ethical outlook, one that creates a closer bond between the Japanese and the other peoples of the world. To be sure, such an international outlook need not be entirely Western in character but instead be one that compromises and blends and strives for harmonious solutions.

In this regard Japan should address itself to such ethical questions as compassion for the peoples of the lesser developed nations. Compassion and sympathy for the underdog have never been strong features of Japanese ethics but if Japan is to continue to sell largely and successfully to many countries, rich and poor, it will have to come to regard those countries as something more than mere market outlets. Instead, they should be treated as partners in a trading relationship founded on good will and understanding.

Economics professor Haruo Shimada of Keio University in Tokyo put it well when he wrote in the September, 1983 number of *Current* magazine, "and (Japanese) industries that have acquired large shares of the world market may not do as well in the future without taking their impacts on other countries more seriously." In other words, profitable long-term business may require ethical behavior.

Take, for an example, the recent case of Tseng-hsing Wang, a 57-year old wealthy Hong Kong businessman who had spent his early years in Japan and knew good Japanese. With an investment of $20 milion, he and his partners had bought 23 percent of Katakura Industries, a Japanese silk spinner. Mr. Wang's 23 percent made him the largest stockholder, the Fuji Bank being second with only 10 percent of the shares.

Mr. Wang thought that Katakura could make more money if it developed land it already owned into a shopping center, but the other shareholders rejected his proposal. Then the Hong Kong investor decided he would try to buy enough shares of the company to give him majority control so that he could force his shopping center proposal through the board.

Just at that time the Japanese government was about to remove the rule that limited foreign ownership in such corporations to 25 percent, but excepted eleven companies from the pending liberalization for what it called "security reasons." Included were six oil companies, two defense industry manufacturers, one pharmaceutical maker, and one aircraft builder. One could understand the "security reasons" for these ten exceptions.

The eleventh exception, however, was Katakura, the silk spinner.

Because he could not see how foreign ownership of a silk spinner could jeopardize Japan's defense, Mr. Wang next took the goverment of Japan to court: a gesture, needless to say, doomed to failure.

Thoroughly discouraged, Mr. Wang then decided to give up all thought of investing in Japan and sell his shares in Katakura. Now, however, securities brokers say they can find no buyers for his stock.

Query: Are such transparent maneuvers on the part of a government truly ethical?

For years it has been said among knowledgeable Westerners that the ethics of the Japanese, like their humor, are not for export, supporting this proposition with numerous examples of how favorable treatment of one kind or another extended to Japanese may often not be given to non-Japanese.

Until recent years, the people of Japan have not had the reputation abroad of being either particularly kind or especially cruel to animals. Nowadays, however, their slaughter of porpoises and their unchecked taking of whales, including some species believed—abroad, at least—to be endangered, have aroused considerable foreign anger, with signature campaigns and proposed boycotts of marine products from Japan now and then being proposed.

Cleveland Amory, the distinguished American who is founder and president of the Fund for Animals, characterizes Japanese treatment of other creatures than man in this way:

"Although the annual slaughter of dolphins off Iki Island was recently halted by the combined efforts of the Fund for Animals and Sea Shepherd Conservation Society, virtually everything Japan does, from the continued slaughter of whales to their treatment of laboratory animals, is on the low end of the totem pole."

The Japanese position seems to be that the whales in question are not actually endangered and that, in any event, this is not really an ethical matter. The porpoises are killed because they interfere with netting of other food fish and most of the whales taken provide the Japanese with an important source of protein.

Opponents aver that those species are endangered indeed and, without limitations on whaling, will become extinct. (Perhaps extinction would be just as well. If there were no more whales, then there would be no more torturous deaths by harpooning, although what effect the whales' absence would have on the marine food cycle is difficult to say.)

One of the justifications for the attempted preservation and conservation of other endangered species of animal and bird life is sometimes voiced by sad-faced persons in American TV commercials who ask us, "What would this world be like if your children and mine could not go to a zoo on Sunday and see a giraffe?"

Well, children today seem to survive well enough without having seen a passenger pigeon or a sloth or a mastodon or any of the hundreds of other species that have disappeared from the face of this earth, so one wonders what good it really does them to see a giraffe in a zoo, anyway?

It is difficult to take sides in the whale debate. One feels sympathy for those magnificent leviathans of the deep and somehow wishes that man would just leave them alone to live out their watery lives—as well as the porpoises who have been shown time and time again to be friendly to man, helping to rescue persons adrift at sea and even fighting off marauding sharks, to save the humans who later sometimes repay the kindness by killing them. Still, when one considers that we Americans kill 630,000 cows every week (more than one every *second*) when we could get more caloric value from devoting that amount of cattle pasturage to the cultivation of grains, it may not be ethical for us who live in glass houses to throw stones.

Although it is no longer true, there was a time in the West when man found it expedient to kill animals in order to live, even though the length of his intestinal tract compared to that of other creatures suggests he was not meant to live on their flesh. Now we eat beef and pork simply because we *like* both, without thought for the number of creatures who die to satisfy our appetites.

This fondness for meat brings up a puzzling dichotomy in American/European attitudes. We claim to love animals and abhor cruelty to them, yet we consume myriads of creatures when we would be better off economically, morally, and probably physically as well—if we ate grain instead.

This manifestation of anthropocentrism has always been with us. To justify it, we point to the Christian Bible that tells us that all other creatures were put on this earth by God to serve man and therefore, by logical extension, we conclude we can do with those animals as we like: kill them, eat them, work them, cage them, hunt them, even bait and badger them.

Or perhaps, in this instance, the cart preceded the horse, and our fondness for meat caused such words to be included in the Bible, to serve a secular purpose. After all, it has been shown that the Gospel according to Mark, with its account of the circumstances leading up to the death of Jesus Christ at the orders of Pontius Pilate, was written in Rome years later in A.D. 71 with the purpose of allaying Roman suspicions of the revolutionary tendencies of the Jewish Christians then in that city.

Writing in *Chūkō Shinshō* No. 92 in 1966, Japanese scholar Toyoyuki Sabata, in an article entitled *Nikushoku no Shisō* or The Meat-Eating Philosophy, postulated the interesting theory that early European sexual conduct and attitudes derived in part from their treatment of animals.

In order not to suffer from nightmares about the animals he was continually slaying for his table, Mr. Sabata implied, early European man had to continually re-affirm the vast differences between himself and four-legged creatures. If animals slept in the open, man would sleep under shelter. If animals went about without covering, man would clothe himself. If animals could not utter coherent speech, man would devise a method of doing so. . . . But then man came to the delicate question of fornication. Animals fornicated; so did man. Could man stop the beasts in the field from promiscuous fornicating? Obviously not. The solution? He himself must refrain from sexual acts.

Manifestly, not all European men and women did so—or we would not be here today. But at least some were persuaded to treat sexual abstinence as an ideal. Thus the celibacy of the Catholic priesthood. Thus the sacrament of marriage ("I will cleave to thee forever. . . .") with its insistence on permanent one man/one woman-*only* sex.

But the point of this discussion is that for many centuries of their development as a people and nation the Japanese treated animals with far more consideration than we have in the West. At least, they seldom *ate* them, not until the advent of "advanced" Western cultures. Even now their consumption of the flesh of four-legged animals is much less than that of Westerners, although we keep pressing them to eat more and import more (from us).

With beef prices so high in Japan (one of the co-authors recently saw *shimofuri* beef on sale in a Tokyo butcher shop window at $52.00 a pound), the day may yet come when the Japanese will revert to their more ethical past and abandon eating the meat of their four-legged animals, delicious though those steaks may be.

With beef prices so high in Japan (and of the co-author,
recently saw sirloin beef on sale in a Tokyo butcher
shop window at $32.00 a pound), the day may yet come
when the Japanese will revert to their more ethical past
and abandon eating the meat of their four-legged animals,
delicious though those steaks may be.

Chapter Three

Morality in Today's America

The foundation of Christian and Jewish religious and moral teachings—the one source of our ethical concepts that must stand shoulders and head and waist above any other—is the Ten Commandments of the Bible—the Jewish Decalogue—which was vouchsafed by God on Mount Sinai. It is a tidy listing of ten do's and don't's that, if followed faithfully, should foster the development of decent men and women found to be admirable in more cultures than one:

1. You shall have no other gods before Me.
2. You shall not make for yourself a graven image of anything on heaven or earth; you shall not bow down and serve such graven images.
3. You shall not take the name of the Lord thy God in vain.
4. Observe the Sabbath, to keep it holy.
5. Honor your father and your mother.
6. You shall not kill.
7. Neither shall you commit adultery.
8. Neither shall you steal.
9. Neither shall you bear false witness against your neighbor.
10. Neither shall you covet your neighbor's wife; and you shall not desire anything that is your neighbors.

Christians—whether 'born again,' non-practicing, or

backsliding—accept these religious directions as the Words of God and either obey them or at least say they wish they could be more punctilious in their observance.

But history has seen its worst crimes committed by men and women with God's name on their lips—from the Papal Inquisition in Spain to the Hindu-Moslem slaughter of hundreds of thousands in post-partition India—and one must wonder at the legendary robber baron who donated gold to the needy from his plush private pew in church on Sunday, then sweated gelt and pelf from widows and children in his sweat-shops on Monday.

It is accepted that as one ages, he becomes more morally conscious and observant, while castigating the young for the same sins of which he was guilty as a youth, and he despairs of the appalling immorality of the age. Even so there seems to be more than a slight validity in the proposition that morals have deteriorated in recent years in America.

Even a generation ago pundit Walter Lippman wrote, "The wisdom deposited in our moral ideals is heavily obscured. . . . We continue to use the language of morality, having no other which we can use. But the words are so hackneyed that their meanings are concealed, and it is very hard to realize that virtue is really good and is really relevant. . . . Morality has become so stereotyped, so thin and verbal, so encrusted with pious fraud . . . that our generation has almost forgotten that virtue derives originally from a profound realization of the character of human life. This is——due directly to the widespread loss of genuine belief in the premises of popular religion. Virtue is a product of human experience: men acquired their knowledge of the value of courage, honor, temperance, veracity, faithfulness, and love, because these qualities were necessary to their survival and to the attainment of happiness."

What Lippman would say about the moral condition today makes for fascinating conjecture, for our liberal intelligentsia has mounted so furious an attack on our traditional social values and morals that some have been turned completely about. Whereas it was once thought immoral to defend the right of homosexualists to make public their sexual preferences, now it is believed to be immoral *not* to defend such rights. Those who advocated the right of all women to abortion were regarded as depraved, but now those who protest the unrestricted right to abortion are under attack. During World War II anyone who supported the country's enemies might well have been lynched by an angry mob or at least charged with treasonable activities, while such public, defiant support of the enemy was commonplace during the conflict in Vietnam and is now beginning to be heard for the communist guerillas in El Salvador.

This inversion of moral values has led to the development of a legal system that protects criminals while paying little heed to the rights of their victims and to a large segment of the public that regards dedicated policemen as necessary evils, to be vilified if not instantly available in emergencies but otherwise not worthy of appreciation, support, or respect.

As Daniel Bell wrote in *The Cultural Contradictions of Capitalism*, "When the Protestant ethic was sundered from bourgeois society, only the hedonism remained. . . ."

Given the eighteen desirable qualities—including such as courage, cleanliness, and responsibility—in the Rokeach Value Survey, the majority of American respondents put honesty at the top of the list, while only 17 percent of Japanese men between the ages of 15 and 24 stated in an *Asahi* newspaper survey that they wanted to be regarded as honest more than anything else.

(Eighteen percent preferred "dependable," 16 percent

"gentle," and 12 percent "commonsensical.")

Yet the November, 1981 issue of the American magazine *Psychology Today*, after tabulating 24,100 replies to a questionnaire raising ethical questions, found that:

One out of three respondents confessed to the deception of a best friend within the past year.

More than half thought that if their tax returns were audited, they would probably owe the Internal Revenue Service money.

Forty-five percent of the married respondents admitted extramarital liaisons.

Other reports from newspapers in recent years included such statistics as these:

One out of every three hotel guests steals some item of hotel property from his room. (In the first 19 months of operation, New York City's Americana Hotel lost to pilferage 38,000 demitasse spoons, 18,000 towels, 15,000 finger bowls, and 355 silver coffee pots.)

Forty-eight percent of supermarket patrons have taken something from the store without paying for it, with residents of Los Angeles leading the rest of the nation by a wide margin. (So much for the new American 'racial melting pot.')

Seventy-eight percent of the nation's teachers confessed to having cheated on a least one examination in school, while nearly half of all students get their passing grades from faked laboratory experiments, examination papers bought from others, or by reprogramming computer tapes.

The American Insurance Association has estimated that 75 percent of all insurance claims are dishonest in some respect.

According to Dr. Hattye Liston, professor of psychology at North Carolina Agricultural and Technical State University, cheating can be addictive and more than a few persons become habitual cheaters. "They cheat," says Dr. Liston,"even when they don't have to."

Still, the Internal Revenue Service estimates that about $4 out of every $5 owed the government in taxes get paid, which is a high figure in comparison to such European countries as France and Italy, where the adroit evasion of taxes is a game played with imagination and elan, and may be higher than in Japan, where many corporations hire as consultants retired tax officials and where taxes are often "negotiated," a euphemism meaning that old cronies reduce the amount of taxes one would otherwise pay.

It is believed by many that the higher the rate of personal income tax over a reasonable level of, say, 25 percent, the more the resistance, protest, and cheating, which may be the wave of the future in the U.S., where efforts have been made to re-distribute the wealth of the nation through the graduated income tax in order to maintain and expand hundreds of social programs and utilize them to gain popular support for the acquisition of political power.

It is a truly invidious cycle, for the more the recipients receive, the more they expect and the more the candidates for public office promise them to enhance their own chances of victory in elections.

In 1947, one of the coauthors (JS) was in attendance at the graduate school of the University of Michigan, where he made the acquaintance of another veteran of World War II: an infantry captain who had been seriously wounded in the China-Burma-India theater of operations and who, after long convalescence, had been separated from the military service and was then studying in the Michigan graduate school. This ex-captain's home was in Ann Arbor, a short distance from the university, and he lived there with his widowed mother.

Then, as now, Ann Arbor was not exactly a "university town" in the sense that the school and its student-faculty population were so large that it completely dominated the surrounding community, but the University of Michigan did have considerable influence on the town's moral tone.

It was against this background that the above ex-captain of infantry, then 27 years of age, was arrested one day by campus police. His mother had been taken quite ill suddenly and the ex-captain had helped her into her car and was rushing her to a hospital when arrested by campus police.

Students—even one who was a 27-year-old graduate student, ex-officer, and wounded war veteran —could not then drive cars on campus or even in the town limits, a regulation designed to prevent them from using automobiles as sites for sexual assignations or as transportation to hie themselves to trysts in outlying motels and forests.

Doubtless the laws in Ann Arbor have changed for the better during the intervening years, but American attempts to legislate sex have always been a crazy quilt patchwork pattern, starting back with some of our early colonists who made the crime of adultery punishable by death. (Even today adultery remains a criminal offense in all of our states except five. Further, almost every sexual activity that can occur between a man and his wife—with the exceptions of caressing, kissing, and missionary-style intercourse—is defined on the law books as criminal in most states.)

Granted, many of these absurd anti-sex regulations are no longer prosecuted, but their very existence on the books allows for their occasional and capricious application.

How much the situation has changed since 1947 is evidenced by the fact some colleges now have coeducational dormitories. Further, if a young male student and a coed wish to cohabit while in attendance, few colleges question their right to do so any longer. Following a long famine of feeling that denied mankind's basic sexuality, a lusty revolution has swept the land, shattering taboos, curbs, and prohibitions along the way. With the divorce rate ballooning and women being given more economic and personal freedom and career opportunities, the singles and the accoutrements of their life-style have proliferated.

In the words of Columbia University anthropologist Herbert Passin, "It is finally becoming possible to be both single *and* whole. For the first time in human history, the single condition is being recognized as an acceptable adult life-style for anyone." Many young working women no longer need the sacred halo of marriage.

Freed from recourse to furtive sex in the back seats of automobiles, many young people have reached the stage in their sexual habits where even the most transitory physical attraction is consummated as a matter of course—and at once.

Still, people continue to marry, with their unions not necessarily ending in divorce. Couples keep on having babies, not all of whom are illegitimate. One international survey of the sexual inclinations and beliefs of young people found that, in America, only 12% of women but 25% of men believed that sex is "all right even without love."

In 1982 a leading newspaper commissioned a study of what makes a good marriage in the U.S. and learned that of the 13 ingredients given, sexual fidelity ranked near the bottom, in 11th place.

The most vital of the 13 listed ingredients turned out to be communication between spouses, in the opinions of the respondents. This finding is not exactly surprising, but when placed next to a 1984 study done by Professor Hans Jurgens, it becomes rather worrisome.

Professor Jurgens asked 5,000 German couples how often they talked to each other and found that after two years of marriage most chatted for three minutes or so at the breakfast table, about twenty minutes at the evening meal, and a few minutes more in bed. Thereafter, communication decreased to ten minutes a day after six years of wedlock and, to "almost complete speechlessness" after eight years of marital bliss.

Chapter Four

Business Ethics and Codes

Business ethics in Japan are no more standardized than they are in the U.S. and where they have been verbalized or set down in writing, they vary with the source; yet certain strong currents run through most and typify the whole.

Where variance exists, it may reflect conflicts within or specific needs of the originator. Such factors as *giri* (a sense of duty and obligation) and *ninjō* (humaneness) may confront each other in the mind of the Japanese entrepreneur so that he must sacrifice either his public or group duties or his obligations to family or friends. Or his ethical decisions may become tangled in the traditional humanities and accepted situational truths of Japan and the progressive rationalism of the West.

The elements of today's Japanese business ethics, varied though they may be, can be traced to several origins (the Confucian Management School or *Jukyō Chūyō Keiei-ha*, Bushidō, Buddhism, Shinto, the spirit of the Meiji industrialists, and to such individuals as Yukichi Fukuzawa and Eiichi Shibusawa, and the postwar ethics of Western individualism), but prominent among them should stand the ethics of the merchant class and the primitive capitalism of the Edo Period, as exemplified in the teachings of Shozan Suzuki and Baigan Ishida described elsewhere herein.

Humility is a powerful motivating force in all areas of ethical behavior, including the conduct of business. The

Japanese see themselves as being debtors to the ages, guided by an overwhelming sense of unpayable debt to myriads of benefactors. Being so burdened by obligations, they must adopt a humble pose. As they say, their heads do not rise (*atama ga agaranai*) under the weight of this debt. The often-heard expression "*o-kagesama de . . .*" reflects this; although it can mean "thanks to you (alone)," it is also often used to mean "thanks to everyone. . . ." Whatever one accomplishes is perceived as seldom being done through his efforts only. The credit for much of his success must be given to the society in its entirety: his teachers for what they taught him, his parents for raising him, the Emperor for symbolizing the national polity, his employees for their loyalty, his supervisors for their parental concern, his acquaintances for their friendship, his progenitors for producing previous generations, and so forth.

This humility is visible in the low public posture of the Japanese and is audible in their choice of honorifics in almost every sentence uttered. The businessman who is not ready to humble humself, to bow and kneel and repeat the verbal formulae of humility over and over again will not do well in commercial activities in Japan. Some years ago when the Coca-Cola company was faltering there due to the odd phenomenon of their glass bottles bursting spontaneously, a new president took over the helm of the Japanese subsidiary, his first act being to visit all the bottlers throughout the country to prostrate himself and apologize most humbly for the inconvenience caused them.

Coca-Cola's fortunes improved significantly thereafter.

This compulsion toward humility on the part of the Japanese can manifest itself in ways that may not be noticed by Westerners. When Prime Minister Nakasone, for instance, is literally given the red-carpet treatment in his travels, it is his practice not to walk down the center of the carpet but along one edge, believing that to walk in the middle would constitute unseemly pride and arrogance.

Japan has been described as a humility-controlled socie-ty. The greater the degree of humility displayed, the larger the chances of getting whatever is asked for. Complete helplessness is often strongly implied in the anguished pleas for succor. Going to this extreme would be demeaning and even repellent to most Westerners, but it is second nature to the Japanese.

Japanese ethical conduct in business is bound not only by this humility but also by the sense of obligation—the operative phrase is *gimu-chūshin* or obligation-preoccupied—to the many described above. When a Japanese chances to meet a friend on the street, his first thought is, "How am I indebted to him? Have I thanked him for taking me out to dinner last week? Did we send him a mark of our appreciation for attending our daughter's wedding? Well, no matter even if we did, I'd better thank him again." The skill and the tremulous fer-vor with which this sense of obligation is expressed are vitally important to one's acceptance in the highly emo-tional social fabric of Japan. And while genuine feelings are no doubt present in these bow-bolstered protestations of gratitude, histrionic ability certainly plays a significant role as well. The Japanese, needless to say, are well aware that the element of play-acting is present, but they seldom mention it or object to it, since it is all part of the game whose rules they tacitly accept by just being Japanese. To be sure, if one's later actions utterly belie the sincerity of his statements on the stage, so to speak, then recrimina-tions, effective even if indirect, may well ensue.

A companion to humility in these Thespian perfor-mances is the institution of the apology, which surely deserves ranking among the *beaux arts* of Japan. This is no casual "sorry about that" as blithely tossed off in to-day's America but an ashen-faced, often wet-eyed pleading for forgiveness, usually accompanied by gifts and deep, multiple genuflections. It can work miraculous cures and heal serious ruptures. In the case of crimes, its manifestation prompts prosecutors and judges as well as the victims to consider amnesty.

Just how the sincerity of such apologies can be gauged puzzles Westerners, but there is little doubt of their efficacy. When one cannot meet agreed-upon payment or shipment schedules, the apology with all its accoutrements is the first expedient to be used. Letters of apology or *shimatsu-sho* are so vital to corporate health that large companies will designate one employee with a good hand and a penchant for apt locutions to produce the vital ones.

The use of the apology in business can sometimes be carried to lengths Westerners would regard as extreme. One of the authors (JS) recalls the occasion when he was having lunch in the roof garden restaurant of a department store in Kamakura where the waitress spilled a bowl of noodles on his trousers. It was regrettable but an accident so JS said little but finished his meal and prepared to leave. At the door were waiting the head waiter and several waitresses, all bowing and making profuse apologies. At the elevator the head-waiter caught up with him and asked for JS's business card and home address.

JS put the incident out of his mind, but that evening the store manger and two of his assistants appeared at his front door, laden with rather costly gifts and effusive with their regrets.

One should not always count on such apologetic excess, however, for some time after that JS was dining in the elegant dining room of one of Fukuoka's leading Western-style hotels when what should appear on the damask linen of the tablecloth among the sparkling silverware but a monster cockroach, which he pointed out to the waiter, whereupon this worthy summoned aid and captured the creature. "Now," thought JS, "my dinner will be, of course, free and one or two fine souvenirs will be delivered to my hotel room later."

But all that he got free was a meager scoop of vanilla ice cream: "compliments of the house." Perhaps they suspected JS had brought the cockroach along with him.

Together with humility and obligation to the nation and people as imperatives in Japanese business ethics rank responsibility to the welfare of the employees and the drive to be sufficiently successful in acquiring market share to be able to repay obligations and fulfill responsibilities. This responsibility toward employees is expressed in an advanced form of paternalism in which corporate officers become surrogate fathers and mothers—sometimes harsh and stern, sometimes lenient and forgiving—to their family of employees. Many employees welcome such paternalism, with polls showing that a majority prefer the employer who takes a keen interest in their personal lives to one who does not. Indeed, the employment group is the most important of groups in Japan. In contrast to the family, the workplace represents a group that the employee joined of his own volition and that recognizes and values his competence, giving rise to a degree of psychological devotion that is perhaps analogous to that of a member of a fanatical religious cult.

The profit motive is given short shrift in business in Japan, and those entrepreneurs who have amassed fortunes are accorded little respect or admiration, especially in comparison to the frugal, spartan, retiring executive. During the Lockheed scandal, revelation in the media that then-Premier Kakuei Tanaka raised, for his personal gratification, carp costing several thousand dollars each did him much harm in the public eye. Profits are by no means scorned or forgotten, but the proper businessman does not exult over them nor does he use them to satisfy a hedonistic bent but rather to upgrade plant, increase R&D, or grant bonuses to employees.

In addition to service to country, society, and employees, the ethical businessman is expected to provide conscientious *sābisu* or service in the form of repairs for whatever products he sells. Assiduous "after-service," as it is sometimes called, is of considerable concern to the consuming public, many of whom remember too well a time when Japan-made paste and pinchbeck merchandise was of consistently low quality resulting in frequent malfunctions that the makers showed little inclination to repair promptly, if at all.

The concept of face—saving one's own and not causing its loss to others—is also an integral feature of Japanese business ethics, though 'professional reputation" might be a more apt description. Every worker is presumed to have certain knowledge and skills and must ward off any aspersions against them, which can be difficult considering the requirement to be humble. While protecting his own face, he must take care not to spatter muddy discredit on the countenances of others. One of the strongest reasons supporting the preference for group decisions and concensus in Japan is the desire to avoid possible loss of face arising from individual failures. The shying away from confrontation, protestation, and high-decibel debate in Japanese business is also part of the face syndrome.

Other aspects of business ethics can be expressed in the following cautions:

1. Avoid hard-sell tactics. Such enthusiastic sales methods do not appeal to the Japanese, since the would-be customer, if he really does not want the merchandise, is placed in the position of having to say No, which is always hard for a Japanese to do.

2. Whenever possible when approaching a company, get

a formal introduction. The people one wants to do business with will feel more comfortable.

3. Develop personal relationships. The Japanese prefer doing business with people whose company they can also enjoy away from office or factory.

4. Gifts at the proper season are important to these personal relationships. Even small gifts tell the recipient he is remembered.

One negative facet of the above need for a proper introduction is the widespread avoidance by the Japanese of answering letters or inquiries from strangers, in whatever language . . . even in Japanese. When bluntly asked why, they usually respond that since they do not know the correspondent, they cannot know if he (or that company) is trustworthy, even in instances when the company in question is large and well-known. What is meant is that the lack of a formal introduction by persons whose trustworthiness has been established, in their eyes at least, does not permit future recourse to the usual Japanese means of bringing a wrong-actor to his senses, of persuading him to act "with sincerity," as they would say.

Speaking without rancor, it would seem easy to arrive at the conclusion that the Japanese do not trust even other Japanese who have come to them without the protection of a formal introduction, which is in itself a pejorative comment on the essence of Japanese ethics. The world at large might well ask, "If the Japanese do not really trust each other, why should foreigners trust them, especially when it appears that Japanese ethical standards, such as they are, are not often extended to include persons outside the group that is Japan?"

Not only do the Japanese seldom reply to business inquiries from strangers but it is also their wont to abruptly interdict a correspondence about possible business matters when they decide, for whatever reason, that it is no longer of much interest to them. Within the past year one the coauthors (JS) was involved in lengthy correspondence with two Japanese companies about rather promising business possibilities. (He had been given formal introductions to both of them.) Considerable time and some expense had been expended at both ends in advancing the proposals to the point where it would soon have be decided whether to invest some capital and recruit a staff or not.

At length, although at different times, both Japanese companies must have decided not to pursue the proposals, probably due to the business recession in Japan, although this is not certain. At this point, correspondence from Japan was discontinued. No reason or even a hint was given. Letters and telexes were sent from the U.S. to no avail. Overseas telephone calls were made, but the Japanese were always "in conference."

> Query: Is this ethical behavior in business? Is the Japanese compulsive avoidance of the confrontation that might result from an unqualified "No" and their ingrained horror of openly embarrassing the other party so pronounced that they really cannot bring themselves to send anyone a negative reply, even when they must know that their prolonged silence inflicts a form of mental torture on the person with whom they have been corresponding? Or, had JS been Japanese, would their behaviour have been entirely different?

If the above are the vectors that characterize Japanese business ethics, how are they inculcated upon workers? Do they spring from a general social awareness requiring little elaboration or exhortation, are they principles taught in schools, or does each employing organization have its own codes and principles which it promulgates in weekly sermons and mounts prominently in the workplace?

Each of this triad has validity, but the third is widely

utilized and is readily identifiable. In large corporations training and indoctrination periods for recruits are lengthy and sometimes extreme. As noted elsewhere herein, the new communicants of one corporation are led into the frigid waters of a lake in mid-winter to encourage them to slough off the lackadaisical habits of their school days. This theme of submersion in cold water recurs often, with the victims being not only recruits but often enough senior staff members as well. Fasting, prayers at dawn—thinly-clad against the morning chill, and other "religious observances" are not unusual, and a sharp lash with a bamboo ferule to encourage mental alertness is not unheard of. Often these training sessions are held in corporate camps in mountain fastnesses and have the ambience of a revival meeting in the red hills of Georgia.

At times these spiritual renascences will so galvanize corporate employees that they will debouch from the camps with the energy of startled grasshoppers to perform deeds of salesmanship unique in the annals of commercial endeavor. For instance, one Japanese manufacture of beds instills such an ambitious, plucky spirit through hour-long chanting sessions under icy waterfalls and other spartan means that his district sales managers soon thereafter arrange all-out "assaults" on buyers of their products. When, for example, Mr. and Mrs. Inoue in Kanazawa buy a new bed, the district sales manager will first set the hour and day for its delivery, then circulate through the Inoues' neighborhood spreading the glad word that the Inoues have just bought a——Bed and that this marvel of all marvels can be inspected at close range when it is delivered at 10:00 o'clock Thursday morning.

On that date with destiny the sales manager gathers a coterie of his salesmen, loads the beribboned bed on a truck, and mounts on the vehicle half a dozen banners that announce to the world such pleasantries as "Congratulations to the Inoues," "The Inoues have just entered the cultured world of beds," and "A new day has dawned for the Inoues!" (It should be remembered that most Japanese still sleep on pallets on the floor.)

And just in case the neighbors are not already sufficiently agog with excitement, he hires a claque from among the town's idlers to run along beside the delivery truck to add to the commotion with boisterous noise and rout and din.

While such instances as that of the——Bed Co. may be extreme, that of a certain bank in northern Japan where an American named Thomas P. Rohlen worked for a spell, is not. In *For Harmony and Strength*, Mr. Rohlen has described an induction ceremony for bank recruits which begins with all employees chorusing the bank song, ending on this rousing stanza:

"Marching forward to the next day
  With strength unbounded
  We continue forward step by step
  Oh, the happiness of productive people!"

While still standing, all the employees then recite the principles of the bank:

"Constantly abiding by the ideas of cooperative banking, we will, together with the general populace, advance in our mission to serve as an instrument of small and medium business enterprises."

"Intent in the spirit of service, we will contribute to public welfare and social prosperity. Emphasizing trust and possessing an enterprising spirit we will advance scientific administration."

"With mutual respect and affection, we will work with diligence, employed in maintaining systematic order. Possessing a spirit of love for *Uedagin*, we pledge to plan for the prosperity of the bank and for the public welfare and to make the bank the greatest in Japan."

(Note: "*Uedagin*" or "*Ueda Ginkō*" is not the true name of the bank in question.)

Warming to their work, the employees next chorus the president's teachings:

> "Harmony (*wa*). The bank is our lifelong place of work, so let us make it a pleasant place, starting with our greetings to each other every morning.
>
> Sincerity (*seijitsu*). Sincerity is the foundation of trust; let us deal with our customers with a serious and earnest attitude.
>
> Kindness (*shinsetsu*). Have a warm heart. Be scrupulously kind.
>
> Spirit (*tamashiii*). Putting our heart and soul into it, let us work with all our strength.
>
> Unity (*danketsu*). Strong unity is the source of energy for our business.
>
> Responsibility (*sekinin*). Responsibility makes rights possible; first let us develop responsibility.
>
> Originality (*sōi*). In addition, let us think creatively and advance making each day a new day.
>
> Purity (*seiketsu*). Have a noble character and proper behavior.
>
> Health (*kenkō*). With ever growing pride let us fulfill the *Uedagin* dream."

Later during the ceremony, according to Mr. Rohlen's book, the bank president relates the history of the bank and outlines the problems facing the nation. Then, his voice becoming vibrant with passion, he tells the recruits that they are now adult members of society and that they must shoulder heavy responsibilities to *repay society for its blessings and their parents for the sacrifice of raising them from infancy*." (Italics author's.)

To the Western mind all this seems puerile and a bit ridiculous, even though it apparently has endowed the Japanese with a very serious attitude toward economic activity, which they elevate to the status of a matter of over-riding civic concern, When JS worked in the main office of a Japanese camera corporation in the 1950's, the scene was reminiscent of the above-described bank. Every morning the employees assembled for a *chōrei-shiki* or 'morning-greeting ceremony' in which the section chief bowed and said "*Ohayō gozaimasu*," whereupon the employees returned the courtesy. Sometimes the chief would make announcements of general interest and even offer a homily or two. Once a week, all sections were gathered in one large room for a company-wide *chōrei-shiki* and hortatory remarks by the president. His exhortations leaned toward the explicit, even telling his employees how to vote in forthcoming elections and how often to visit the barber shop. A spiffy dresser himself, he was keenly interested in the dress and appearance of all his people and would sometimes stand in the entrance in the morning and inspect the *soles* of the shoes of the employees as they came in off the street. Of course, there was a company song—more a hymn, really—with all the usual platitudes and bromides and tedious cliches about the "morning sun" and the "glorious future" and a "prosperous Japan."

JS felt somehow that he was once again eleven years old and attending a Cub Scout meeting in Dallas, Texas. On one occasion when the company president gave a martini testimonial to celebrate the completion of his new domicile, the company hymn was sung after the second round of drinks, which JS found to be a hideous embarrassment. Shortly thereafter he requested an early transfer to the company's office in New York.

These *chōrei-shiki* and weekly assemblies and *bōnen-kai* (forget-the-old-year parties) are all examples of the corporate rituals so beloved—at least by management—in Japan, and they make good use of the emotionalism of collective or group acceptance to sermonize and to vivify their codes of business ethics. *Shakun* or corporate moral teachings are posted throughout most companies and tend to be pithy and sometimes a little enigmatic, like simply "*Isshin*" or "One Heart." And of course, many of the larger companies have their own specific codes of ethics which are promulgated in such documents as the company outline (*kaisha annai*), which all but the very smallest business organizations seem to have for distribution.

Among the objectives given in the code of Nippon Steel Company (*Shin-Nippon Seitetsu K.K.*), the world's largest maker of steel, are such items as:

1. Service to the nation through industry. Our goal shall be to contribute to the progress and welfare of the community and the nation.
2. We shall be fair and just in all our business and individual dealings. Without this spirit, no man can win respect nor can he respect himself, no matter how wise and capable he may be.

In addition to general principles such as the above, some companies will use their codes of ethics as a curative device for specific problems facing them. For instance, the code of the above Nippon Steel Company states the following goal:

"Harmony and cooperation: Alone we are weak, together we are strong. We shall work together as a family in mutual trust and responsibility. An association of talented men is but an unruly mob unless each member is imbued with this spirit."

On the surface this sounds like still another bromidic precept, the writing of which gives men more pleasure than the observance, but it actually had a specific and rather urgent purpose. After World War II, SCAP Headquarters in Tokyo had sundered the *zaibatsu* so that the above corporation, then called *Dai-Nippon Seitetsu K.K.*, was split into fragments which had tended to coalesce over the succeeding years until at last only two mammoth entities remained: *Nippon Seitetsu* and *Fuji Seitetsu*. By then, however, so much time had intervened that the two were almost complete, competitive strangers to each other. When the decision was made to amalgamate them into the *Shin* (for 'new') *Nippon Seitetsu K.K.*, hostility and friction between the two parts ensued, so the above portion of the corporate code of ethics was inserted in an effort to tone down this rivalry and replace it with harmonious cooperation.

Another company, *Shōwa Bōeki K.K.*, or the Showa Trading Co., of Osaka offers a company hymn quite similar in general purpose to most of the others, its last stanza being,

> "We hold aloft this banner, the rally point for all,
>   To always strive for leadership in the far-flung business
>   world.
>   Joining hands to work together for the good of all,
>   Dilligently giving forth the products of our toil,
>   Sharing our joy, we give forth this call:
>   Oh, let us create an ideal company.
>   *Shōwa, Shōwa, Shōwa Bōeki*, our own company,
>   *Shōwa Bōeki*.*"

The three key words in Showa Trading's code of ethics—faith, sincerity, and perseverance (or diligence)—are given emphasis in all three of the song's stanzas. 'Faith' is explained by the company president, Akira Sueno, as the desire to lead a worthy life supported by one's inner convictions, harking back to the *honshin* concept of Baigan Yoshida. 'Sincerity' means doing without fail what one has promised to do and being honest and truthful. And perseverance, of course, is diligence in performing one's duties.

Other than these admonitions, however, this company president provides little formal training in ethics to his employees, preferring instead to give guidance on an ad hoc basis, as the appropriate opportunities arise.

In regards to commitments to truth professed by the Japanese, it should be remembered that two definitions of the word are possible. While a Japanese of a more international or Westernized persuasion may mean truth as it is defined in the West, another more steeped in traditional beliefs may very well define truth and honesty in the *honshin* sense of Baigan Yoshida and Shōsan Suzuki, who preached that the believer should be truthful and honest with his *honshin* or 'heart.' Following the dictates of one's *honshin* would foster ethical (in the Japanese sense) conduct, even though "at times that required lying to others," in the words of Shichihei Yamamoto, noted philosopher and author of the *Spirit of Japanese Capitalism*, reflecting the belief that "truth is uncertain and probably plural."

In contrast to the above norms, attention should be focussed on the *sarakin* (loans for salaried employees) because it is so revealing about how business ethics work—or don't work—in Japan.

These loan agencies are a relatively new phenomenon in Japan, but by 1978 they numbered 15,000, of which 10% were controlled by criminal elements. Because it has been hard for the man on the streets to borrow money from banks or to get credit in any form in Japan, these agencies sprang up to answer a glaring need by providing short-term loans, without collateral or credit checks—but at usurious rates of interest as high as 109.5%, but averaging 70%.

Often enough the borrowers were desperate persons with other pressing debts and with a weakness for horse and dog races who were attracted to the *apparently* low interest rates advertised by the *sarakin* agencies. When their bets did not pay off to enable them to repay their other obligations, the borrowers sought out other *sarakin*, to whom they were required to show only their driver's license, and there plunged ahead with their reckless borrowing.

At length the ineluctable occurred, the borrower could not meet his repayment schedules, and one or more of the *sarakin's* myrmidons would set out in relentless pursuit of the hapless debtor. In a recent case three of these Sons of Belial broke into the wake of the just-deceased wife of a man who levanted and threatened to rip to shreds the ceremony unless all the condolence money proffered by the grievers was turned over to them in repayment of the outstanding debt.

Backs against the wall, those unable to repay their rapidly mounting debts resorted to single and family suicide, so that in the first three months of 1983 alone, 19 murders, 408 suicides, and the loss of their homes by nearly 7,000 families were reported as traceable to *sarakin* excesses. In tragic fact, all of 1983 witnessed 1,155 such suicides.

Despite these shocking abuses of business ethics, the government of Japan delayed taking corrective action until 1977 when it at last lowered the barriers to allow the entry into the Japanese market of a wholly-owned American consumer finance company, in the hope that the much lower rates of interest offered by such American companies would force the *sarakin* to lower theirs. And if some of the *sarakin* chanced to go bankrupt in the resulting scuffle, well, then the foreign competition could be blamed.

By 1979 nine other foreign consumer finance companies gained approval to enter the Japanese market, offering loans at an annual interest of between 18 and 29% in lieu of the 70% average among the *sarakin*—and with no strong-arm methods of collection.

In response to this competitive pressure 170 of the largest *sarakin* agencies formed the Japan National Consumer Finance Association and lowered their interest rates, agreed to quote those rates on an annual instead of a daily basis, promised not to wear sun-glasses (to foil easy identification) to work, and vowed to stop making collection calls in the middle of the night or very early in the morning.

After a late start, the Ministry of Finance pressed ahead with other corrective measures and issued administrative guidance (but not orders) to the banks to be chary about lending money to the *sarakin*, which was a proper step— except that they (intentionally?) included the "good guys" of the scenario—the American consumer finance companies—in the same category with the native *sarakin*, making it more difficult thereafter for the foreign companies to obtain from banks operating funds with which to carry on their business.

An anomalous note in the *sarakin* story was next struck when it was learned that foreign, including American, banks were the source of more than half of the money lent to the *sarakin* agencies and other Japanese consumer finance companies by the commercial banks, insurance companies, and other financial institutions. In short, the American consumer finance companies could not borrow money as easily as the much more unethical *sarakin* even though the source of the money may well have been in their own country.

At about this time the Japan National Consumer Finance Association of the 170 leading *sarakin* used their unified strength (the *sarakin* earned almost $80 million in profits in 1982) to force some of the communications media to allow them to advertise—something that had not been permitted before. But the advertising privilege was extended only to members of the association, which rejected applications for membership from their foreign competitors.

According to *Focus Japan*, a JETRO publication, a new law governing the actions of the *sarakin* went into effect on 1 November, 1983 that makes it a criminal offense to lend money at the maximal interest rate of 109.5% set 30 years ago. The permissable rate is now 70% and will be gradually lowered over a period of years until at last it reaches the final maximum of 40%.

The National Police Agency also promulgated new regulations to prohibit strong-arm collectors from demanding payment of debts at weddings, funerals, and other ceremonies and from hounding debtors in their sick-beds in hospitals.

The next act in this Drama of Ethical Values took place in February, 1984 when a senior official of the above Japan National Consumer Finance Association's Tokyo branch was arrested on the charge of pocketing money deposited by members of the association. Later in the same month an ex-official of the Ministry of Finance was given the job of Executive Director of the Consumer Finance Association at the very high (for Japan) annual salary of ¥15 million or about US$65,000, with a chauffeured car, a secretary, and a partitioned office (the last being quite unusual in Japan).

What is revealing in all this about how Japan really works is that this ex-official's appointment was arranged after a year of conferences between the Association and the Ministry. Lawyer Shinsuke Kimura stated publicly that this appointment amounts to overt collusion between the two organizations, against the public interest.

Since they could not advertise in many of the major media and were limited in their access to loans even though the money applied for may have originated in the U.S., the American consumer finance companies found themselves, despite their more ethical rates and methods of collection, at a growing disadvantage. Seeing this, the *sarakin* increased their contributions to malleable politicians who agreed to make efforts to weaken the Ministry of Finance's earlier attempts at reform.

Perhaps, after all, the central truth of life everywhere is the vast gap between rhetoric and actual experience.

When the authors first broached the idea of a book on business ethics to their American literary agent, his quick reaction was, "It'll be a mighty short book, won't it?"

Another acquaintance, hearing about the work in progress, told the following story:

Two business executives were having lunch one day when the first executive, Bill, asked the other, Joseph, how Joseph had chosen the auditors who did his company's books.

Joseph explained that he had interviewed the representatives of three auditing companies and as a test, asked each of them how much two plus two equalled. The first two representatives replied "four" and were crossed off the list. "So we called in the third representative," Joseph explained, "and later selected his company."

"Why?" Bill asked.

"Well, when we asked him how much two plus two added up to," Joseph explained, "he said to us, 'Just what figure did you gentlemen have in mind?'"

Such views are legion. A *New Yorker* cartoon shows a board of directors' meeting with one of the directors making the comment, "Of course, honesty is one of the best policies."

Another cartoon pictures a businessman haled into court

on a breach of contract charge, with the clerk holding out a Bible and asking, "Do you swear to tell the truth, the whole truth, and nothing but the truth—as you see it?"

TV programs harp on the theme of unethical businessmen. Whereas in the Thirties, movies often depicted the lives of the affluent as an exercise in escapism and as a palliative for the economic distress of the Great Depression, present-day TV treatment of the rich, and especially rich business people, leans toward the perception that they are largely dishonest, lecherous, spiteful, cunning, conniving, and immoral vulgarians.

A study of 263 prime-time TV shows done by George Washington University professors Linda and Robert Licher disclosed that "a stock criminal type is the businessman whose selfish pursuit of profit leads him into illegal activity. TV businessmen and their underlings account for almost one in four lawbreakers with identifiable occupations."

The Lichers also learned that TV criminals tend to be middle and upper-class white males over 30 years of age and that the villains are more than five times as likely to be rich as poor. Clearly TV programs emphasize the "avarice of the middle and upper classes in an ambience in which the barest suspicions are elevated to incontestable truths." Yet statistics show that upper-class white males over 30 years of age, including business executives, have far lower crime rates than most other separable segments of the population.

The profitable TV series *Dallas*, which epitomizes this estimation of rich businessmen, is widely viewed in many, but not all, foreign countries, to varying reactions. At a recent meeting sponsored by their government, French intellectuals presented arguments that the disintegration of their culture was a result of the *Dallas* series. In Japan, however, *Dallas* failed to capture much audience attention because, as one Japansese source relates, the Japanese people could not accept that the upper-class group portrayed in the series could be so consistently treacherous, boorish, amoral, and predatory. Score one for the apperception of the Japanese.

There is much resentment in the city of Dallas over the unfair treatment given business in the TV show of that name. On 13 July 1984 the *Dallas Times Herald* carried the following story: "Mobil Oil's media mogul, Herb Schmertz, who dishes out company funds for public television's 'Masterpiece Theater' and other British imports, denounces American TV for exporting 'trash' like 'Dallas' and 'Dynasty.' Schmertz complained that the nighttime soaps' 'peculiar views' especially misrepresent business, the police, and other authority figures."

To be sure, *Dallas* may credit its reputation in part to geographical location, for, since the Kennedy assassination there, the rest of the country as well as much of the world has been only too ready to believe the worst about that city and its people, although the assassin was not a native Dallasite. And beyond that, there has long been in the U.S. a better-than-thou attitude toward all of Texas, especially on the part of the so-called media elite, most of whom are left-leaning, non-religious liberals who come from that sector of the nation bounded by Chicago on the west, Boston on the east, and the Mason-Dixon line on the south.

In a 1983 TV portrayal of the "true" events surrounding the shooting by Houston police of an out-of-town youth every native Houstonian in the film was shown to be crass, ignorant, sneaky, and generally disreputable, while the 'white hats'—including the quasi-heroine in the local prosecutor's office—were all out-of-staters who had migrated to Houston in the recent past or had gone there just for the trial.

Why the success of such programs as *Dallas*? Four identifiable groups are involved in their promotion: the audience, the producers, the networks, and the sponsors.

The apparently valid theory behind the audience support of, for instance, *Dallas*, is that is clearly demonstrates to the average viewer that the rich too have more than their share of troubles and assuages fire-in-the-belly plebeian ambitions to possess great wealth.

How about the writers and producers? A lawyer and journalist by the name of Ben Stein, in doing the research for his book *The View from Sunset Boulevard*, found that most of Hollywood's producers and writers of TV programs have a deep-seated dislike for those who are successful in business. In the author's words, ". . . one of the clearest messages of television is that businessmen are bad, evil people, and that big businessmen are the worst of all."

And the major networks? At least two of the triad are seen to lean leftward to liberal inclinations to restructure American society but despite this are highly profit-motivated organizations. If the writers and producers bring them proposed series that tend to defame the business establishment and if similar series are known to be popular and profitable, the networks apparently feel no compunction about airing them.

So much for the first three of the four on the list. Their motives are not difficult to ascertain. The fourth group, however, presents a paradox. Why do the sponsors earmark their advertising dollars to broadcast programs that defame and malign themselves? Is their sponsorship prompted by their ad agencies, most of whom are nestled in the heart of liberalism in the U.S.—New York? Or are their advertising managers afflicted with the perceptions of the ad agencies? Or do the major corporations that sponsor such programs feel it their duty to do sack-cloth and ashes penance for the robber barons who cut such a wide swathe through American capitalism before the turn of the century? Or are they just as profit-motivated and money-grubbing as many of the unsavory characters portrayed in the programs they sponsor and will they knowingly contribute to the demise of their own class, as long as it does not occur within their tenures in office?

But whoever is to blame, it seems regrettable that the white Anglo-Saxon Protestants, who predominate in the cadres of command of the business establishment, do not have an anti-defamation league to spring to their defense against insupportable attacks, to sue, picket, boycott, and deluge the Congress with a paper storm of protests.

The fabric of our business ethics, viewed from the standpoint of such TV series, would seem to be coming apart at the seams.

Yet this extreme view of businessmen is new only in its vehemence and its degree of diffusion. If we go back not so many years, we find President John Kennedy telling U.S. Steel representatives that his father had always said that all businessmen were S.O.B.'s. And long before that, in 1776, Adam Smith wrote in his masterwork of capitalist economics that businessmen "seldom gather except to conspire against the public interest." Smith believed the motive force of a capitalist economy was "self-concern," and in his defense of capitalists, he held that their "individual acts of avarice came together to promote the public welfare, although few of them had any concern except their own self-enrichment."

While the opinions of Smith and Kennedy are not necessarily among the eternal verities, it must be granted that self-concern or a desire for self-enrichment is a strongly motivating force in a capitalist economy since its proponents and opponents alike agree that the desire for a materialistically-blessed life style does spur individual businessmen upward to levels of exertion not often achieved when their own proceeds are limited and they must strive only for some abstract ideal like the public weal: at least, in the Western industrial democracies. In Japan, however, the public weal as a motivator appears to play a larger role.

How to achieve peaceful and cooperative coexistence between what Adam Smith saw as the self-concern of the capitalists and the ethical imperatives that are receiving increasing attention, if not all-out support, in today's America is a dilemma confronting most businessmen. It seems that their desire to climb the ladder of success to increasing wealth and influence must somehow be adjusted to cohabit effectively with the essential precepts of the Codes of Ethics their own organizations have been announcing and promoting increasingly in recent years, especially since some highly publicized scandals raised ethical questions to a higher level of interest in the eyes of the American people.

That self-interest is present in force cannot be effectively gainsaid, nor need it be, for it is one of the healthiest elements in the capitalist system. The problem more deserving of examination than self-interest is the question of whether or not the very nature of commercial activity—buying and selling in a market place—really lends itself to completely ethical, e.g., honest, truthful, and fair, behavior.

In the May, 1983 issue of the *Journal of Business Ethics*, James H. Michelman tackles this question in an excellent article entitled "Some Ethical Consequences of Economic Competition." Michelman, who is president of Mainzer Minton Co., Inc. of New York, makes the following observations:

"In their (e.g., his coworkers) dealings with me, they are truthful and faithful. . . . Yet in our dealings with customers and suppliers neither our truthfulness nor our fidelity can be assumed. If we are truthful and faithful it is because of (economically) rational or sentimental reasons, not because we are determined by moral law. . . . We are seldom kind. When large sums are at stake, kindness is irrelevant."

Mr. Michelman goes on to point out that the very nature of business negotiations is such that any obligation to tell the truth is expunged. If the would-be buyer reveals early in the negotiations the highest price he is willing to pay, then the contract will be signed at that figure. Nor can the would-be seller open the bidding with the lowest price he will take. The corporate *duty* of the buyer is to convince the seller that his top bid is lower than it actually is, while the obligation of the seller is to persuade the buyer that his bottom price is higher than it actually is. By leading the other to infer what is not true, both are practicing an unethical deceit. The responsibility of both the buyer and the seller to their own employers makes a casualty of truth.

Mr. Michelman's conclusion is simply that business competion is amoral.

The most recent repetition of one extensive periodic poll of business excutives has found that while four out of five of the respondents stated that people in business should endeavor to "live up to an absolute standard rather than the moral standard of their peer group," nearly half of them agreed that the American business executive tends not to apply the great ethical laws immediately to his work but is chiefly preoccupied with gain."

The survey in question suggested two explanations for this failure. One, that ethical conduct is not necessarily rewarded. 50% of the respondents felt that one's superiors in business often do not want to know how results are obtained, as long as they achieved the desired outcome. Second, that the pressures from competition push ethical considerations into the background. 43% of those responding believed many businessmen are forced to resort to shady practices in order to survive.

In *The Cultural Contradictions of Capitalism*, Harvard sociologist Daniel Bell diagnoses the ills of contemporary American society as being partly, at least, traceable to unbounded and often irrational hedonism set loose by the disappearance of the Protestant ethic from bourgeois society and by the vain struggles of the body politic to cope with the rising demands for entitlements by those segments of society that cannot afford a comfortable life-style.

Mr. Bell apparently recognizes the self-interest inherent in the capitalist entrepreneur but argues that it was kept within bounds by the Protestant ethic which limited expenditures to reasonable personal needs. With the withdrawal of that ethic from its restraining role, however, only hedonism remained, and this pursuit of pleasure as the primal goal in life was galvanized by the invention of installment plan purchasing, credit cards for instant gratification, and mass-marketing techniques. The villain of the piece is what Bell calls the "disjunction of realms" or the tensions among the cultural, economic, and political portions of a society where impulse has been substituted for restraint and feelings triumph over thought. The "extension of vulgarity," Bell says, "threatens to overwhelm serious society," and argues that the "foundation of any society is the willingness of all groups to compromise private ends for the public interest."

All this is not meant to derogate from the theorem that there are indeed many businessmen who strive mightily to obey self-imposed or company-directed ethical imperatives within the limitations placed on them by the very nature of commercial endeavor. In earlier times it was no doubt easier for a small-scale merchant to buy at a fair price and sell at a fair profit and in so doing provide a decent living for himself and his family but as society became more and ever more complex, the question of which master to serve first and most fully became increasingly vexing and troublesome. With so many claims being made on his profits by family, tax office, church, environmental interests, and charity to orphans in Brazil, it must have seemed to many that the only solution was to increase those profits. And as long as he seemed to be footing the bill for welfare payments to the unemployable, poor, and idle, for a navy to protect Taiwan, and for no-interest or low-interest loans or financial grants to nations that continually thwart and traduce his country in the forum of the United Nations, why not use more of his profits for his own self-gratification?

Against this flood tide of hedonism and of widely publicized instances of corporate skulduggery, numerous organizations—local, national, and international—have risen to the challenge and are working to promote ethical conduct in business through the promulgation and enforcement of their own codes of ethics.

One such organization is the Rotary Club, which was founded in Chicago in 1905 and soon expanded to include affiliated clubs in foreign countries, with the first Rotary Club in Japan being organized in 1921. By 1984 there were 900,000 Rotarians belonging to 20,000 clubs in 150 countries. Membership is made up primarily of businessmen, physicians, dentists, educators, lawyers, and government officials, and all Rotarians, regardless of nationality, are expected to adhere to its codes of ethics. The first ethic learned is the Four-Way Test, which Rotarians hang in their offices, where it serves as a tacit invitation to every customer or supplier or patient who sees it to measure the performance of that Rotarian. This Four-Way Test reads, "1. Is it the Truth? 2. Is it Fair to all concerned? 3. Will it build Good Will and Better Friendships? and 4. Will it be beneficial to all concerned?"

The Rotary Code of Ethics contains eleven paragraphs each describing a principle to be followed. Examples are: "It is my duty as Rotarian to realize that I am a businessman and ambitious to succeed but that I am first an ethical man and wish no success that is not founded on the highest justice and morality. . . . To consider no personal success legitimate or ethical which is secured by taking unfair advantage of certain opportunities in the social order that are absolutely denied others, nor will I take advantage of opportunities to achieve material success that others will not take because of the questionable morality involved."

Many trade associations have their own codes, much as the one unveiled in July, 1983 by the National Association of Accountants for the internal accountants of companies. Among the items adopted in this code was one that requires "that an accountant should report any improper behavior to supervisors within the company." Although the code did not require that the accountant publicize the questionable practices outside company, it did suggest that he tender his resignation if the abuses were not corrected.

The Accountants' Code of 1983 listed fifteen standards of behavior under such categories as competence, confidentiality, integrity, and objectivity. It required that members know the laws, regulations, and technical standards governing their work, avoid actual or apparent conflicts of interest, and report both favorable and unfavorable information fairly and objectively. Although no sanctions were listed for violations of the ethics code, the Association may ask its members to sign a statement with their membership renewal each year asserting that they had adhered faithfully to the code. The Association could suspend members found in violation of the code.

Sometimes it is difficult for an organization to issue a code of ethics that will satisfy the interests of both its members and the public. An example is Rule 502 of the Rules of Conduct of the American Institute of Certified Public Accountants, which reads: "A member shall not seek to obtain clients by solicitation. Advertising is a form of solicitation and is prohibited." While it might be thought undignified for CPA's to hustle after business in the manner of certain salesmen, restrictions on advertising and solicitation would reduce competition with the result that the public could pay higher accounting fees.

At the same time excessive competition can do much damage, as demonstrated in recent years when an industry previously regulated by a government agency was opened to competition. Domestic airline companies became very aggressive when deregulated, with price wars resulting in which none turned a profit. Bankruptcies resulted and in some instances regular commercial service to small cities was terminated.

Among other organizations in the United States that have achieved good reputations in promoting truth in advertising and fair business practices are Better Business Bureaus. Nearly one hundred of them are in operation, linked by a National Council. Being non-governmental, they receive support from private businesses.

In 1976 the Organization for Economic Cooperation and Development (OECD), after much study, published a list of twenty-nine rules of behavior that it recommended be followed by multinational corporations throughout the world. Among these rules are such as:

1. Multinational corporations should not involve themselves in any way in the political processes of the countries in which they operate.
2. In no form is bribery to be countenanced.
3. Multinationals should make public the activities of their principal affiliates in their major areas of operation.

4. All forms of predatory behaviour toward competitors is unethical.

5. All taxes due should be paid honestly without resort to accounting techniques that transfer ledger profits to lower-tax jurisdictions.

6. The right to form unions and engage in collective bargaining on the part of all employees should be recognized and protected.

In 1979 the OECD Ministers reviewed these ethical imperatives and reaffirmed their governments' commitments to the 1976 declaration. It should be kept in mind, however, that the OECD codes are strictly advisory and are not backed by laws except in a few instances: for example, the United States Foreign Corrupt Practices Act of 1977. This act makes it a criminal offense for American enterprises to offer illicit payments in business transactions abroad. Since no other nations have followed suit with similar legislation, U.S. companies have been put at a disadvantage, and the huge and ever-growing foreign trade deficits suffered by the U.S. are to some extent the result of losses of orders to competing countries with no compunction about bribery.

In Third World countries in particular, many officials either demand or suggest under the table payments in exchange for the approval of contracts, custom clearances, etc. Payments such as these are clearly forbidden under U.S. law, but foreigners often make them with impunity. Many of the Third World countries where bribery and corruption are rife are among those most critical of the U.S. in United Nations Assembly debates.

Chapter Five

The Influence of Religion on Japanese Business Ethics

"The Western visitor to Japan who asks a Japanese acquaintance what his religion is (a question not often asked among the Japanese) would be puzzled if the Japanese should answer that he is at once both a Shintoist and a Buddhist. Perplexed, the visitor might then refer himself to a reliable book of statistics and learn that while the population of Japan is only slightly more than 120 million the number of Japanese who say they are Shintoists is 79 million and the number who say that are Buddhists is 66 million.

"As this same visitor travels around Japan, he will be impressed by the outward evidences of religion, e.g., 180,000 buildings of worship in an area the size of the state of California, which has only 25,000. In addition, he will see myriad roadside gods, *torii*, altars, stone lanterns, and other odds and ends of statuary with religious significance, not counting the millions of altars in homes. Yet, if he pursues his inquiry, he will be informed that the National Character Study Committee (organized by the National Institute of Statistical Mathematics) reported that as a conclusion of an extensive survey, 69 percent of the Japanese people do not consider themselves 'religious' and that for the young this percentage should be raised to 90.

"Many years before this survey was made, however,

Westerners had already agreed with this assessment and had characterized the Japanese as 'irreligious,' 'indifferent to religion,' 'undevotional by temperament,' and even outright 'agnostic,' although it should be borne in mind that these descriptions were offered from the standpoint of the Western world of Christianity, with its God who tramples out vengeance from the grapes of wrath and who reportedly keeps a sharp-eyed accounting of our many sins.''

The above three paragraphs from *The Japanese* written by one of the coauthors (JS), is pertinent to our present discussion, for the Japanese do leave the impression with foreigners that they are not deeply religious and that what few such inclinations they have be shared, within the soul of only one person, by three beliefs: Buddhism, Shintoism, and Confucianism, although the last, Confucianism, is probably more accurately viewed as a social ethic than as a proper religion. For our purposes herein, however, we will treat it as both.

Although what Westerners regard as the outward manifestations of religion (church services, a universal Messiah, TV sermons, evangelists et al) are in short supply in Japan, a number of prominent corporate leaders are nonetheless zealous adherents of one religion or another, fashion their companies' ethical practices around their beliefs, and deal with their employees as a pastor deals with his congregation. Also the promotion of such beliefs appears to deepen in times of economic distress, reflecting what the Japanese call "*tsurai toki no kami-danomi*" or "calling on the gods when times are hard."

The Mitsuyo Manufacturing Co. of Tokyo, for instance, holds a monthly service to honor ancestors, with all employees participating. Flowers are offered; candles are lighted; all sing the Buddhist hymn "Mountains of the

Law." Similar services are celebrated monthly in Mitsuyo's plants in the U.S., Brazil, and Germany.

Chairman Numata of Mitsuyo explains, "We build mutual confidence by having a religious experience as a group."

Chairman Benzakuro Kato of the Kyowa Hakko Kogyo Co. offers daily prayers before a large statue of Buddha in his office. His religion having taught him that all human beings are alike and equal, he initiated in 1946 his company's labor-management consultations to enhance unity and cooperation by teaching that the rank-and-file worker is on the same footing as the president and the chairman.

Among the many high-ranked executive officers who are known to inject religious beliefs into corporate and organizational management are Honorary Chairman Doko of the Federation of Economic Organizations, President Maruta of Kao Soap, President Hiraiwa of Tokyo Electric Power, Chairman Saeki of Kinki Nippon Railways, President Fujisaki of Sumitomo Metal Mining, Chairman Atsumi of Kajima Corporation, Honorary Chairman Sakurada of the Federation of Employers' Associations, and President Kadokawa of Kadokawa Publishing Co.

In Yamaichi Securities Co., *all* the executives are said to be firm believers in Shinto, with its representative director travelling annually to the Ise Shrine, which is regarded as the Holy of Holies of Shinto, to offer the company's homage to the Sun Goddess Amaterasu Omikami.

Not content with this measure of religiosity, some corporations extend the 'crib to casket' concept even farther—to the grave, and beyond. Such corporations as Sagawa Express, Bank of Osaka, Kajima Corporation, and Shiga Bank have built memorial towers for the repose of the souls of their deceased employees in such parks as that of the Enryakuji Temple on Mt. Hiei, while others like

Kyoto Ceramic (Kyocera), one of the world's front-running high-tech companies, have laid out actual cemeteries for the eternal rest of the faithful on their payrolls.

Although Kyocera's employees profess to several different persuasions, including Christianity, the company expects their unity and loyalty to employer to be, in effect, a religion in itself standing above other beliefs. It is a "corporate religion: the heart of which is the group ethic", and as commentator Shuichi Kato has written, ". . . the group is all; no universal value, whether Confucian or Shinto, can transcend it."

The Kyocera cemetery accepts not only deceased employees but their wives as well, with the inscription on the main tombstone, which is dedicated to all, reading in part, "Let us keep on doing good and cleanse our souls in this life and when we are no longer here, let us get together now and then to drink sake and have a friendly chat. . . ."

Another corporation, the Suzuya Co., uses what it calls "unusual experiences" of a religious nature to form a "strong spiritual bond and a sense of loyalty to the company." In their Employee Training Center on Lake Kawaguchi, they dress their new female employees in pure white, put lighted candles in their hands, and have President Suzuki lead them into the waters of the lake when it is cold enough for a thin layer of ice to have formed. According to the president, this ceremony helps the recruits forget their "lukewarm student days" and plunge with all their hearts into the rigors of corporate life.

Professor Yukio Cho of the Tokyo University of Foreign Studies believes that the rising popularity of these corporate religions in Japan is attributable to the changes that have recently taken place in the management structure as the period of rapid growth came to a close and to management's resulting fears about the future.

Even though Confucianism is, as noted above, more a social ethic than a religion, it has wielded greater influence on economic and commercial conduct in Japan than either Buddhism or Shintoism, because the educational policy of the Tokugawa government, throughout its two and a half centuries of omnipotent hegemony, ardently emphasized the Confucianist virtues of filial piety, a sense of unity between the rulers and the ruled and between the employers and the employed, respect for elders, benevolence, loyalty to the state, and respect for the harmony that arises from proper relationships.

As the Pax Tokugawa began to take hold, the numerous samurai class fell idle and were given employment as Shogunate officials, teachers, and clan administrators. Soon after the Meiji Restoration of 1868, the samurai were abolished as a class altogether, adding impetus to the trend toward bureaucratic employment. It was at this stage that modern Japanese capitalism was born under circumstances that helped form its present-day character. There being no strong middle class on which to rely for such entrepreneurs, the new government had to raise capital through taxation and the issuance of paper currency with which to build a modern industrial base. This was followed soon thereafter by an early form of recession which prompted the goverment to sell its factories cheaply to retired bureaucrats, mostly samurai, or to favored samurai/bureaucrats who hastily retired and set up private companies for that purpose. (Oddly, the old trading houses, some of which had been in existence a century or longer, showed little enthusiasm for purchasing the government's industrial facilities, perhaps from a long tradition of cautious business practice and perhaps from resentment of the scorn the samurai class and the nobles had always shown toward them.)

The men who bought the factories had to raise the

capital for their purchases and while the government accepted lenient compensation schedules, they still had to go to the banks for part of the payment, there being no widely accepted concept of public stock companies at that time, as well as for money for immediate operational costs. These considerable loans involved the banks intimately in corporate operations from the beginning, so that the typical company founded at that time depended heavily on bank financing with resulting bank participation in or at least close supervision of its management. Additionally, such a company was probably owned and run by ex-bureaucrats and ex-samurai steeped in a tradition of loyal, selfless service who were greatly beholden to their government for a corporate means of livelihood that was often almost a gift.

All this stood in sharp contrast to the West where the industrial base was constructed more slowly and mostly through the efforts of individuals with no particular bureacratic background and with little if any help from the state.

Later, after the Pacific War ended in 1945, in a country that had been at war on the continent since 1931 and throughout the Pacific since 1941, those men who came back to work to rebuild Japan's shattered industry had long years of service to their government, in uniform, and so while retaining part of their loyalty to their government, also found it easy to transfer a part of it to their new civilian employers.

And behind it all, like a seldom-enunciated yet subconsciously felt rationale, stood the religious and social precepts of men like Shosan Suzuki and Baigan Ishida, whose teachings infused commercial and, later, industrial actions with a moral purpose and draped them in robes of respectability as well as the Shinto teaching of an unquestioning devotion to the nation: a silent, common value among the Japanese that facilitates group communication.

Shosan Suzuki, who preceded Ishida, was a samurai who lived in what is now Aichi Prefecture, of which Nagoya is the largest city. He fought for the founder of the House of Tokugawa, Ieyasu, later became a Shogunate official in Osaka and finally a monk of the Zen Sect. His contribution to the work ethic of the Japanese, together with that of Baigan Yoshida, is mentioned elsewhere herein. Equally important was his formulation of religious principles that serve to guide Japanese business ethics even today.

In Suzuki's time, the daily work of the peasants, artisans, and even the merchants was arduous, the hours long, with little if any time left for religious observances and contemplation.

How could they save their souls, they asked the Zen monk. With the cruel necessities of mere survival filling their hours, how could they achieve Buddhahood?

In response Suzuki propounded an answer that became the fundament of his system of ethics. Also, it was perhaps the only answer he could have given.

In effect, he said that *work itself equalled religious observance*:

> "You must work in extremes of heat and cold——work with all your heart and soul. When you toil, your heart is at peace. In this way you are always engaged in Buddhist practice. . . ."

Suzuki further glorified work by stating that the peasants and other toilers were more virtuous than priests, of whom he was one, who did little useful work at all. To the farmers he preached,

> "As a farmer, you are Heaven's gift to the people of the world, your mission being to feed them. . . . Serve Heaven through your labors in the fields. . . . Celebrate

Buddha by raising the five grains. Work earnestly and your fields will be purified with every stroke of your sickle.''

Next the artisan asked, ''But I have no fields to plow or grains to raise. What about me?'' To which Suzuki replied,

''Every kind of work is Buddhist practice. Through work we can attain Buddhahood. There is no occupation that is not Buddhist.''

A merchant said to Suzuki, ''I follow my humble trade in the hope of making a profit, but I fear I may never achieve Buddhahood. Please show me the way.'' Suzuki told the merchant:

''Pursue your calling with honesty, and even as fire burns and even as water flows down the hill, the blessings of Heaven will follow you and your every desire will be fulfilled.''

Honesty was a central element in Suzuki's social ethic. An honest profit was permissable, but the merchant must not take delight in his profits or use them to arouse the envy of others or permit himself to become luxury-loving or idle or forgetful of his obligations to society and, most of all, to the ''Buddha within.''

''Pursue your trade with all your heart and energy,'' Suzuki advised merchants. ''Distribute the produce of your prefecture throughout the nation. Travel everywhere to bring people what they need. Such activity is a religious exercise that will cleanse you of an impure heart. If you cast aside all attachments and work hard, the gods will favor you and your profits will be considerable. You will become a person of virtue and wealth but *you will care nothing for that wealth*.''

This Zen monk's dictum against delighting in profits and material wealth sank roots into the consciousness of the people of his day with the result that even the richest merchants often donned robes of cheap, coarse cloth and allowed the exteriors of their dwellings to take on an unkempt, humble appearance. The inner linings of those coarse robes, however, were often made of the finest silk while the interiors of their shabby-appearing domiciles were luxurious to the verge of hedonism. This "poor on the outside, rich within" syndrome can be observed in several facets of Japanese life even now.

Japanese businessmen of the late 20th century are often repelled by the frequent emphasis placed on profits by Western businessmen, with Suzuki's philosophy accounting for this attitude. They feel instinctively that it is wrong to set out with the primary purpose of making profits, even if those profits accrue to stockholders rather than themselves, but they will accept profits that result as a natural consequence of an unbendable commitment to honest service to customers and to providing dependable merchandise at a reasonable price.

Elsewhere Suzuki advised merchants to pursue profits wholeheartedly but not to enjoy those profits. Instead they should use them for the benefit of others or to build up capital to invest for socially useful purposes. In the words of Suzuki, "Those who think nothing of the people but give consideration only to their own profits will surely incur the wrath of Heaven, meet with ill fortune, and be scorned by all."

To say that many Japanese businessmen do not today live up to the ideals propounded by this Zen monk is only to state the obvious—and the regrettable.

Shosan Suzuki spoke frequently of the "Buddha within," it being his belief that the natural or cosmic order of things not only encompassed all but breathed within the hearts of everyone, not exactly a unique view in Oriental religions. If men and women could avoid entanglement with the "three poisons" of anger, greed, and discontent, they would need only follow the dictates of their hearts—in which shone the light of the cosmic order—in order to attain Buddhahood:

> "Believe with all your heart in yourself," he told his followers. "If you really want to become a Buddha, you need only believe in yourself. Believing in yourself is believing in the Buddha, for the Buddha is inside you. Those who are ignorant of the blessings of our Buddha-nature, who fail to value themselves and the Buddha-nature with which they enter this world will lose their way in this life and fall into Evil."

When Suzuki talks of believing in oneself, he is not, needless to say, speaking of having confidence in one's own ability to surmount difficulties, to prevail against odds, to climb mountains, to "do great deeds in Hungary to pass all men's believing." Rather, he means that men and women should believe in the natural goodness that is—we hope—within us all, unless we have allowed it to become "overgrown by the dank foliage of the 'three poisons.' "

As noted in the beginning of this chapter, today's people of Japan have often been characterized, even by themselves, as non-religious, but in one sense at least, "anti-clerical" might be a more apt adjective, for why offer alms to non-productive (although some shrines engage in commercial activities aside from their collection boxes) priests when one can commune with the Buddha dwelling in his own breast at no cost? This tendency is fortified by their natural disinclination to endeavor to grasp abstract ideas that have no clear limits, things too distant in time and space. It is far easier, they find, to follow a religious credo that holds that being religious and eventually achieving Buddhahood consist only in working hard and following the dictates of one's heart.

It is from this concept of religion that comes the Japanese penchant for work and much of their business ethics. This is why they dread retirement and despise idleness. While obviously necessary, even sleep—the ultimate idleness—is not surrounded there by the admonitions we hear in the West. ("Be quiet, your father's asleep. Don't wake him up." "You must get a sound sleep." *Inter alia*.) And this is why so many Japanese nap on their commuter trains. Sleep is permissable—even laudable—since there is little work the sleeper could otherwise be engaged in while riding a train.

When we see a Japanese employee listening with rapt attention to a lecture on management or watch a group of their bright-eyed businessmen silently and intently walking though an American factory with cameras at the ready or hear of a Japanese salesman trekking through the jungle to follow a sales lead to an isolated African community, we should remember that all of them are doing more than just earning their daily wage.

They are following the dictates of a religion.

ing Buddhahood consists in ... working hard and follow-

... the distance of one's heart.

It is from this concept of ... that ... come the immense pressure for work and much of their craziness rules. This is why they dread retirement and despise idleness. While obviously necessary even sleep—the ultimate idleness—is not surrounded there by the admonitions often ... Don't waste time ...? You must get a sound sleep. the rich ... and this is why so many Japanese nap on their commuter trains. Sleep is permissible—even laudable—since there is little work the sleeper could otherwise be engaged in while riding a train.

When we see a Japanese employee suddenly jerks rapt attention to a lecture on pharmaceuticals or watch a group of them high-awed businessmen slowly and intently walking though an American factory with cameras at the ready I hear of a Japanese salesman trekking through the jungle to follow a sales lead to an isolated African community, we should remember that all of them are doing more than researching their daily wage.

They are following the dictates of a religion.

Chapter Six

The Work Ethic in Both Countries

A Japanese businessman in his late thirties was visiting one of the coauthors in his Houston home last fall. It was a Sunday afternoon and his sons were watching a pro football game on television. A beer commercial appeared on the screen and caught the visitor's eye. It showed several American men throwing aside their tools and running from their work-place to their pickups as the five o'clock bell was ringing. Surprise was evident on the visitor's face when he turned to JS and asked, "Don't American workers feel any sense of obligation toward their employer? They act as if they can't wait to get away from where they work."

JS explained that perhaps the beer vendors responsible for the TV commercial had overstated the workers' eagerness to leave in order to enhance the irresistible taste of their beer, but he had to admit that such a commercial would be unthinkable in Japan. In any event, put on the defensive, he went on to point out that Americans believe they owe their employers an honest eight-hour day's work, in return for which the employer owes them the amount of wages he agreed to pay when they signed on. And if he wants them to work long past closing time, he should expect to pay for that extra time.

The Japanese visitor shook his head in disbelief. "I would be ashamed to leave work so abruptly. If I did it often, my fellow workers would become very cold to me. Besides, I feel that I have entrusted my life to the president of my company."

Having spent twenty-five years in Japan, JS thought that he was fairly familiar with the Japanese work ethic, but this was the first time he had heard it expressed in such bald terms.

Yet when he was first in Japan shortly after the close of the war in the Pacific, nation-wide disillusionment had eroded the foundations of loyalty to most forms of authority, and few of the Japanese employees of the Occupation Forces worked as fast or as efficiently as persons doing the same job in the U.S. For instance, the construction supervisors on U.S. military bases gauged the work of their Japanese employees against standards obtained from labor unions in the U.S. and often found the Japanese sadly wanting.

Perhaps this should not be surprising when one considers that those Japanese were working for foreign military forces occupying their country, but similar observations were often made of work gangs on road and rail repairing projects not related to the Occupation Forces. The laborers all swung their pick axes in unison and shouted, enhancing the appearance of arduous activity, but closer scrutiny would reveal that each pick axe seemed to move a few small rocks a couple of inches in one direction, only to move them back to their original location with its next leisurely swing.

To be fair, of course, one must bear in mind that the Japanese, as a nation, were then not only disillusioned but also tired and undernourished and working for pittances.

It has taken nearly forty years, but now the pendulum has swung to the other extreme, and today frequent panegyrics are heard about the intensely loyal, industrious Japanese worker, together with criticisms of him that imply that he is a grim workaholic and that it is not ethical to work so hard, that hard work somehow constitutes unfair competition.

In 1981 the Ministry of Labor in Japan found that workers used only about half of the vacation time they were entitled to. The percentage of Japanese taking off two full weekends a month was fifteen, while sixteen percent took off only one full weekend. Staying home for four two-day weekends was considered scandalous. Many factories like the Mazda facility near Hiroshima have repaid such loyal industriousness by never having laid off a worker, nor do the workers necessarily pay for this job security by accepting significantly lower wages.

In Japan, a lazy person is regarded as untrustworthy and morally unsound, because Japan's history has transmuted necessity into virtue and the busy man has become the good man. One is congratulated when he says he is "very busy," not commisserated with, and being called a *hatarakibachi* (workaholic) is a compliment of a high order. Missing work is not just a matter of losing pay; it lays the worker open to the suspicion of being downright disloyal.

So devoted are the Japanese to improvements at their place of work that fifty-four percent of them participate in suggestion programs, compared with only fourteen percent in the U.S.

In both the U.S. and Great Britain, employees leave their communities in the morning to travel to their work-place, whereas in Japan the Japanese employee goes to his community, e.g., his workplace, in the morning and returns, usually late in the evening, to where he sleeps. (To be sure, those below *kanrishoku* or managerial level receive overtime pay that adds a welcome 10–15% to their salary.) At times it seems that although the Japanese male is dedicated to the continuation of his family line, home life is no more natural to him than a cage is to a bird.

A recent poll asked Japanese workers whom, in the event an earthquake derailed the train they were aboard, they would inform first: their company or their home? Most answered their company, by a large margin.

Not only do the Japanese work long overtime hours but they are also zealous about getting to their work place in times of emergency. During a transportation strike a couple of years ago, many even arose as early as four a.m. to walk two or three hours to get to their offices. In times of business recession it is not so unusual for many of them to accept reductions in bonuses in order to help their employer through the hard times. In contrast, consider the Greyhound Bus workers who are striking in the U.S. as this is being written: Greyhound announced it had to reduce salaries in order to survive and proposed to the union that their drivers, whose average pay was some $35,000 annually, accept a reduction to $29,000. (The industry average was $27,000.)

Enraged, the drivers together with other workers struck the company in protest.

Similarly, in a recent labor dispute at Continental Air Lines, many of its pilots refused to accept pay cuts to a level of about $40,000, saying they could not live on that amount, which is almost twice the average family income in the U.S.

When one of the coauthors (JS) was in Tokyo recently, he went at 10:45 one evening to the coffee shop of the Aoyama hotel where he was staying. The coffee shop was empty of customers and only dimly-lit, but JS sat down at a table, under the impression the shop stayed open until eleven. In a moment a smiling waitress bustled up to him and took his order. When the sandwich and coffee were served, JS commented that the shop didn't seem to be doing much business. "Oh," the waitress explained, "that's because we closed at ten o'clock."

En route home JS stopped over in Seattle and spent one night in a motel near the airport, where again he went at 9:50 one evening to the snack bar. When the waitress who was wiping down the counter refused him service, JS pointed to the sign on the door that gave 10:00 pm as the closing hour. "Well," the waitress told him, "we couldn't serve you and get you out of here by ten."

About the working habits and inclinations of the Japanese, three prominent and readily identifiable bodies of opinion appear to exist in the U.S.: The first body accepts such reports of Japanese industriousness and sense of workplace obligation as completely true and, admiring them, urges that Americans emulate this facet of the Japanese culture. A second also accepts these reports as true but is critical of such loyal efforts as being somehow unfair and excessive. To this group, which includes many labor unions and politicians seeking scapegoats to draw attention away from mismanagement and excessively high wages in such industries as steel, autos, and the airlines, the Japanese have become 'economic animals,' joyless robots living in rabbit hutches, grim automatons, secret connivers in the Japanese conspiracy, conscienceless dumpers, their leaders mere 'transistor radio salesmen' who are guilty of industrial planning—a legitimate device when used at home but sharp practice when resorted to by others.

A third group attributes Japan's success to sweat shop labor practices (believed by forty-six percent of U.S. college graduates, according to a recent opinion poll), bare survival wages, and the employment of children. But on 18 January, 1984 a Cable News Network Special Report stated that New York City alone had some 3,000 sweat shops with 50,000 workers, many of them paid only $1.00 an hour with little or no protection from safety devices and health insurance.

Further, because of loose controls on migrant families

working in agriculture, the employment of children may be more prevalent in the U.S. than in Japan, where it exists only marginally in family-owned shops and in the form of chores on farms.

Such beliefs range up and down the scale from complete validity to utter buncombe, so it seems that a closer examination of the Japanese work ethic is in order: its roots, its stability, its validity, as well as to what extent it is responsible for Japan's economic success in the Seventies and Eighties.

The analogy between the samurai of yore and Japan's businessmen of today has become a popular one of late. An article in *Harper's Magazine* of November, 1982 states the case succinctly, telling its readers that business journalism in Japan never gets weary of the military theme, 'offensives' being launched, foreign markets being 'invaded,' and 'bridgeheads' being protected against 'counter-assaults.'

Certain rigorous schools for businessmen are described, sounding—for all the world—like infantry basic training camps.

Yet the curious observer of the Japan scene is hard put to detect the same formidable essence in both the fierce, rather overwhelming depictions of the samurai and the often rather small, humble, self-effacing company employees of today's Japanese business world. The observer is compelled to ask himself, "If this 150-lb. man across the conference table from me were to don armor and grasp a sword, would I *really* believe him a menace?"

Still, one cannot deny that the ideal of today's Japanese man does hark back to the samurai, even as an American ideal—perhaps seldom achieved any more—harks back to the mountain men and the Texas Rangers and the town marshalls of the pioneer period.

Just as many Americans may subconsciously long for

that ideal of the mountain men—however dissimilar they may be, so the Japanese businessmen of today yearn after the ideals of their far-off ancestors: those top-knotted, two-sworded warriors for whom life was nothing but "service, service, service" to their lords and masters and to whom death but the glorious culmination of a short life, often compared to the cherry blossom: blooming briefly in pale glory, then quickly descending to the dust.

Ah, but it is *how* the blossom falls! Therein lay the essence of samurai existence, with its code that taught that the first thought of each samurai on arising every morning should be to prepare himself for death that same day, that death was the climax of life, and that by dying properly, in accordance with his code of *Bushido*, one could perhaps accomplish more than in all his years of living. Hear these words from the *Hagakure*, a classic work on samurai life:

"I am but a servant of my liege lord. Let him be cruel to me, or kind, as he pleases. Or let him ignore me entirely and not even know that I live. It is all the same to me. For my part, not a minute goes by without my heart overflowing with the bliss of having him as my master. At the thought of my dear lord, my eyes swim in tears and I am filled with thankful ecstacy."

The samurai were ranked beneath the nobility in Japan, followed by the farmers, artisans, and merchants in that descending order and were the models of loyal service for the others to emulate. Superimposed on a backdrop of such ready receptacles were the philosophies of Confucianism, Shinto, and Buddhism, each vital ingredients in the developing work ethic.

The principal sculptors of the work ethic in feudal times were Sontoku Ninomiya, who told the farmers to "Work hard, earn much, and spend little," Shozan Suzuki, who fought for Ieyasu Tokugawa and later became a Zen master, and Baigan Ishida, a man of merchant stock who also founded a school of religion. Where Ninomiya aimed his maxims of hard work, savings, and thrift at the farmers, Suzuki and Ishida transmitted to the merchants and artisans a greater sense of self-respect by urging them, as well as the warriors, to pursue excellence in all they undertook, to seek enlightenment through the glory of work well done, to regard work as its own reward. For many, no doubt, the preachments of Ninomiya, Ishida, and Suzuki served as justifications for what they were all already practicing of necessity if not of personal conviction, and therefore all the more welcome.

After the end of feudalism and the restoration of the Emperor Meiji to his throne in 1868, the man who transformed the feudal work ethic of Japan into a philosophy to guide businessmen and workers in a country faced with the necessity of modernizing and Westernizing itself was Viscount Eiichi Shibusawa, founder of what is today Japan's largest bank and involved in the establishment of at least 500 other companies. An ex-samurai himself, he set out early to make the image of the businessman a respectable one and to industrialize Japan.

Called the "conscience of Japanese business," Shibusawa strove to demonstrate that profit should not be the primary motivation for business activities, that profits would come in due course to those who took the long view of business planning, who treated their employees justly and recognized them as the real strength of any enterprise, who dealt with their customers honestly, and who tied the progress of their commercial endeavors to the progress of their country. "Productiveness is virtuous" was his belief, and the inculcation of a proper work ethic upon the people was his highest aim.

Yet as influential as Shibusawa was, he nevertheless had to vie with more avaricious entrepreneurs intent on building their own empires and filling their own coffers so that the work ethic as it is seen today in Japan did not come into flower until after the close of World War II when the dissolution of the conglomerates, the shock of defeat, the breaking up of a value system designed to support imperialist military purposes, and the partially successful superimposition—by laws and codes—of American ethics of fairness and equal treatment revived and strengthened Shibusawa's ideals.

The Japanese work ethic that has contributed largely to Japan's economic success in the postwar era can be viewed as a coincidental replication and extension of the Calvinist work ethic, "Work. Save. Forego pleasure," to which has been addended the precepts to workers, "Give loyal service to your employer" and "Place the interests of your group above those of yourself" and the admonition to employers, "Cherish your workers above all else."

Although at times quite similar to that of Japan, the work ethic of the West and in particular of the U.S. has developed in different ways and for different reasons. In the earlier days of Western civilization, the Greeks looked upon all work as a curse and waged wars to win slaves to do their work for them. One Greek philosopher wrote that "Leisure is the purpose of all work—and its only justification," while the ancient Hebrews thought physical work was a punishment from God for man's original sin: an idea that was transmitted to early Christians as well.

For centuries thereafter, the traditional view of work was that people labored because they had to—in order to survive—but that the work itself held little intrinsic value.

St. Thomas Aquinas changed the general view of work somewhat when he propounded his theory of work as being morally neutral, neither good nor bad but just essential. Selling one's labor and buying the labor of others was likened to buying and selling wheat or cooking oil, an economic transaction that had its place as long as a just price characterized the transaction.

Western civilization either held work in low esteem or viewed it as morally neutral until Protestantism and Martin Luther came along to propound the idea that it was leisure that was immoral and that labor was morally worthy for its own sake, regardless of what one gets in return, thus forming the very core of the work ethic that is still alive today. (Both Martin Luther and Shōsan Suzuki lived, although at different times, in the 16th century, with Luther preaching that work was the way to serve God and Suzuki teaching that by doing his daily tasks, the worker was doing Buddha's work as well. Suzuki was born not long after the death of Luther and while there is no indication that he ever heard or read Luther's name or the thrust of his thesis, one wonders if that bit of religious intelligence might not have somehow trickled in through Japan's half-open doors of the time to play a role in the formulation of a work-ethic that is causing hardships in the largely Protestant U.S. today.)

John Calvin, a Frenchman, joined the Protestant movement and extended Martin Luther's premise with his hypothesis that it was God's will that all men should work, that work belonged to the Lord and that nothing was as sinful as idleness, thereby sublimating the Protestant work ethic into what was thereafter often called the Calvinist work ethic.

In order to follow the development of the American work ethic since the early days of our republic, it is necessary first to note that a work ethic can be distinct from work behavior and also to define high-discretion and low-discretion work as pertaining to jobs in which the workers have a considerable measure of autonomous control over how they function in contrast to, in the case of the latter, a minimum of such control, workers in such routinized, low-discretion jobs being called colloquially 'machine-minders.'

Workers in both high-discretion and low-discretion jobs may believe in a work ethic whereas their work behaviour may suggest that they do not.

The work experience in the U.S. can be roughly divided into three eras, the first or preindustrial period lasting until about 1870. The second—the American industrial revolution—extended from then until the late 1960's or early 1970's, while the third, set against a background of a post-industrial high-technology economy, is just beginning.

Work in the pre-industrial period can be characterized as highly discretionary, since more than three-quarters of the work force was self-employed, in contrast to less than ten percent today. These were artisans, farmers, and independent merchants who held autonomy over the tempo and the quality of their work. While believing in the virtues of long hours and high-quality work, they could, in theory at least, work slowly and produce meager crops or shoddy merchandise, if they chose to do so, but the stern realities of existence in those early times precluded much use of these discretionary powers. In short, both their beliefs and the force of necessity inspired them to work hard and work well.

When the industrial revolution began just over one hundred years ago, the economy began to shift from agriculture and the small shops of craftsmen to large-scale, smoke-stack manufacturing industries. Along with revolutionary techniques of making goods came a new approach to organizing work. Management planners such as F.W. Taylor argued that discretionary efforts, if allowed, would hamper productivity. Specifically, he wrote that "any improvement which the workman makes upon orders given to him (by management) is fatal to success."

Specialization of work was introduced so that a worker made, instead of an entire product such as a rifle or cart or watch, only a nut or pin or bolt or spoke of a wheel. Or maybe he only sanded the spoke. It was found that such specialized, repetitive-motion work largely improved productivity and profits although making the work itself more boring and emotionally unrewarding. The new system reduced reliance on motivation, loyalty, and even peripheral skills. Little did it matter if the worker was devoted to an ethic or not. If he put in his eight (or ten or twelve) hours on the assembly line and produced his quota, little else was expected of him. Indeed, if he produced much more than his quota, his efforts might well be rebuked by his coworkers as a cause for embarrassment to them while seldom producing any additional income for this one ambitious workman.

Even so rural folk quit their high-discretion work on farms to pour into factory towns and apply for such jobs because it was becoming increasingly evident that the new levels of productivity so achieved provided such workers with a higher standard of living in the form of consumer goods. At the same time, as if in compensation for the tarnishing of the traditional work ethic, a new ethic—that of self-denial for the sake of one's family—was being born. By sacrificing autonomy and discretion, the factory worker could give his dependents a "better way of life," materialistically speaking at least. That his job was unpleasant and unsatisfying received recognition, and the respect accorded him as breadwinner and provider of a home, the children's education, and a share of the crescive output of the new consumer conveniences increased both at home and in the community.

As this recognition and respect for the factory hand's sacrifice mounted, the moral value of doing good work for its own sake decreased and became an abstraction not in consonance with the stern realities of the factory floor. As the second period of the national work experience moved well along into the 20th century, the American traditional work ethic moved away from the burgeoning industrial facilities and began to flourish instead in an important symbolic role. In the words of Daniel T. Rogers, "As rhetorical commonplace, as political invective, or as moral shibboleth, the equation of virtue and work continued to pervade the nation's thinking long after the context in which it had taken root had been all but obliterated."

Important changes, however, were beginning to take place. At the close of the first World War, only about one quarter of all jobholders worked at white-collar jobs, but by the early 1980's this figure had grown to over one-half, with half of them reporting that they have a "great deal of freedom" in deciding how best to do their jobs. Advances in technology have also served to make jobs less routine and more interesting, and the workers more autonomous within the scope of their roles.

At the beginning of the second World War, the length of education received by the average American worker was a little more than eight years but in the subsequent forty years, this figure grew to almost thirteen. Entitlement programs increased from 27 percent of the national budget in 1967 to half of the budget in 1982, providing a safety net in the form of various transfer payments against the punishments of the workplace. So while the loss of a job is still a traumatic experience its impact has thereby been somewhat alleviated.

And, importantly, the ethic of self-sacrifice that was such an essential feature in the industrial success story underwent change so that by 1980 only about 65 percent of the population defined a "good man" as an ample provider who sacrificed his own job satisfaction for the welfare of his dependents, in comparison with the 86 percent who so defined the term a mere twelve years previously. More Americans have come to regard having a job as a right than as a privilege while a solid majority do not believe that extra efforts on the job will be rewarded.

As a result of all these changes, only about one in five of today's workers views himself as a holder of a low-discretion job, and this shift to a high-discretion workplace has endowed the traditional work ethic with renewed strategic importance.

Yet while a majority (fifty-one percent) of workmen believe they are working harder now than in the past, sixty-two percent of the public, according to the Public Agenda Foundation, believe that *others* do not work as hard now as they did five to ten years ago.

In 1980, at the behest of the U.S. Chamber of Commerce, the Gallup organization did a study that found that almost all (eighty-eight percent) working Americans feel that it is important to themselves that "they work hard and do their best on the job," which is generally supported by other such studies among them, one conducted under the auspices of the Connecticut Mutual Insurance Co. In contrast, in 1981, almost exactly the same percentage (eighty-seven percent) of the nation's business and government leaders, according to a study done for Motorola by Yankelovich, Skelly, and White named a lack of work motivation as a prime reason for the diminished competitiveness of the U.S. This apparent contradiction can be explained by showing that two terms—work ethic and work behavior—have been confused. The former still manages to stay well and alive while the latter has admittedly deteriorated, with nearly half the work force saying that they put little more effort into their jobs than minimally required.

In fact, one study by D.J. Cherrington measured work

behaviour by the clock for two years and concluded that forty-nine percent of work observed was given over to idle time: breaks for coffee, water-cooler conferences, waiting for others, and late arrivals and early departures. What apparently has caused the decline in actual job performance on the part of workers who nonetheless say they feel an inner compulsion to do a good job is that the growing trend toward more discretion in the work-place has outpaced the ability of management to keep up with and utilize the inner desire of the majority to do a good job that has grown with work discretion.

The expansion of work discretion and the concomitant revitalization of the work ethic of the past—that survived more in the form of proud words of exhortation in the mouths of politicians and defensive protestations in the mouths of labor union officials than in actuality—has given the United States a fine and perhaps unique opportunity to take advantage, through innovative managerial skills, of this conviction on the part of most American workmen that they should each put outstanding efforts into their job performance.

Yet the current structuring of the work place undermines the effectiveness of the work ethic. In the Gallup study mentioned above less than ten percent of workers believe that they would be the primary beneficiaries of their own efforts to increase productivity. (In Japan, the comparable figure is nine out of ten.) Additionally, three out of every four American workers say that managers in general do not know how to motivate employees, but that they themseves would respond positively to the right kind of initiatives on the part of management.

The three areas where management should focus its attention if it is to effectively guide its work ethic resource into higher levels of productivity and quality workmanship are:

1) promotion of higher quality standards,
2) a broader system of both monetary and non-monetary awards in recognition of extraordinary efforts, and
3) an enhanced sense of vital participation in the corporate entity with management surrendering some or even many of its prerogatives in order to shorten the perceived distance between themselves and the factory (or shipping room) worker.

Closed-off luxurious offices, reserved parking spaces, weekend access to company vacation houses in the Adirondacks, and executive bonuses in seasons when workers are protesting giveback proposals are not at all conducive to fostering a dedication to corporate unity.

Instead, they only enhance the feeling on the factory floor that "it's us against them."

In defense of such prerogatives and of often excessive emoluments, many ambitious American managers point out that they often work, at their desks or at home, three or four hours longer every day than their office and factory subordinates, most of whom abandon the ship while the five o'clock whistle is still blowing.

As these changes were taking place, another American ethic—the Puritan ethic of government spending ("Balance the budget, stay out of debt, live within your means") had entered upon a declining curve as politicians sought to expand their base of voter support through massive welfare programs and redistributive tax programs.

Okurezu, Yasumazu, Hatarakazu

The question has been fairly asked, "Since Japan seems to have followed the lead of the U.S. in so many other fields, will a diminution in work behavior not also appear there as well?"

Indeed, the above three words in Japanese, meaning

"Never be late, never take a day off, but never work" is a cynical reflection of a Japanese observation of certain laxity in their own present-day work habits. A study done by Tokyo's Rikkyo University found that while Japanese worked longer hours than Americans, they did not work as intensely.

Granting that part of their enthusiasm for complete identification with their employer and his interests is dwindling, some forty-six percent of Japan workers in 1982 still looked upon their jobs as their "primary reason for living, " although this figure is down from fifty-eight percent in 1975.

What is happening is that the younger generation of workers, perhaps under the influence of life-styles viewed in Western movies and read about in translated books and in some instances experienced first-hand, is dismayed at having to come home almost every night often at ten p.m. or even later and being unable to spend much time with their families on weekends because they must go to the office or play golf with their colleagues.

Even so, in contrast, almost eighty percent of college seniors say, according to a 1981 Ministry of Labor survey, that they "would not mind working for a company that required them to work on Saturday." To be sure, this question was asked just before graduation from college, at a time when many are ready to make any commitment, even to themselves, to insure their entry into a company that will offer them job security.

Many of these polls and surveys must be analyzed with care before being swallowed whole, for here are to be found the *tatemae*, what one says for public consumption, and the *honne*, what one truly believes privately. And it is these two forces in conflict that will make the Japanese work ethic an increasing puzzle to the casual observer henceforth. The writer (JS) has had numerous young

Japanese company emplyees tell him, after three or four "*mizuwari*" (highballs) in a Ginza or Akasaka bar, that they would like nothing better than to leave the office at five o'clock or so, but the glares of their coworkers prevent them from doing so. Nor did they confess to any burning obligation to go to the office on Saturday, but were admittedly afraid not to do so.

Also hesitant if not actually afraid to return home as early as 7:00 p.m. are many employees, particularly among the young managerial class, but for a reason not connected with the cold stares of their coworkers. Rather, the neighbors would assume that their jobs were not very important or they would not be able to return so early, thereby causing loss of face to their families.

This is reminiscent of a book by Philip Wylie in which a medication that vastly prolongs life is developed, with the one demerit that it turns all who take it green. At first there is resistance to the medication and resentment against the "Greenies," but as time passes, more people opt to swallow the potion when faced with the likelihood of their own demise. At length the Greenies come to outnumber the Non-Greenies, who, now the minority, begin to feel the prejudice they themselves had earlier directed at those whose skins had turned green and to realize a diminution of their own influence.

This is what will almost surely happen in Japan as the younger generation becomes more influential and as they are joined by the generations who follow them.

For the present they are still shamed into a certain degree of compliance by the pressure of their seniors, says Atsuko Toyama, Director of Intermediate Education in the Ministry of Education. She warns the managerial class, "You will have to eventually accept that most younger workers, once the time comes to go home, will want to do exactly that."

Recognizing this "danger" and determined to counteract it, many companies are now promoting and refining means to instill the desired degree of loyalty to employer in their young recruits—meditation sessions, company slogans pasted on walls, chorusing of company songs, taking vacations as a group, early morning group jogging in lockstep, and group calisthenics at noon on the company roof or by their desks being just some of these measures.

All that said and suggested, there seems little doubt that, on balance, the average Japanese works longer hours and is more loyal to his employer than his American counterpart, although Prof. Taira of the University of Illinois asserts that the American is still thirty percent more productive (productivity being more a function of investment in plant than of sweat and long hours). Assuming this to be true, how valid are their work behavior and their loyalty to employers as reasons for their success? Will the dominant industrial power of the early twenty-first century be one guided by the Western ethic of individuals or by a feudal ethic of relationships?

Although high productivity is more often found in larger Japanese companies with the reason usually cited being that more money is invested in their machinery, there are instances where even a large company will be unable to get as much production out of its workers as desired, despite investment in production line equipment. An example was a factory in Otsu which obtained a license from a Massachusetts company to produce the identical product turned out in New England. The production line in Otsu was in every respect the same as that in the U.S., and the work hours were the same. Despite this, the Otsu plant was never able to get as large an output as in Massachusetts. After years of strenuous effort, visits to Boston by Japanese, and visits by Americans to Otsu, the Japanese finally had to admit that their workers were simply not as productive. The writer (HFZ) found only one real difference between the two operations. The average age of the Otsu workers (those on the line were all female) was about 23, whereas that of those in the Boston area was about 32.

If toil and dedication are not to be thanked for the Horatio Alger-like success of the Japanese, should the view of the late president of the Pioneer Electronics Corporation, a major Japanese corporation, be considered? He wrote in *Business Week* of 23 May, 1983 that the Japanese system is founded on economic power held by a cartel of banks, corporations, and government and is one of excessive discrimination, little personal freedom, strong nationalistic tendencies, workers who are willing captives, savers who expect little in return for forgoing current consumption, and shrewd negotiators who ask much and give nothing in return. It is, he went on, a system capable of producing more goods and services of higher quality and at lesser cost than any other in the world. He predicts that it is just a matter of time before the Western economic democracies collapse in the face of this highly successful economic performance from a state-guided communal capitalist system.

Or is the story behind Japan's postwar rise in international commerce an even more complicated one—and being complicated, a story with little demotic appeal to the many who want one or two but not more than three handy villains (or heroes) to whom they can point?

In any event, there *are* a considerable number of reasons for Japan's success, and they should be listed, not necessarily in order of importance, for consideration:

1. At the close of World War II Japan's industrial plant was in various advanced stages of destruction, their marine transport on the sea-bottom, their credit low, the stock of good will owed them zero, and their past sources

of raw materials cut off and future sources uncertain. At such a time when few if any would have given them an iota of a chance of future economic prowess, a small group of outstanding strategic thinkers daringly determined to build a future place for Japan in the world by creating and substaining a flourishing industrial economy. These few elite planners of Japan's meritocracy raised their eyes above the ashes and rubble piled around them and developed a sophisticated and rational economic policy, one that they held to tenaciously. This far-sighted policy has always emphasized the importance of global market share, which leads to lower costs because of experience gained and economies of scale, and the transfer of resources from low-productivity industries to those with higher technologies. Its planning provided management and labor alike with useful guidelines for structural change so that both could adjust to dynamic shifts in comparative advantage and the press of technological advance. In contrast to the regulatory function of the U.S. government, Japan's meritocracy played more of a developmental role in its relations with business.

The relationship between government and business was not one of suspicion and hostility but an instinctive cooperation in reaching a commonly agreed-on goal. It was not a sinister conspiracy of unlawful trade pacts and secret subsidies (although subsidies were and are given, just as the U.S. massively subsidizes its number-one export earner: agricultural products.)

Japan developed a pattern. Sighting in on a target industry, she first bought the needed technology, then built the plants. She protected that fledgling industry until its costs became competitive, then began exporting its products to Third World countries. This increased her global market share and enabled her to further reduce costs, after which she entered the U.S. market. From there Japan would move on to industries in higher technology levels and repeat the pattern.

"Aha," think some. "There it is, out in the open. Central planning in the style of the deep-dyed Communist countries. Or the new buzz-word: 'targeting.' Like hard-nose Russian trade commissars, the dictatorial bureaucrats at MITI and the Ministry of Finance are issuing stern edicts about production quotas and mandatory personnel utilization. They brook no dissent nor disobedience. They are the chief executive officers of monolithic Japan Inc. and rule with steel fists."

An industrial policy is the sum of the efforts of a country to influence its own economic growth and to shape its own commercial activities. It is tantamount to a corporation's long-term strategy. In the case of Japan, it is without doubt a significant reason for that country's economic success, but it can be and, at times, has been overemphasized, for Japan's planners made little or no contribution to some of Japan's most outstanding industrial successes.

For instance, according to the U.S. Federal Trade Commission, Japan's governmental subsidies to its steelmakers averaged a mere forty-six cents a metric ton throughout the twenty-four year period ending in 1975, when Japan gained world dominance in steel.

Again, in the chip industry, Oki Electric is the fastest growing 64K producer and the first maker in Japan to test the state-of-the-art 256K chip. Yet Oki did not participate in MITI's R&D project in chip research.

Nor, in an earlier and well-known example, did Japan's auto industry heed MITI's guidelines aimed at strengthening that industry's base through selective amalgamation.

In the words of Rep. Jack Kemp (R-N.Y.), "In 1950 Sony was making coffee pots, and MITI told them to stay in the coffee-pot business and stay out of electronics. MITI told Honda to keep making motorcycles and not go in to the automobile industry. MITI told Mazda to go out of business.''

So it is evident that the bureaucrats do not always get their way. When the private sector disagrees, they disagree loudly and often effectively. Even so both parties know they are in the same boat, rowing in the same general direction. So MITI continues to offer *gyōsei shidō* or administrative guidance hoping that their advice will be followed and not ignored. For instance, MITI is now engaged in 'urging' seven industries to shut down outmoded factories, to enter into joint ventures, and to generally become more competitive by 1988. Note, however, the verb 'urge': *not* ''order'' or ''direct'' or ''demand.''

2. Muted labor strife is surely a factor in Japan's success, as has often been commented on. Japanese labor-management relations are characterized by the three elements of lifelong employment, salary increases based on seniority, and enterprise unions as against industry-wide unions.

These have been called the Three Sacred Treasures, but there is some element of myth in their image. Lifelong employment, for instance, is practiced only by the larger corporations and government agencies and then only until a comparatively early retirement age, when the employee is either retired or shifted to a lower-pay, less secure job. Then, too, ten to twenty percent of employees leave their companies every year, although admittedly these turnover rates are higher among female employees and workers in small companies. The age-wage profiles for Japanese workers of different levels of education are quite close to those of their American counterparts, except for younger workers. And labor union activities in Japan, which function in accordance with a law patterned on the U.S. labor relations law, are dedicated to the improvement of the working conditions of their members, just as they are in other industrialized countries, although, to be sure, Japanese workers seem to be more willing to moderate their annual wage demands than jeopardize their company's market share and competitive position.

The major contribution of industrial relations to Japan's success has actually been in three contiguous areas: One, there is greater wage flexibility, as seen in the bonus system—an employee's income may drop as much as forty percent during bad economic times—and greater flexibility in transferring workers from one activity to another. Two, joint consultation groups between managers and labor union officials discuss management policies, fringe benefits, production plans, working conditions, etc. (This effort at information sharing and enhancement of worker awareness is an activity distinct from collective bargaining.) Of 5,000 private corporations with at least 100 employees, more than seventy percent have such joint consultation groups. And third are the famous quality-control circles and the first-line supervisor or foreman system, both adopted from the United States. By 1980 Japan had some 115,000 QC-circles with more than one million participants.

These contributions changed industrial relations in Japan from the hostile and adversarial confrontations of the immediate postwar period to the more harmonious and cooperative relationships that fuel industry today.

3. In the industrial world today, Japan has one of the smallest discrepancies between the lowest and the highest wage scales, resulting in a middle class that forms the huge majority of the population. For this reason there are probably few Japanese today who are seriously discontented with their lot, or at least not enough so to man the barricades or plant bombs in the main offices of major corporations.

Granted, such has happened in the past, for there is still

among the Japanese what was once called their 'assassination mentality,' but the students who rioted in the streets in the late Sixties are now, for the most part, steadfastly climbing their way up corporate ladders so that such disruption is no longer a significant element in Japan's business climate, which must, in part, be due to the comparatively few extremely affluent and extremely indigent in Japan.

4.   Japan is blessed with a societal discipline that is lacking in the multi-ethnic culture of the U.S. and even in other Western economic democracies, with the exception of Germany. The Japanese have accepted lower standards of personal comfort and sacrificed personal ambitions and desires—almost instinctively, it seems—for the collective good more willingly than any other people in the industrialized nations. Observers and commentators on the Japan scene who spend only a short while in the comparative comfort of Western lodging there can never appreciate what the middle-class Japanese company employee or factory hand endures in his daily round, for it is seldom revealed to them, and many are beguiled by an apparent evidence of comfort and plenty. Ninety-nine percent of all homes, for instance, have refrigerators, the same percentage have color TV-sets, ninety-eight percent have washing machines, and over half have microwave ovens. In fact, the abundance of appliances is such that one-fifth of Japanese living space is given over to them.

But behind all this glitter and electrical modernization stand grimly the cramped quarters, the one-to -three hours of commutation time aboard impossibly crowded trains and subways, the mind-wracking problems and costs of getting a child into a decent school, the concern of how to cope upon enforced retirement at fifty-five or fifty-seven without an adequate retirement base, subsistence mostly on rice, pickled vegetables, and occasional fish, screen-less windows, the relatively few homes with flush toilets and central air conditioning, and so on *ad infinitum*. It may be true that Americans are too comfort-loving, but surely the Japanese are a long way from reaching that stage.

Their willingness to accept this degree of discomfort in personal living arrangements may not be fully realized by most of them either, having no basis for comparison, but it is nevertheless a tremendous factor in their national success, as is their haunting memory of many years of scarcity.

Another facet of this societal discipline or national attitude is the willingness of the Japanese to accept, without significant demurral, basic changes in organization, personnel utilization and so forth.

5.   The massive destruction inflicted on Japan by American bombers in 1944-45 provided Japanese industries with both the opportunity and the incentive to build newer and more productive plants than their foreign competitors.

6.   Japan has fewer restrictions and barriers to inter-company joint research and development projects than the U.S.

7.   Tough competition in Japan's domestic marketplace provides excellent training for product rivalry abroad.

8.   The ownership of Japanese corporate debt is mostly in the hand of financial institutions. With easier credit accessibility, firms are more likely to incur debt to expand their market share, increase their productive capacity and growth, and invest in new, longer-term, riskier projects with less rapid payback and lower profits—all this with foreseeable results.

9.   As noted elsewhere herein, the distance between the top echelon and the factory floor in a Japanese corporation is much shorter than in many in America, resulting not only in better communication but also a heightened sense of corporate unity. In the example cited in another chapter, Ford has twelve layers of organization in contrast

to only seven at Toyota, a similar company. Also, because there are fewer private offices even among the higher ranks in Japan, the lower-level employee feels less constraint in approaching an executive's desk and saying whatever is on his mind. For example, the office of the president of Honda's Ohio plant has no door, and any employee can talk directly to him at anytime.

One of the writers (JS) remembers when he was in the export section of a Japanese company in 1956-59. All of the thirty-five or so staff members of that section had their desks in one large room together with a senior managing director: the number two man in the corporation. This director had no secretary, and the employees could approach him at any time. Indeed, because all the desks were so close together, he would often overhear conversations at nearby desks and join in them himself or ask the participants to gather at his side.

When there was reason for a formal discussion involving the president of the company, the staff would use the corporate conference room, but when someone wanted a private talk with another member of the staff, they would usually retire to the tea shop several doors away.

10. According to the *Economist*, most of Japan's growth since 1973 arises from the investments by their private corporations in energy-efficient machinery.

11. Another important element in Japan's success story is the absence of any legislation, such as the Glass-Steagall Act, which prevents banks from owning stock in private corporations, and the role played by Japanese banks in such owned companies has been delineated above.

12. The limited Japanese budget for defense is important. By restricting money spent on defense, it is true that the Japanese can thereby earmark large sums for other useful purposes, but this is a complicated situation and by pressing the Japanese to re-arm, the U.S. may be opening

a Pandora's box. Given the deep-seated opposition of the Japanese people to war and to military forces, one must wonder just how strongly they would support and participate in a defense effort if they were forced to don the panoply of Mars. Most of them still seem to feel that Japan can be the Swizerland of the East: always the observer, never a participant. How farfetched this desire may be is another matter but one certainty is that possessing a cannon is not the same thing as being willing to fire it with deadly intent.

13. Next come a grab-bag full of reasons, each with its own role to play in the success story:

a. Japan's low birth rate.

b. A transportation system ideal for their topography and the relative nearness to each other of all their most important domestic points of shipping and receiving.

c. Among the industrialized nations, the world's lowest crime rate.

d. A stable and relatively mild climate. Although much is made of their earthquakes, typhoons, and tidal waves, the total effect of these, in terms of crops damaged and lost, is less than the havoc that can be caused by an extended drought or major flooding in such land masses as the U.S., Russia, and China.

e. A relatively simple national diet. For all the fancy foods that can be had—at extravagent prices—in the cities, Japanese dietary requirements are relatively modest and bear a certain analogy to the spartan wartime diet of their soldiery: a few balls of rice. Of course, this would be inadequate by today's standards, but when one sees the bowl of instant noodles or the rice, pickled vegetables, thin soup, and a small piece of broiled fish which many Japanese regard as a quite plentiful meal, one cannot help but think of the contrast with what Americans consider an adequate meal, with all its trimmings and especially its emphasis on butter, bread, fats, and sugars.

f. The manual dexterity of the Japanese.

g. Their racial homogeneity and comparative lack of genuine racial disorder.

h. Japan has no land borders through which millions of illegal aliens can infiltrate to partake of its bounty and thereby lessen each legal resident's rightful share.

i. Although Japan takes decent care of its truly indigent and physically handicapped, it has few of the social welfare systems that are emasculating the U.S.

j. The percentage of Japanese who are gainfully employed is significantly larger than the equivalent American figure.

k. Surely the Japanese willingness to learn from foreign sources is one of their greatest strengths. The Japanese will go to amazing lengths to study. An illustrative incident that JS recalls is that of a Japanese ear, nose, and throat specialist, who—when in his 70's—received an invitation to attend a convention of ENT doctors to be held eight months later in Philadelphia. Like most Japanese doctors of his age, Dr. Kurosu had studied German in medical school so his English knowledge was limited to what he could remember from his high school days.

Even so, he hired a tutor and studied English three evenings every week during the intervening eight months in order to learn as much as he could at the medical convention, which was to last only one week. To JS, this elderly doctor has long typified the eagerness of the Japanese to learn.

14. In 1980 the savings rate in Japan was about twen-

ty percent of personal income, more than three times the U.S. rate and the second highest in the world, after Switzerland. Americans not only do not save significantly, they prefer to spend before they earn, which is why the average American is several thousand dollars in debt while his Japanese counterpart has as much or more tucked away drawing interest that is largely tax-free. (A 1984 Sanwa Bank survey of 1,000 company employees in the Kinki Region found that couples had an average of five million yen—about $21,270—saved.)

This leads, of course, to a high rate of capital formation, which spurs industrial growth.

15. One important element in the attitude of the Japanese wage-earner toward savings is the design of his tax system, which permits him to exempt much interest from taxes. For instance, in 1981, the tax-payer who saved part of his salary through his company savings plan paid no tax at all on the first $22,600 of his savings. Also tax-free is interest from the first $13,600 in a postal savings account, and one can seemingly have as many accounts as the number of post offices he cares to visit, since there are twice as many postal savings accounts in Japan as there are people.

The U.S., however, encourages borrowing, rewards consumption, and taxes interest on savings. No other country permits unlimited tax deductions for interest paid on loans, and its total taxes on purchases are the lowest in the industrialized world, according to David Wyss of Data Resources, Inc.

A tax system that encourages growth is a most important element in the story of Japan's success. During the nineteen years from 1951 to 1970, Japan's real GNP grew at the average rate of nine percent a year, but during that period, local and national taxes decreased from twenty-two percent of national income to eighteen percent, while those of the U.S. *rose* from twenty-eight to over thirty-one percent. It should be noted, however, that for any one in Japan making over $210,000, the income tax rate rises to 78%.

In any case, the average tax burden in Japan is $2,634 per person, in comparison to $3,832 in the U.S.

Further, the inheritance tax in Japan is considerably lower than in the U.S., especially since their tax codes greatly undervalue real estate.

16.   Another reason that deserves a place in this listing is the one given by the late Kurt Singer, a German economist and sociologist, who explained that Japan works so well not because of the "rationalized perfection of its mammoth organizations" but because of the "dense tissue of its small social relationships."

Chapter Seven
Foreign Trade

The issue of the trade imbalance between Japan and the United States—who between them account for 25% of all the trade of the world—is a thorny and complicated one, with large numbers on both sides seeing their own position as essentially correct and that of the other side as unreasonable, self-deceiving, or unethical.

Many Japanese see themselves as scapegoats whom American politicians and labor unions want to use to camouflage their own inadequacies and unwillingness to take steps that would be unpopular with their constituents or members. Many Americans, on the other hand, are convinced that the Japanese will stoop to stealing trade secrets and designs, dump products when it suits them, undersell other countries only because they pay low wages, and pursue commercial advantage with a dedication and ruthlessness that is utterly unethical in a community of nations supposedly bound to each other by treaties of friendship and mutual understanding and assistance.

In the face of such criticisms, the typical Japanese reaction is to say little, adopt what they call a *tei-shisei* or low posture, and either extend a "voluntary" export quota for another year or protest that their own market is now "completely open" or at least "as open as that of any of the other industrialized nations."

Faced with such protestations, Laurens Jan Brinkhorst, a senior European Community representative in Tokyo, was quoted by the *Japan Times* of 5 January, 1984 as responding, ". . . . under the surface, formidable barriers to imports still remain, such as Japanese attitudes—especially the 'behavioral mentality' of Japanese bureaucrats and customs officials—the complexities of the distribution system, or the almost complete dominance achieved by Japanese products before tariffs and import restrictions were largely removed."

Brinkhorst later added fuel to his charges by pointing out that Japan's imports of manufactured goods, as a percentage of their gross national product, has remained at about 2.5% for the past 20 years.

A further American perception of Japan these days is that of a nation ungrateful for postwar aid and leniency that has taken advantage of American good will and generosity with unethical trade practices.

Ethical standards in both countries, however, are somewhat different, with an example of our differing perceptions being the question of reciprocity. Americans have tended to take the view that what is fair for one side is fair for the other, while the Japanese doubt that there should be true reciprocity between any two nations when one has twice as many people and twenty-five times as much land. Moreover, the Japanese attitude of *amae*—to presume on the good will of a stronger party—has characterized their attitude toward the U.S. throughout most of the years since 1945. No matter how the Americans bluster and threaten, the Japanese have not been able to bring themselves to really believe that the U.S. would put into effect its own threats of protectionism, which have been increasing as the levels of self-justifying rhetoric rise on both sides of the Pacific. Besides, the Japanese planners know very well the disastrous effects of the highly protectionist Hawley-Smoot Tariff Act of 1929 and how hesitant the U.S. administration is to support protective tariffs or other such measures for that reason.

However, Japan has practiced protectionism in many glaring forms during most of the four decades since 1945 without suffering any of the unfortunate consequences brought on by the Hawley-Smoot Act. Part of their technique was to raise their barriers quietly, without fanfare, in hundreds of little-noticed ways, but if the U.S. tried to raise such barriers, American importers would flood Congress with their protests.

Another Japanese attitude that may explain to some extent their seeming recalcitrance to lowering trade barriers is the traditional feeling that when a weaker man wrestles with a stronger opponent, the former should be allowed to employ any means, fair or foul, to compensate for his weakness.

In any event, in defense of their own position, the Japanese have raised certain questions that are thought-provoking. The following are from Japanese sources:

a. In November, 1983, General Motors announced a record annual profit of $3.7 billion, followed in February, 1984 by Ford with $1.87 billion and by Chrysler with $701 million, both records. These profits, which helped America's car industry recover from its three previous years of losses, were possible because Japan refrained from exporting its lower-priced models. The American car buyer paid more than he would have otherwise, and these additional payments went into the coffers of the Detroit manufacturers.

Now the United Auto Workers are demanding that the car makers give back to them, from these record profits, all the salary increases and benefits they believe they deserved but did not receive during the previous bad years, in addition to demanding increased benefits and raises for the future.

The result is that the extra money from the pockets of the American car buyers went to the manufacturers, who now may have to turn most or all of it over to their labor union members, who are already the highest paid in the world ($25 an hour in wages and fringe benefits).

b. If Japan's barriers to imports are so difficult, why is it that the European share of Japan's total imports has been rising while the U.S. share has been declining—or remaining about level?

c. In 1982 the U.S. sold 36,000 tons of beef to Japan and now demands that such imports be freed entirely. But if the dollars that the U.S. would earn from the sale of that much or more beef is so important to the U.S. economy, why does America *import* seventeen times that much (low-grade) beef from other countries such as Australia and Argentina?

d. For 1983 the U.S. announced a $21.7 billion trade deficit with Japan (although Japanese sources figured the deficit at $18.1 billion). For 1984 the U.S. trade deficit with Mexico, which is selling more oil to the U.S. while the devaluation of its peso has lessened its ability to import American merchandise, turned out to be $6.3 billion and the deficit with Canada added up to $20.4 billion. In other words, on the North American continent alone, America's trade deficit was more than $26 billion.

What the deficit with Japan for 1985 will be remains to be seen, but for 1984, at least, it was less than $37 billion. Why then is little heard about these other deficits? Would it not be wise for the U.S. to spend some of its energies on exports to its neighbors? We Japanese understand that the Americans are glad to have sources of oil and natural gas so near to home, but after all it is the *overall* trade deficit that should be addressed, not just the one with our country.

e. According to *American* sources, if all Japanese barriers to trade were done away with immediately, U.S. exports to Japan would increase by only $1.5-$5 billion. And if *all* barriers to trade in *both* the U.S. and Japan were completely dismantled, "the Japanese trade balance would benefit—not ours," according to C. Fred Bergsten, director of the Institute for International Investment.

f. Even when Americans who know the Japanese language and are familiar with its culture, history, psychology, negotiating practices, geography, and customs, are available, they are seldom utilized by either the U.S. government or by private corporations. The U.S. Department of Commerce and to a lesser degree, the Department of State, for some unaccountable reason, rarely assign culture and language experts to handle their business dealings with Japan. Japanese government agencies, including the Ministry of Foreign Affairs, the Japan External Trade Organization (JETRO), and the Japan National Tourist Organization and private corporations assign their best English-language speakers to their offices in the United States. There are more than a few Americans who study Japan in colleges and who are familiar with our language and culture; yet they can't get jobs with either the U.S. government or private corporations. Instead U.S. government agencies and firms send out to Tokyo people who, though expert in U.S. law or engineering or business methods, lack the ability to communicate well with the Japanese. If Japanese government organizations or companies followed U.S. practices, there would be no trade surplus and Japan would sell very little in the U.S. Japanese like to do business with and are greatly impressed and flattered by Americans who truly know their country, its language, culture, and customs.

g. In October, 1983 Potomac Associates, an American survey and research organization, released the results of a poll that found that nearly half (47 percent) of American citizens blame the U.S. trade deficit with Japan mainly on their own country, with only 37 percent laying the blame at the door of Japan.

Like domestic commerce, foreign trade is desirable only as long as it is conducted in such a way that both the buyer and seller benefit. Although there may be periods when one country sells substantially more than it buys or purchases much more than it sells, this cannot last too long or a government will intervene.

The United States has suffered trade deficits with Japan since 1968. These have soared in recent years, growing from over $5 billion in 1976 to $36.8 billion in 1984. And at present projected rates of growth, they will rise to $50 billion in 1985, to $65 billion in 1986, and to $75 billion in 1987.

Common Market deficits grew enormously as well, rising from $9.5 billion in 1982 to $12 billion in 1983. Japan also enjoys trade surpluses with many other countries, including its neighbors: Taiwan, South Korea, Hong Kong, the Philippines, Thailand, and Singapore, with Taiwan trade being in surplus from 1952 to 1982, except for 1955. Most of these nations were able to buy from Japan because they enjoyed large surpluses in their own trade with the

United States. Taiwan, for instance, had a trade surplus with the U.S. of $4.2 billion in 1982 but a deficit of $2.3 billion in its trade with Japan, so it was the dollars it earned from the United States that enabled it to make purchases from Japan.

Theoretically, when one country buys more from another than it sells over a long period of time, a correction in foreign exchange rates will result: As foreign suppliers accumulate more of the buyer's money than they require, it drops in value, making prices of the seller's products more expensive and forcing the buyer to reduce his purchases and increase his sales.

The United States suffered a deficit in its world merchandise trade in 1982 that amounted to almost $32 billion, fifty-three percent of which came from trade with Japan. The deficit rose to $69.4 billion in 1983 and topped $120 billion in 1984. One of the reasons for these huge deficits was that the U.S. dollar was overvalued in terms of foreign money, making American goods and services relatively expensive and foreign goods cheap.

Inflationary effect of U.S. government borrowing
The question would naturally be asked: "Why wouldn't normal foreign exchange market adjustments drive the dollar down in terms of foreign currencies and thus lead to a balance in trade?"

This has not taken place because of another factor: inflation in the U. S. leading to higher interest rates. When the American government suffers from deficits in its revenue-expense budget, it must borrow money to cover them, and the interest rate must be set sufficiently high to attract lenders. Much of the money comes from the huge accumulations of dollars overseas that were built up from U.S. trade deficits. Foreigners are attracted by the high interest rates and the comparative stability of the United

States. As long as the money continues to pour in from overseas, there is no pressure to revalue the dollar downward.

It might be asked: "Why does the U.S. government spend so much more than it takes in through taxation, thus leading to inflation and high interest rates?"

The answer lies with the enormous social welfare budget, to which American politicians are committed to get popular support, and the defense budget, to which the U.S. is committed in its endeavors to protect itself and its allies from the ever-growing inroads of Russian Communism. The defense budget alone for 1984 was only slightly less than the overall budget deficit of some $200 billion which itself was the largest in history.

It is generally believed that were it not for American military prowess, aggressor nations would take over much of the free world and impose on it their social and political systems. Therefore, Americans feel that the beneficiaries of U.S. military power, of which Japan is one, should, as a matter of fairness, do what they can to share the burden.

Japan's defense policy

The Japanese suffered from the aggressiveness of their *gumbatsu* (military clique) from 1931 until 1945 and do not want to see a recrudescence of that militarism. For this reason the Diet refuses to allow its defense budget to be raised to a level where its armed forces might again dominate domestic politics and become a menace in the Far East.

Japan's military forces, according to the U.S. Department of Defense, are extremely outdated and insufficient even for the defense of the sea lanes within a 1,000-mile radius of the country, and the U.S. feels compelled to carry this defense responsibility for Japan. Many believe this is inequitable and that Japan is getting what they call a "free ride." They point out that the U.S. could save tens of billions of dollars each year if it could considerably reduce the size of its air force and navy in the Far East. They remind their Japanese friends that the oil lifeline from the Persian Gulf to the Inland Sea is patrolled by U.S. warships. They ask, "If the Diet is unable to get public support to increase the size of the naval forces, couldn't Japan at least bear part of the cost of the U. S. fleet?" A suggestion has been made that Japan build and then lend-lease aircraft carriers and other vessels to the U.S. Navy. The lease rentals would be small, for instance, $1 million a year per vessel. Considering that the United States spends $3½–4 billion to build a single aircraft carrier, the significance of having Japan construct and lend-lease to the U.S. such ships becomes apparent.

Japan's military procurement practices
Japan's Self Defense Forces, small though they are, spend a good deal of money on modern equipment, and much of what they require has been developed at great expense by the U.S. Department of Defense. Instead of buying this equipment from the United States and thus reducing the trade deficit, the Japanese instead insist upon manufacturing it is their own factories. This policy appears to be basicly unfair, for the Japanese not only pass up the chance of helping the country that is spending such huge sums to defend them, but they also insist upon learning relevant U.S. manufacturing and design secrets so that they may build an arms industry competitive with the American.

As an illustration, in testimony before the Sub-Committee on International Trade of the Senate Committee on Finance on March 6, 1973, Andrew J. Biemiller, AFL/CIO Director of Legislation, declared: "The AFL/CIO has learned that the Thor-Delta launch rocket and its entire missile launch system are now in the process of being sold to the Japanese by McDonnell-Douglas Corp., a multinational firm. . . . The basic system was developed at (American) tax payer expense and cost millions of dollars in research and development funds before it became operational . . . launching work provided the U.S. with millions of dollars in funds helping offset the balance of payments deficit . . . but this sale, which of course benefits the U.S. balance of payments this one time, will adversely effect the U. S. balance of payments for years to come.''

Mr. Biemiller then added: "In military aircraft too, American industrial leadership is being rapidly sold off and exported abroad. McDonnell-Douglas has licensed Mitsubishi of Japan to build 91 F–4 fighter planes, the famous Phantom fighters. . . . The result is a heavy loss of employment amongst highly trained U.S. aircraft technicians . . . the loss of an export industry, and the transfer of a total military production facility to another nation. Earlier the F–104 Starfighter followed the same export route. When Japan wanted the F–104 Starfighter, then built by Lockheed in California, it arranged to have it built in Japan. . . . Now, of course, Japan has the technology as well as the plane. Other commercial and military exports—with resultant job losses—are the production in Japan of the Sikorsky S-61 helicopter and the Pratt & Whitney JT S D turbofan engine for the C-1 U.S. military transport.''

Japan's Self Defense Forces also require the U.S. P-3 C antisubmarine patrol planes. Instead of buying them from the U.S. maker, Lockheed, and thus helping reduce the trade imbalance, the Defense Agency in Tokyo demands that approximately 90% of the planes be manufactured in Japan, an extreme example of a 'local content law' that the Japanese find so objectionable when the shoe is on the other foot.

In late July, 1983, the United States Special Trade Representative, William Brock, accused Japan of unfair conduct in the procurement of F-15 fighter planes. He pointed out that instead of buying them from America, and thereby helping reduce the trade imbalance, the Japanese insisted upon manufacturing them under license from McDonnell-Douglas. If this would have saved the Japanese money, it might have been less distressing, but the cost of manufacture in Japan ranges from $20 million to $40 million more per plane than if they were built in the United States.

In the words of an American aerospace executive, "When a U.S. corporation enters into a joint venture with a Japanese company, the Japanese always come out of it having learned more than us Americans. We build the first generation ourselves, the second generation with them, and then they build the third generation without us—and better."

Japan's aircraft industry

William Brock complained further that the reason Japan wanted to make the planes at home was in order to gain technology and experience so that it could further expand its own domestic aircraft industry, which suspicion is supported by MITI's announcement that the creation of a strong domestic aircraft manufacturing industry is one of its prime targets. That the U.S. government eyes with doubt and caution, therefore, cooperative ventures between U.S. aircraft and Japanese manufacturers should not be surprising.

An article by Howard Banks in *Forbes* magazine in its September 13, 1982 issue states that America's largest export earner outside agriculture is commercial airliners and the fan jet engines that power them. The *Forbes* article goes on to predict that this industry is about to be infiltrated by the Japanese, and when discussing U.S.-Japan cooperation in building a 150-seat plane, asserts it is folly to share crucial export-earnings technology with the Japanese.

It is highly probable that when Japan builds more planes and exports them to world markets in competition with U.S. makers, the trade imbalance will rise even higher. In spite of this, U.S. manufacturers continue their march into commercial oblivion.

The Martin Marietta Corp. in late 1982 signed a basic technology licensing contract with Nissan Motors by which the U.S. firm would provide Nissan with design and manufacturing technology on space rockets and the various missiles it had developed. The *Nihon Keizai Shimbun* correspondent, in reporting Nissan's entry into the defense aerospace business under this license, predicted that this arrangement would alarm the U.S. administration, which had become increasingly nervous about the continuing outflow of aerospace and military technology to Japan.

The Long Term Credit Bank of Japan in its *Research Bulletin* of April, 1983 reported that through participation in five major military and civilian aircraft production projects with America, Japanese manufacturers would probably acquire advanced technologies in design, forming and processing of new materials, as well as engine production know-how, the latest break-throughs in avionics, and other technical aircraft production information.

U.S. assistance in helping Japan build its own civilian aircraft manufacturing industry goes back many years. Mr. A. J. Biemiller of the AFL/CIO, in testimony before the Senate Committee on Finance on March 6, 1973, said: "Recently the Boeing Company entered into an agreement with the Japanese government to develop a new wide-bodied air bus. Technology for the short-haul airliner will come from Seattle. The work will be done in Japan by employees of three manufacturers—Mitsubishi, Kawasaki, and Fuji. . . . At the same time, United Aircraft is helping Mitsubishi produce gas turbine aircraft engines. The technology comes from East Hartford, Connecticut, an area with very high unemployment."

In 1981 Boeing and Alitalia joined the three Japanese firms to produce the B-767. Production was started in 1982 and plans call for the completion of 1,000 planes during the 1980's. Then in March, 1983, the Boeing Company reached an agreement with the same three Japanese companies to develop the next generation medium-range 150-seat jet passenger aircraft called the YXX series. A month later the Douglas Aircraft Co. proposed joint production of airliners with Mitsubishi, Kawasaki, and Fuji. Specifically, it offered to consign the manufacture of parts for its DC Super-82 and Super-90 to the Japanese airplane makers on a subcontract basis. It also proposed a tie-up to produce its subsequent plane, the MD 100, and split sales of assembled planes on the basis of the production sharing ratio, and lastly, it expressed the wish to undertake development, production, sales, and maintenance of its planned D3300 jointly on an equal footing.

The cost of developing aircraft is enormous. Howard Banks in his article in the Sept. 13, 1982 issue of *Forbes* stated that it "costs around $1.5 billion to launch a new airframe today, followed by another $1.5 billion to put it into full production. For an engine derived from an existing one the cost would be a mere $750 million while an all-new engine could cost twice that."

The American engine maker, Pratt & Whitney, which had spent almost $1 billion over the previous three years developing an engine called the PW2037 for Boeing's new 180 seat B-757 airliner, proposed in early 1982 that they tieup with Rolls Royce and a consortium of three Japanese firms. The Japanese asked Pratt for a guarantee of access to the American market if they joined. Howard Banks, in his article in *Forbes*, posed the question: "If the engine uses Pratt's American technology, how will the Defense Department react? Secretary Cap Weinberger is known to regard the Japanese as suspect when it comes to technological secrets."

The United States is already having problems in another aspect of aircraft manufacture. The so-called general aviation industry, which manufactures small private and executive-type aircraft, is having difficulties because of foreign competition. The General Aviation Manufacturers Association reported that in 1981 imports of general purpose aircraft were valued at $913 million and exports fell to $749 million.

The obvious reason that Boeing, Douglas, Lockheed, Pratt & Whitney, etc. are licensing the Japanese and then sub-contracting is that the financing costs for developing new aircraft and engines are greater than these private concerns can afford. Under present circumstances, it would appear that the U.S. companies should have obtained aid from the American government in financing the research and development costs, considering that MITI as a general rule is willing to provide fifty percent of the total development expense of new aircraft and engine programs undertaken in Japan.

U.S. aircraft makers and engine manufacturers, because they have licensed Japanese firms or sub-contracted or entered into joint ventures with them, may have created competitors who will in time devour them.

Questions to be considered are:

1. Were the American airplane and engine makers naive in facilitating the entry of the Japanese into their industry?

2. Were the Americans so eager to find short-term solutions—licensing, sub-contracting, etc.—that they

overlooked the potentially disastrous long-term implications?

3. Was the Japan Defense Agency unfair in compelling U.S. manufacturers to license Japanese firms rather than importing the planes and engines from America and thus helping balance trade between the two nations?

4. In the early 1970's MITI labeled aerospace, along with computers and alternate energy technology, as one of the three main pillars for the nation's future economic growth. Was it equitable to include aerospace considering that even as far back as the early 1970's the U.S. was suffering from a large trade imbalance and badly needed to nourish its aerospace industry?

5. Many of the world's civil airline companies are now suffering heavy financial losses. Under these circumstances is it really necessary at present to develop costly new aircraft in any country?

6. What can the American and Japanese governments do to solve such problems before they become unmanageable?

Unfair trade practices
Even though Japan has enjoyed a surplus in its foreign trade since the mid-1960's, it continues to exclude by varied means foreign products and services that, if allowed into the country, would help in solving the increasingly worrisome trade imbalances.

a. The Narita Airport pipeline barrier
In August, 1983, a new pipeline was opened to deliver fuel from Chiba barges in Tokyo Bay to the airplanes flying in and out of the Narita Airport. The story of its possible effects on foreign airlines using Narita was related by Clyde McAvoy in the June, 1983 issue of the *Journal of the*

American Chamber of Commerce in Japan in an article entitled "The 35-Mile Tab."

All air carriers using Narita were, of course, expected to buy their fuel from the tanks at Narita that were filled from this source, but the problem was that the pipeline charge was 17¢ per gallon. By international standards this is extraordinarily high. At New York's Kennedy Airport, for instance, fuel is delivered for 3/4¢ per gallon over a 32-mile pipeline. Hong Kong delivers it for 3¢ per gallon, and Chicago's O'Hare Airport charges only 1/4¢ per gallon. The explanation for the high cost at Narita lies in the expenses incurred in building the pipeline, which were $468 million or 2,340% more than one recently constructed in Europe of similar length.

The 17¢ per gallon charge is one which the airlines cannot well afford. As Clyde McAvoy described it: "To meet just the pipeline costs, airlines departing Narita would have to find an additional five passengers per flight. To understand the magnitude of the task, it is helpful to know that one U.S. airline chief executive estimated that if his company could have boarded just one more passenger on each of its flights in 1982, he would have been able to report a profit instead of a multimillion dollar loss. . . . Of the 35 airlines operating there (Narita) this year, five or fewer will be in the black, even at current operating costs. If the new pipeline costs are enforced, there will be none."

McAvoy indicated in his article that the effect of the high pipeline charge would be to stunt the operations of airlines already flying into Narita and discourage any others who might think of coming in. But what about Japan's flag carrier?

JAL will have to pay the same charge as the others, but it is 41% owned by the government and is not going to quit flying in and out of its home airport regardless of the loss since the government stands behind it.

Foreign airlines not owned by governments—including all American carriers—are in no condition to absorb such losses and in time may have to stop calling at Narita. If they do, JAL and such others (mostly government-owned) that can remain will sell enough extra seats to make a considerable profit and recoup previous losses.

The questions may be asked: Is the high fuel cost fair? If it is exorbitant, should the Japanese government absorb some of the cost so that foreign airlines will not have to stop flying into Japan?

b. Automobile imports into Japan

Without doubt, the most successful and controversial export from Japan is the automobile. Much less discussed, however, is the import of foreign cars into Japan. Japan's automobile industry is the world's largest. In 1982 it produced 11,353,751 passenger cars and commercial vehicles. Of these 6,204,817 were exported, including the 1,800,611 that went to the United States.

But imports of foreign cars in Japan totalled a mere 35,000, of which number only 3,484 came from the U.S. Sales of Japanese cars, trucks, and buses in Japan itself amounted to 5,261,431 in 1982.

Japan's strategy in shutting out competition is well expressed in an article by Glenn Davis in the May, 1983 *Journal of the American Chamber of Commerce in Japan*. Davis quoted Mr. Luder Payser, president of the German automaker BMW's Japan operation: "I believe that the total domination of the Japanese market by local manufacturers nowadays is historically a result of effectively closing this market by fiscal, technical, and administrative measures for many years until the time Japanese car makers achieved their current strength."

Considering that Japanese automobile manufacturers have a firm grip on foreign markets and do not need to worry about an invasion of their own, it might be expected that all the barriers to imports of cars into Japan would be removed. An obvious reason for doing this would be to avoid provoking the erection of retaliatory barriers against imports of Japanese cars in those countries most injured by those imports. Although some barriers to such importation have been removed, many still remain.

Payser of BMW described some of the remaining barriers: "... BMW Japan—like other foreign auto importers—still faces substantial barriers in penetrating the Japanese market. The government insists on 30 modifications to each BMW before it enters Japan, and a lengthy inspection process takes about two months ... a 22.5% commodity tax on landed cost, sizable dealer markups and inspection and freight costs severely reduce the competitiveness of foreign imports. For example, a BMW 3181 that sells for the equivalent of ¥2.7 million in West Germany is priced at ¥4 million in Japan. Passing individual type approvals on all models once they arrive in the Japanese market seems an unnecessary form of red tape to foreign companies. Although these models, in BMW's case, have already been (officially) approved in the company's factories in West Germany before they are exported, it does not cut any ice with the Japanese authorities. Each model then has to be inspected individually before it can be licensed. This practice contrasts starkly to locally manufactured vehicles which require only a 'final inspection' before they can take the road.''

The damage being done to the United States automobile manufacturing industry by the huge volume of imports from Japan has been widely discussed. Several hundred thousand workers have been laid off, and the industrial cities of Michigan, Ohio, and Indiana that live off the automotive business have been shaken badly. Imports of cars rose 41.5% between 1979 and 1982, while employment fell by 46.9%. With unemployment so high, the damage to the morale of the people in those areas has been incalculable. In 1984 Detroit, Michigan—the heart of the car business—had the highest crime rate in the country, totalling 141.6 per 1,000 residents of that city.

The following questions should be asked:

1. Why are the officials responsible for processing foreign cars at ports of entry in Japan still applying non-tariff barriers to keep them out?

2. Why have the auto workers' unions in America pushed wages and fringe benefits up so high that they have literally priced themselves out of the market?

3. Is the Japanese strategy mentioned by Payser of BMW, namely keeping competitive foreign products off the Japanese market until the domestic industry became strong enough to be unassailable at home, being followed in many other Japanese industries as well?

4. If this be true, will other industrialized countries start following Japan's lead and use the same strategy?

5. If so, will this ultimately reduce world trade to mere exchanges of raw materials?

c. Shipping by ocean vessel

According to an article by Karen Sugiyama in the May, 1983 issue of the *Journal of the American Chamber of Commerce in Japan,* Japanese shipping lines carry about 65% of all conference cargo moving from Japan to the U.S. The American shipping lines have perhaps a 30% share of the conference cargo, and about 20% of the total. Of shipments from the U.S. to Japan, the Japanese lines carry some 50%, while the Americans account for only 10%.

A number of non-tariff barriers handicap foreign shipping lines. As an example, in transporting leaf tobacco from the U.S. to Japan, until 1982 only Japanese lines were permitted to carry this product. The reason given by the Japan Tobacco and Salt Monopoly Corporation was that only the experienced Japanese shipping companies could be relied upon. This unfair trade practice exacerbated Americans, who felt that U.S. firms know how to ship tobacco very well, having done so much longer than the Japanese. One of the American shippers was, in fact, a subsidiary of a tobacco company and unquestionably skilled in handling the product.

Another problem concerned freight rates. Karen Sugiyama, while describing the under-the-table kickbacks granted chosen major accounts in Japan, wrote, "This practice is illegal in the United States but is said to be a common part of doing business not only by Japanese lines, but by other foreign lines as well."

Question: Was the Japan Tobacco and Salt Monopoly Corporation directly influenced by Japanese ocean shipping lines to deny foreign firms the right to transport tobacco—or was this merely an act based on a sincere belief that only Japanese could properly handle the product?

d. Other barriers.

Besides those listed above, there are countless other barriers. In the May 31, 1983 issue of the *Japan Economic Journal,* the president of the American Chamber of Commerce in Japan, Lawrence F. Snowden, raised several points. He stated that while the Japanese government had made many promises to facilitate importing, some of them could not be carried out until changes were made in laws and regulations by the Diet. In the previous sixteen months, the Japanese government had committed itself to adoption of three trade liberalization packages, but actual implementation of the first two had been so painfully slow that they were still more air than action. Snowden added: "Widely publicized liberalization measures have been, in many cases, form without real substance; too little or too late; or bureaucratic maneuvering to resolve a detail without addressing the basic cause.''

Some Japanese attribute the failure to actually carry out these promises to liberalize to lifetime employment practices in the bureaucracy. They explain that even after a high tariff is reduced or some other barrier to imports is removed, the government officials who were in charge of applying the restrictions are still on the job. They cannot be dismissed or retired, and since many departments have a redundancy of workers anyway, it is difficult to move them to other slots. Since most of them feel it is patriotic to be protectionistic, they find new and devious ways to carry on with the old restrictive policies.

The *Nihon Keizai Shimbun* senior staff writer based in New York, Soshichi Miyachi, in an article dated 25 January, 1983, in the *Japan Economic Journal,* declared: ''I would also like to point out that the gaping divergence between the Japanese government's formal stand on market opening and its actual application is proving a serious obstacle to the entry of foreign commodities into the Japanese market. Cases in point are a notorious variety of non-tariff barriers. Extraordinarily intricate inspection standards and procedures on foreign commodities which can be described as 'super-red tape' are courting criticism even within Japan.''

Miyachi was correct in stating that there was ''criticism even within Japan.'' On April 19, 1982, the *Mainichi* published an opinion poll that disclosed that while 48% of the Japanese queried agreed with the statement that ''Many of the U.S. demands are unjustified,'' 46% believed, on the contrary, that justice was on the side of the U.S.''

Nearly half of Japan's people, therefore, agree with the stand of a foreign country.

Examples of "other barriers" to open trade exist in abundance in Japan. To mention a few:

Item: American and European cosmetics manufacturers were told that they would have to increase the size of the spray nozzles in their aerosol cans by an infinitesimal 0.015 millimeters before their products would be permitted to enter Japan.

Item: Any importer of foreign soap must have a full-time pharmacist on his payroll.

Item: Companies that import gold for use in dentistry must be able to prove that none of their board of directors is a drug addict.

Item: After an exhibition of pharmaceutical equipment in Japan, the Ministry of Health and Welfare informed the exhibitors they would have to send out of Japan the sample equipment imported for display at the exhibition and then apply for an import license, before it could be sold domestically.

Item: High schools in Japan were not permitted to use aluminum baseball bats made in the U.S.—the home of baseball–until as late as January of 1982.

Item: Even though U.S. suppliers could profitably sell soda ash to end users in Japan for $185 to $200 a ton, they are not permitted to market it since this would compete with the four major Japanese producers, who sell their soda ash at $250 to $300 a ton.

Item: Such Japanese banks as the Bank of Tokyo, Sumitomo Bank, and Mitsubishi Bank have taken over banks in the U.S., while American banks are not permitted to acquire banks in Japan. When the Bank of Tokyo, for instance, bought the California First Bank, it thereby acquired 100 branches in California, with full power to accept deposits and act as any other U.S. bank.

Item: The Japanese company Green Cross bought

Alpha, America's second largest collector of blood, but no American company would be permitted to do the same in Japan.

Item: When Fujitsu, Japan's largest computer maker, sought a stronger foothold in the U.S. market, it bought stock in Ampahl, but no U.S. corporation would be allowed to do the equivalent in Japan.

Item: Learning of his company's newly-designed bottles for use with salad dressing, the American representative in Japan cabled his home office to send him some of the new bottles to show to his buyers. The U.S. maker sent a case of the bottles, all full of salad dressing. The Japanese Customs Office—which has been called the "most archaic and stultifying edifice in the Japanese bureaucracy," refused to approve the entry. Hearing this, the American representative offered to empty all the bottles in front of the Customs inspector and take only the bottles, but this was rejected. The case of full bottles was sent back to the U.S.

Item: When importing cosmetics, shampoos, and perfumes, the Ministry of Health and Welfare demands not only a list of the ingredients of each product but a detailed description of how the product is made. If such trade secrets were ever to be shown to competitors, severe financial harm could be done to the owner of the formula.

Item: Then there was the infamous Potato Chip Fiasco to illustrate that the Japanese Customs Service is not above collusion with Japanese manufacturers. When the potato chips were first imported into Japan, Customs classified them as "vegetables prepared or preserved," which carried a duty of 16%. Then sales of the imported potato chips increased, offering serious competition to similar Japanese products. It was then that Japanese Customs decided to reclassify the imports as "pastry, biscuits, cakes, and fine baker's wares," which were dutiable at the much higher rate of 35% and which priced the imports out of the market. (Eventually, after strong protestations, the old rate was re-instated.)

Item: Complying with Japan's testing and certification procedures has been one of the highest barriers to free trade. At the heart of the matter is the fact that until recently Japan would not accept foreign test data, although the U.S. accepted Japanese manufacturers' data as well as the results of tests conducted in hundreds of authorized laboratories in Japan. Indeed, some of the tests done in Japan are themselves highly dubious. Japanese testing labs are faced with backlogs of up to six months, while the tests themselves may take another three or four months, thus seriously delaying the introduction of the imported products to the market and losing vital competitive advantage.

Food exports to Japan

A major cause of contention in U.S.-Japan trade relations is the protective curtain Japan has established to protect its farmers from import competition. The United States argues that Japan's restrictions deny America its best chance of reducing the trade imbalance. Japanese political leaders, on the other hand, explain that it would be risky for Japan to increase its dependence on foreign countries for more of its food. Also, they point out that the farm lobby wields great influence.

The barriers to the importation of foodstuffs are on the whole more clear-cut than those which hamper the entry of manufactured products. While there are twenty -two categories of farm and marine products that are flatly denied entry, many other categories are excluded through devious ways. An example is the importation of cherries.

a. Cherries for the land of cherry blossoms

Although Japan is justly famous for its cherry trees in blossom, the fruit from them is inferior to cherries grown in America. Efforts to import U.S.-grown cherries have, however, been strongly opposed by Japan. In the August 20th, 1979 issue of *Forbes* magazine Anthony Spaeth tells the story. He explains that although the importation of cherries was "liberalized" in 1960, when U.S. growers actually tried to ship them, Japanese officials refused them entry, saying they feared their possible infestation by the codling moth. American cherry experts denied ever having seen a codling moth on a cherry, but an experiment proved that under certain highly unlikely circumstances these moths might lay eggs on cherries.

To solve the moth problem, U.S. cherry growers spent three years devising a fumigation system that would satisfy the Japanese bureaucrats, but what should be kept in mind is that these three years gave the Japanese a face-saving way to postpone the "liberalization."

Finally, the officials in Tokyo agreed to accept some U.S. cherries, but then raised the spectre of cherry fruit flies. When this too was at last laid to rest, they set quotas on cherries: 140,000 boxes for the first year (1978) and 225,000 for the next.

But that wasn't all. These officials decreed that no American cherries could be admitted before 5 July of each year to keep them from competing with Japanese cherries which are harvested a month earlier. The 5 July requirement immediately put all California-grown cherries out of the running because they are harvested at the same time as the Japanese and would spoil if held off the market for a month.

For cherries from other parts of the U.S. that were harvested later and would therefore be in satisfactory condition to enter Japan after 5 July, the Japanese bureaucrats built another barrier: the requirement that the cherries be fumigated at a temperature of 70 degrees, which proved to be difficult because the cherries were generally picked and fumigated on mornings when the temperature was cooler than 70 degrees.

Then the Americans tried using electric heaters in their orchards to raise the temperature, but this artificial heat gave the cherries an unsavory appearance.

There was more to come. The Japanese authorities next insisted that one of their own inspectors oversee the picking and fumigation process. One was dispatched to America, where he demanded to see *each and every* cherry before he would pass it, and sometimes a week would pass between the time the cherries were picked and the inspector got around to looking at them. Finally the inspector relaxed somewhat and mollified his insistence on examining each individual cherry.

Obstacles such as these are not untypical of what foreigners face when trying to get their products into Japan to compete with locally produced items.

Japan's reasons for opposition to food imports

Japan has several reasons for not wanting to increase its imports of agricultural products besides the obvious one: opposition from their farm lobby. The Ministry of Agriculture, Forestry and Fisheries is concerned about possible (1) interruption of sea transportation because of strikes or war; (2) crop failures abroad; (3) poor diplomatic relations with supplier countries; (4) worsening of Japan's foreign trade, leading to a shortage of foreign exchange with which to pay for such food; and (5) global food shortages as a consequence of the high population growth rates in developing countries as well as the flow of immigrants and refugees from those countries into the developed countries that are major sources of food for Japan . . . and the subsequent over-populating of the developed countries by the extremely fertile immigrants and refugees.

How reliable is the United States as a supplier of agricultural products to Japan?

How dependable is the United States, Japan's largest single source of food? How dependable will it be in the year 2,000 or in 2,020? These are questions that concern the Japanese, for the safety of their race may depend on the right answers.

A U.S. government publication "Where Have the Farm Lands Gone?" released in 1979 quotes an article by George Nathan, who makes the following predictions for the year 2,000:

"All food produced in the United States will be consumed here.

"Food exports no longer will be available to help offset massive trade deficits, such as payments for foreign oil. This almost certainly would have a major negative effect on the national economy.

"The hungry people of other nations will be on their own for food supplies."

Mr. Nathan qualified his predictions by stating they would come about only ". . . if farm (land) losses continue." He was referring to the taking out of cultivation of some 3 million acres of farm land each year and its conversion into highways, factories, military bases, stores, office buildings, residential areas, etc.

a. Erosion

Erosion from over-cultivation presents a serious problem in many areas. Some of the richest soil in the country—

top soil that was 25 or 30 inches deep at the beginning of the century—has been eroding so badly that less than 3 inches remain. According to a 188-page report compiled by the Cornucopia Project of Rodale Press of Emmaus, Pennyslvania and reported in a United Press International article of Nov. 26, 1981, the United States is losing about 25 square miles of cropland every day from soil erosion. Considering that it could take as much as 2,000 years to replace just one inch of top soil, it is shocking that Americans have permitted this erosion to take place.

b. Water depletion

A serious depletion of underground water has also taken place. The world's largest subterranean lake is being sucked dry for irrigation purposes. The 177,000 square-mile part of this lake that is drying up most rapidly lies under the farming regions of west Texas, Oklahoma and Kansas and eastern Colorado and New Mexico. Since World War II Texas has drained off 23% of its portion of the water-bearing layer under the ground and New Mexico more than 16%. Unless positive conservation steps are soon taken, a fertile land mass larger than the state of Massachusetts will be lost to cultivation through irrigation by the year 2020.

c. Fertilizer shortage

Essential to soil fertility is the use of proper fertilizer, but it has been predicted that phosphorous for use in fertilizer will be in short supply about the year 2000.

Population growth and immigration control

Many measures are being considered in the United States to forestall a shortage of food. The most important of these is stricter control of immigration, for if foreigners continue to pour into the U.S. at the present level (over 2 million a year), the country will not be able to avoid shortfalls in its food production, and ultimately famines such as are experienced even now in India, Bangladesh, and sub-Saharan Africa will result.

Japanese policy makers watch with close interest the efforts being made in America to stem the inward flow of refugees and immigrants, both legal and illegal. Only if the United States takes prompt action, including the erection an effective barrier along the Mexican border from the Gulf of Mexico to the Pacific, will there be any hope that the country may continue to serve as a reliable source of food.

If the influx of immigrants and refugees is slowed to less than 400,000 per year, the rate of population growth will begin to decline both for this reason and because of a drop in the birth rate. At present the birth rate of the native white population is about equivalent to that of Japan, and is declining. As it declines, the need to convert more farmland to factories, houses, pavement, and office buildings will diminish. Erosion too will be restrained as it will no longer be necessary to plow up marginal land. The drying aquifer under the states of Texas, New Mexico, Oklahoma, Colorado, and Kansas will be given a chance to refill as the demand for irrigation water will decrease as population pressure on the food supply is lessened.

What does all this mean to Japan?

Japan is suffering from some of the same problems faced by the United States. Urban sprawl is taking about 81,000 acres of farmland each year for use as factories, homes, highways, schools, and the like, plus more for afforestation and other purposes. Erosion too is taking its toll, and a growing shortage of freshwater will become serious late in the 1980's. Japan has wisely prevented immigration, so that its population growth rate is low and getting lower.

Nevertheless, just feeding its own people will require adding about 125,000 acres of farmland annually even if food imports remain at present levels. But if food imports are reduced substantially, as they will be if the United States continues to allow itself to be overwhelmed by immigrants from prolific developing countries, then Japan will be faced with a serious problem indeed. Although other countries could conceivably supply Japan with some of its requirements, the problems facing most of them make them even less reliable and more costly as sources than the U.S.

Foreseeing the problems that would arise, Konosuke Matsushita proposed in 1977 that Japan level about 20% of its mountainous area and dump the earth and rock in the adjacent ocean as land for development and agricultural self-sufficiency.

Some possible countermeasures to solve the trade imbalance problem without increasing food imports from the United States

Because of obvious dangers in increasing Japan's dependence on foreign countries for its food supply, other steps must be considered. The trade imbalance with all its attendant troubles will not disappear without prompt and effective corrective measures.

a. A Japan export surcharge

A study group sponsored by the Ministry of Finance tackled the problem and began its investigation in October, 1981. The group was composed of seven academicians, officials of several concerned government agencies, and private citizens. Their recommendations were summarized in an article in the *Japan Economic Journal* of May 4, 1982, viz. ". . . since the floating exchange rate system is not working to effectively adjust trade and the international balance of payments, the establishment of an export surcharge system is necessary to complement the adjustment mechanism.''

The group proposed that the export surcharge be adopted as an interim measure until the floating exchange rate system recovered an adjusting capability in both trade and overall balance of payments. The group drew attention to one of the basic causes of the trade imbalance problem: ''The high American interest rate is a policy measure adopted to control inflation which has weakened the automatic adjustment mechanism of the economy. However, the high interest rate level in the U.S. made it difficult for Japan to expand its domestic demand and almost impossible to rectify the bilateral trade imbalance.''

A second point made by the study group was that ''If an industry in a certain country cannot adapt to the changing international economic environment and fails to make the needed adjustment because of too strenuous pressures from imports, a voluntary restriction measure through bilateral consultations is justifiable.'' They then proposed that the voluntary restrictive measures be permitted for up to three years, during which the necessary industrial reforms would be made in the protected country.

These daring recommendations exhibited an understanding of the problems besetting Japan's international trading partners. Political and economic questions would naturally have to be answered before the export surcharge could be applied. If the U.S. dollar-yen exchange rate of, say, $1.00 to ¥245.00, was considered unrealistic, then a decision would have to be made as to what rate would be proper. If $1.00 to ¥190.00 appeared about equitable considering the purchasing power of the two currencies, then the export surcharge on Japanese exports to the United States would have to be about 27 1/2%. No doubt this would reduce the movement of automobiles, motorcycles, machine tools, steel, *inter alia* across the Pacific, and

American factories could then call back their unemployed workers.

The question arises: Would the labor unions in the U.S. understand that the export surcharge was a temporary measure and refrain from quickly demanding higher wages and benefits that would offset the competitive advantages? Would both labor and management realize that they must take strong action without delay to improve productivity?

b. JETRO Import Educational Program

Several Japanese organizations are promoting an increase in imports. An example is the Japan External Trade Organization (JETRO) where, through its offices overseas and in Japan itself, efforts are being made to educate foreigners in what products would be likely to receive a welcome in Japan, and how to go about marketing them.

c. Shame Project

One proposal that could possibly help in reducing non-tariff barriers and thus opening the Japan market wider would be to publicly bring shame to those who try to keep foreign products and services out of Japan by devious stratagems.

Such a shame campaign was effective in the 1950's and early 1960's in reducing the number of cases in which Japanese companies copied foreign designs and products and sold them in Japan without paying royalties. The campaign took place in response to resentment in foreign countries of the Japanese practice of "*sarumane*" or "monkey-copying."

Those chiefly responsible for the shame campaign were MITI and the Patent Office working in cooperation with major department stores. The modus operandi was to display copied articles in store show windows alongside the originals from abroad with signs saying it was shameful for Japanese manufacturers to stoop to design *"tōyō"* or design "stealing." In one department store in Tokyo alone 150 such articles from all over the world were displayed in its windows.

The campaign was successful, for the number of instances of Japanese companies imitating foreign products without paying royalties dropped dramatically. The Japanese public accepted the MITI-Patent Office shame campaign because they basically disapproved of unethical copying.

The time has come when such a shame campaign should again be initiated, this time against those responsible for the numerous non-tariff barriers. If the devious means employed to keep out foreign products could be given sufficient public exposure, as with the shame campaign of the 1950's and early 1960's, the Japanese might well become sufficiently indignant to force official corrective action.

d. Freeing Japan's money market

It has long been Japan's habit to keep close control over its currency and internal interest rates so that it could freely determine its own domestic monetary and economic policies. Now, at last, Japan is beginning to take a few faltering steps in the direction of internationalizing the yen by agreeing to permit a yen futures market, to make it easier for foreign banks to raise yen, and to sell yen denominated securities in foreign countries. Still, complete de-control will require much more than these three steps.

On the far side of the Pacific from them, the U.S. has an over-valued currency (the dollar is up 40% in value in effective trade terms since 1978) that is the result of a strengthening economic recovery, high interest rates, and international uncertainties that give rise to a "safe-haven" dollar demand, with the high interest rates, of course, being linked to mounting federal deficits.

Reference was made earlier to America's huge and ever-growing international trade deficit. Additionally, the U.S. government is suffering from domestic fiscal indigestion. At the end of 1984, the national debt was $1 trillion, 577 billion. Estimates for the future are gloomy indeed. According to *Budget Briefs*, the Federal debt will rise by $237 billion in 1985, by $239 billion in 1986, and by $257 billion in 1987.

It might seem reasonable to ask why the yen is not freed to supply part of these needs, especially since interest rates in Japan are much lower than what they are in the U.S. The Japanese tried removing most of their restrictions on the yen's international movements between 1980 and 1982 and found that their currency was sucked out of the country as if by a huge vacuum cleaner, with $23 billion leaving in 1981 and $28 billion following in 1982. The outflow was then cut off sharply, but if it had been allowed to continue, Japan's own interest rates would have climbed steeply as governmental and private borrowers competed with American and other interest offerings for a share of the supply. This would have led quickly to a revaluation of the yen, an increase in the imports of U.S. goods and services, and a decrease in Japanese exports to the U.S. But it would also have pushed Japan into a cycle of inflation, which the administration there is determined to prevent.

Japan has a heavy national debt, and its government fiscal deficit is the source of much concern. One of the reasons—perhaps the principal one—for not freeing the yen is worry lest interest rates in Japan would shoot up, and make it ever more difficult to pay the interest on the public debt. The concern shown by Japan's government leaders in protecting their own interests, even though that protection may simultaneously cause injury to Japan's trade partners, is a reflection of the frankly admitted policy of looking after Japan's own welfare first. Many

Americans admire this attitude on the part of Japan's government officials and wish their own govermental leadership would copy the Japanese and put America's interests first.

Americans would be grateful indeed if really effective measures were adopted and if the Japanese market were actually as open as many of the government leaders would like to have them believe it is. For years their officials have been saying that what was needed was only greater sales efforts by foreigners—a diversionary argument designed to direct attention away from the real problem: Japanese protectionism. If the non-tariff barriers were actually removed, foreign businessmen would put forth whatever sales effort was appropriate.

The balance of payments has tilted much too far in Japan's favor—for much too long. And that one incontrovertible fact must be dealt with by men of goodwill on both sides of the Pacific, as well as in Europe, as soon as possible.

Of late another diversionary argument has been voiced. Some Japanese say that American protests against their foreign trade practices are racially motivated, that similar complaints are not being made against the Europeans. In the case of Europe, however, the U.S. is enjoying a trade surplus in its transactions with many of its nations, so the urgency to remove such obstacles to free trade as remain is not as great as it is with Japan, whose trade surpluses with both America and the European Common Market have reached enormous and unprecedented levels. American businessmen are a hard-headed lot and few if, indeed, any of them would allow racial considerations, even if felt, to stand in the way of successful commerce.

Some Japanese point out that other countries also have tariffs, quotas, and barriers to imports, but while this is true, many of them have been raised because Japan has been too slow in opening its doors to imports and foreign trade imbalances had reached unacceptable levels.

In consideration of all the above, Japan makes a formidable competitor, doubtless the most formidable the U.S. has ever faced in the arena of international trade. And it is regrettable that circumstances have arisen that cause Americans to think of them as competitors instead of partners in trade. If only our commerce were in approximate balance, then each could, within those limitations, produce what he is best suited to produce with each market complementing the other.

There is no question that the Japanese have adopted an *amae* attitude toward the U.S. and taken advantage of assumed American benevolence towards them, as protegés, and will continue to do so until forcible measures are taken to reduce their economic incursions to a more reasonable level.

This can be done. Little or nothing has been gained in holding several high-level conferences every year asking, even begging the Japanese to import more from the U.S. in order to correct the trade imbalance. They have merely agreed in principle, moved a few pieces here and there on the chess (or '*go*') board and then watched the imbalance grow in their favor for still another year. The imbalance is much too high to permit this kind of insincere trickery to continue.

Another proposal that should be considered emanated from the chairman of the Liberal Democratic Party Policy Affairs Research Council, Rokusuke Tanaka. Tanaka asks that Japan truly open its markets by eliminating all the numerous barriers to free trade. He calls it a Naked Japan policy. Under this policy all tariffs would be abolished, as would quotas on agricultural imports and the countless devious non-tariff barriers.

Chapter Eight

Corporations

In recent years, as Americans have watched with growing interest, wonder, and sometimes suspicion and resentment the success of the Japanese economy, we have focussed much of our attention on the management practices of their corporations. Those who admire the Japanese wish to learn their methods and emulate them; those who are suspicious and resentful study them as if more than half convinced that sooner or later they will come upon unethical and cunning connivances that will reveal the Japanese as the malefactors they must be.

The theories proliferate. They go up like trial balloons, some to be shot down quickly, others to be scarred and left to drift aimlessly off to uncharted realms. The reasons concomitant on each theory include cheap labor, extensive U.S. post-war aid, Korean wartime procurement booms, protectionism, Japan Inc., targeting, and so on and on. (More about the reasons for Japan's economic success elsewhere herein.) Like bird dogs in the field, we range from one clump of bushes to the next, sniffing out other possible causes to which we can attribute Japan's productivity and growing exports, lack of labor strife, and the apparently contented workers of its post-industrial, high-technology economy.

While both of our economic systems are of the capitalist persuasion, theirs is far more people-centered and state-guided than ours. In fact, the utilization of personnel and the attitudes toward governmental guidance are two of, but not the only, major differences between American and Japanese corporations.

The Japanese corporation, which has been called a human art form, is an extension of the feudal village and of the later *tonari-gumi*, (the neighborhood associations), a closely-knit organization of human beings working in an atmosphere that encourages them to feel they are vital, permanent parts of the whole. They hire recent graduates, expecting to keep them till retirement, and then let them absorb the corporate atmosphere while doing trifling tasks for several years. (One of the writers knows a young man who was hired recently as a sales clerk by Sears, Roebuck in Houston, Texas. He was given only eleven hours of training before being put out on the floor on his own, but after that short time, he was completely incapable of handling the computer and learning the merchandise. In despair, he quit his job. Yet, with the high turnover typical of such retail outlets, Sears evidently believed they could not afford to invest more than eleven hours of training in this employee. —In Japan, even 110 hours of training would possibly have been thought to be totally inadequate.)

By offering the young recruit job security and wages based on seniority and being a member of a large corporation, with its crib-to-casket care, they weld onto the corporate corpus his lasting loyalty and free themselves of all the demerits of frequent personnel turnovers.

Management also takes a similar long-term view of capital investments since their financial institutions, usually more far-sighted and patient than the individual stockholder—own most of the equity and often leave the managers relatively unencumbered to work out their long-term business plans, which emphasize people and product quality and pay less heed to short-term profit goals.

In contrast the American corporation tends to hire a person for one specific function only, thus forming a transient bond that can be easily broken by either party when the employee moves on to what he perceives as more verdant fields or when the company believes it can find skills of a higher order or at a lower wage or both in the abundant seas of the unemployed and discontented. In the Fifties American corporations began to become so complex and diversified that their managers started organizing by profit centers rather than functions. They ceased being managers of men and became instead manipulators of numbers and symbols more intent on short-term returns than on product quality, long-term technological superiority, and market share. Not all industrial managers, needless to say, are so shortsighted, the long-term goals of the high-tech industry, for instance, pointing to a notable exception.

The ethical question is whether or not our present concept of the corporation as an organization devoted to the maximization of the value of its shares—often at the expense of employee welfare, community good, and the national economy–is flawed.

Ownership of Japanese corporations

The characteristic of Japanese corporations mentioned above—that much more of their capital is borrowed than supplied by shareholders–is a post-World War II phenomenon. In 1950, for instance, 61% of the capital of large Japanese manufacturing companies was "owned" capital, but by 1980 this figure had dropped to well under 30%. The comparable U.S. figure, which has been declining since the 1960's, was 49.6% in 1980. Smaller Japanese firms have an even lower debt-to-equity ratio: 15% or below in many instances. Historically, for corporations to be in a sound financial condition, it has been generally believed that owned capital should be over 50%.

The shares not held by Japanese individuals are mostly

owned by banks and other financial institutions. Customarily individuals put their savings in banks and post offices, and the former buy stock or lend money to companies. In 1975, for instance, about 80% of the financial assets held by individuals were in the form of deposits in those institutions.

In the case of the *keiretsu* (financial-industrial groups like Mitsui, Mitsubishi, Sumitomo, Fuyo-Fuji, Daiichi Kangyo, and Sanwa) the member companies hold shares in one another. On the average any one of the member companies owns stock in about half of the firms in its group. These holdings may amount to control in the case of the old *zaibatsu* companies—Mitsui, Mitsubishi, and Sumitomo—where in some instances they hold collectively somewhere between 66% and 76% of the stock. The other three major *keiretsu* hold about 35%.

In addition to owning shares in each other, the *keiretsu* also exchange directors among themselves, amounting to 9% of all the directors of the group's companies. Other than these, however, Japanese companies do not have many if any outside directors.

Since individual shareholders do not hold enough stock to have much of a voice in the management of companies, it is left to the major stockholding groups, such as the banks and financial institutions, and, in the case of the *keiretsu*, other "cousin" firms to watch over management. In view of the reciprocal stock-holdings of the *keiretsu*, the end result is that there is not much criticism of the way member firms are run, and as for the other corporations, neither is there much control by outsiders over the way they are managed. Directors meet monthly in good-sized firms but less frequently in smaller corporations. The careers of inside directors being largely dependent on the good will of the president, it is rare that an inside director will challenge his judgment or criticize his actions, this being one of the prices that must be paid for having few or no outside directors.

Shareholders' meetings

If an investor in a Japanese corporation wants to voice his disapproval of company policy or challenge actions taken or contemplated by the company, he can do so while attending a meeting of the shareholders. These meetings, however, are poorly attended, mainly because they are dominated by the so-called *sōkaiya*: professional attendees at general meetings. These obstreperous thorns in the side of management may own only one or two shares in a company but will demand large fees or contributions from management in exchange for speeding up or at least not hampering the progress of the meetings. In a typical scenario, after the president or chairman of the corporation has read his report, a *sōkaiya* will move that it be approved. Then fifty or more other *sōkaiya* in attendance will shout their agreement. A shareholder not connected with the *sōkaiya* will find himself shouted down if he attempts to ask management a question or if he tries to present his reasons for opposing a motion.

These *sōkaiya* are quite expensive. A large company may pay in fees or subscription payments as much as the equivalent of one million dollars in a single year to dummy consulting or publishing firms set up by the *sōkaiya*. The average large Japanese corporation will be approached by a hundred or more *sōkaiya* in a year. Some will be paid to help facilitate the shareholder meetings, but more are given money just to stay away and not cause trouble.

The writer (HVZ) recalls an experience he had when he was a director of one of Japan's largest manufacturing companies. At one of its shareholders' meetings, after the president had started to read his report, a man entered the room, presented his proxy, and proceeded up one aisle.

As he passed each row, he sharply elbowed the man on the end. When he got to the front row, he found three people sitting there. Pushing all three off their seats and onto the floor, he sat down, glowering at the directors sitting about five feet in front of him. When the meeting was over, the company official in charge of *sōkaiya* relations apologized for the disruption. Later he met with the roughneck in order to make financial arrangements so there would be no further trouble.

By the beginning of 1983 there were over 6,300 *sōkaiya* in Japan, and by police estimates, they extort some $400 million annually. A veteran *sōkaiya* can make as much as $4,500 for attending, or agreeing *not* to attend a single meeting. A study made by a broadcasting network revealed that some 40% of large corporations each dealt with more than 100 *sōkaiya*. About 10% had relations with over 500 of the extortionists, and 2.4% with over one thousand. It is believed that somewhere between 25% and 60% of all *sōkaiya* are mobsters, termed "*yakuza*" in Japanese.

In November, 1982, the Commercial Code was revised, raising the par value of a share in a listed corporation from ¥50 (equivalent to 21¢) to ¥50,000 (equivalent to $210). This meant that a *sōkaiya* would have to spend 1,000 times more for a share than before. It was hoped that this revision—together with stepped-up police surveillance—would help eliminate *sōkaiya* extortion, although it has not yet proved effective.

Ownership of corporations in America

Most of the stock in U.S. corporations is held by individual investors, mutual funds, and institutional investors, and each of these three classes, of course, follows the prices of shares quoted on the stock market with interest. Investment analysts study in depth the activities of companies listed and are quick to draw attention to anything they think notable, whether good or bad. U.S. corporations try to show an improvement in their earnings each quarter in order to raise prices on the stock exchange. In order to show improvement, many financial devices are used. If results for a particular quarter are going to look especially good, the management may delay some transactions so that only a modest improvement will be announced. Then if the results for the next quarter are disappointing, they can be enhanced by a carry-over of transactions from the previous period. To keep steadily showing improvement requires more than a little sleight of hand skill in the Finance Department. Such contrivances, although legal, are of dubious ethical stature, at best.

There are many outside directors in U.S. corporations. Although the inside directors are, as in Japan, under the thumbs of the president, the outside directors may chastise and harass when they feel criticism is deserved. Unfortunately, the outside directors are usually paid only small fees for their services and thus cannot afford to devote much time to a close inquiry into internal operations. They have to rely on reports prepared by department heads, and if these are self-serving, there is little that can be done about it.

Annual meetings of shareholders of American companies are, by comparison with those in Japan, reasonably well attended. Management as a consequence tries to make them interesting and useful. General Motors Corp., for instance, on November 3rd, 1983, held its Stockholders' Forum in Dallas, Texas. Its purpose, as described in the letter sent to stockholders was to "... allow your management the opportunity to review with you our product quality, and the potential for U.S. and worldwide growth. . . . The major portion of the meeting will be set aside to answer any questions you might have on your company's policies, programs, or operations. . . ."

U.S. corporations happily do not have *sōkaiya* to intimidate and rush through management-sponsored motions at shareholders' meetings. Instead, professional attendees of meetings try to assure that management is reasonably fair and ethical. Messrs. Lewis D. Gilbert and John J. Gilbert of New York make motions at meetings of many major American companies. Their motions and the questions they put to management have done much to keep firms in line. Among the matters they raise for discussion are "Why does the corporation pay excessively high salaries and bonuses to some of its executives?" and "Why are exorbitantly high pensions granted to officers?" They also object to having shareholders' meetings convene in small country towns that are inconvenient to most stockholders. The Gilberts have been promoting better ethical conduct in corporations for several decades.

In spite of the efforts of the Gilberts and others like them, it is not easy to get enough votes at shareholders' meetings to pass measures that will correct some managerial abuses, so much of the success of the Gilberts and others has been in raising the issues and shaming management into behaving in a more ethical fashion.

Some of the proposals presented to shareholders' meetings by churches and other religious bodies who wish to impose their concepts of what is right and wrong are political in nature. Usually these are voted down.

Among the differences between corporations in Japan and the U.S. is the rate of return on investment, with Japanese firms usually paying a lower dividend than is paid by American companies. Part of the reason is that Japanese companies traditionally pay out in dividends a smaller portion of what they earn, with the rest being reinvested in the company. A study made by the Nikkei Economic Electronic Databank Service for fiscal 1980 showed that the self-financing ratio, an indicator of the share of owned funds to total equipment investments, stood at 106.5% for Japanese corporations and 81.5% for American.

Ethical questions about ownership of corporations

1. Are American managers so intent upon short-term financial results that they fail to weigh the long-term implications of their acts? Instead of issuing quarterly earnings reports, might it not be better to release them on an annual basis?

2. Have Japanese companies expanded too rapidly on borrowed money? Because the debt to equity ratio is so high, it is probable that many firms will default on their debts and bring down banks and other financial institutions when a real business depression occurs and depressed sales will not permit them to maintain loan repayment schedules. Might it not be better now if Japanese corporations slowed down their expansion to pay off enough of their borrowings so that they might be in a less risky position?

3. Is the Japanese custom of packing their boards of directors with inside directors—with few or no outside directors—a wise one? Might it not be better if there were enough outside directors so that they could openly register opinions critical of management, when deserved?

4. Might it not be enlightened for both Japanese and U.S. corporations to hire outside directors who are not beholden in any way to management, and pay them enough that they can afford to give sufficient time to learning more about the companies they direct?

5. If, as appears probable, the *sōkaiya* continue to extort money, would it not be wise for managements to

realize that by yielding they are building up the strength of organized crime? Is it fair, just, and morally right for managements to pay out huge sums to *sōkaiya*, thus depriving shareholders of amounts that could be passed on as dividends?

6. Would it be possible for annual shareholders' meetings to be well attended by ordinary stockholders if management cooperated with the police and testified against *sōkaiya*? If shareholder meetings were made more interesting and shareholders were encouraged to ask questions and make suggestions, would this increase purchases of stock by ordinary investors?

7. If the *sōkaiya* were suppressed, would it not encourage Japanese shareholders to attend meetings and make motions that would improve the ethical behavior of management, as has happened in the U.S. due to efforts of Lewis and John Gilbert and others like them?

Acquiring ownership of corporations through mergers and take-overs

There has been a strong movement in the United States in the post-World War II period for corporations to grow by merging or by taking over other firms. One result has been the growth of conglomerates, that is, companies that are in many diverse kinds of businesses. Evidence is lacking that a conglomerate can manage the affairs of an acquired firm any better than the previous owners. Every year many conglomerates find it desirable to divest themselves of properties that they had previously purchased. These divestitures often follow a period of heavy losses, and the properties themselves are frequently sold at a price far below what was paid for them.

In many instances conglomerates acquire family businesses or family farms that have to be sold to pay inheritance taxes. The professional managers in the conglomerates often do not have the skills of the entrepreneurs who previously owned the properties. Also, the officers of the conglomerates usually have so many diverse businesses to supervise that they cannot devote enough time to the acquisitions when they get into trouble.

Although most acquisitions are made because the present owners have to dispose of the properties for inheritance tax reasons or because they lack capital, etc., some acquisitions are made against the desires of the owners, these being called "Unfriendly take-overs." Often they are made because the purchased property has a large amount of liquid assets, including cash. The buyer liquidates the company by selling off the assets and taking the cash, although some states have enacted laws that help owners fend off these "raiders."

In Japan, mergers and acquisitions are far less common than in the U.S., and some of those that do take place are the result of pressure from MITI. Unfriendly acquisitions are virtually impossible to consummate, the feeling being that they are unethical.

Another negative factor in mergers and acquisitions is the waste of money, the sum required to acquire another company often being enormous. During the period 1981–1982, when business was poor in America and the inflation rate high due to a shortage of capital, there was criticism of the diversion of funds from productive use to acquisitions. Mr. Lee Iacocca, Chairman of Chrysler Corporation, for example, stated: "Some 83 billion dollars was sucked out of the banks by those conglomerates and not one new job was created. . . . Corporations are squandering valuable resources on take-overs instead of reinvesting the money in new equipment." (*Dallas Morning News*, February 18, 1983.) Iacocca in a speech in Dallas on November 3, 1983, complained that the U.S. Steel Company, protected from imports by a price triggering mechanism, purchased an oil company for $4.3 billion instead of investing that money in modern basic oxygen furnaces to be competitive with the Japanese. (*Dallas Morning News*, Nov. 4, 1983.)

Also the fear of corporate raiders has resulted in some companies keeping their cash and other liquid assets at as low a level as they can to avoid being targets. This policy is in many instances damaging to these companies, for it diminishes their strength to face recessions or competition.

Also to be considered is the treatment of employees of a company by those who are selling it—and those acquiring it. In Japan, employees regard themselves as being such integral parts of the corporation that even if they own no shares, they still feel that in some way it belongs to them. Japanese managers are usually more loyal to the employees than to the owners. Under these circumstances, a forced unfriendly take-over would leave the workers as well as managers in a state of shock. Even where a merger does take place, as for instance the formation of the Nippon Steel Corp., the employees of each of the component companies remained loyal to their own group, and it proved to be quite difficult to integrate the formerly competitive groups into a new cooperative relationship.

A phenomenon of the "take-over" age in America is the defensive position taken by executives of the target companies. When it appears that a company may fall victim, the officers will often band together and vote themselves lucrative termination agreements, to be paid if they are fired or demoted. An example was the acquisition of Bendix Corporation in 1982 by Allied Chemical Corp. Twenty-two key Bendix executives were covered by what had come to be called "golden parachutes;" the chairman's agreement entitled him to receive his annual salary of $825,000 for six years: hardly a miserly amount.

Finance policies

If, as Mr. Lee Iacocca pointed out, it is improper use of capital for banks and other financial institutions to lend money for corporate acquisitions, then the question may be asked: "Was it ethical in the 1970's and early 1980's for U.S. and Japanese banks and corporations to lend money to developing countries where the probabilities of default were considerable?"

Worldwide, some $700 billion were lent to Lesser Developed Countries (LDC's). Of this enormous sum, about $300 billion came due in 1983 and 1984. The international debts of the LDC's have quadrupled in the last ten years, while there has been a widening of deficits.

It is probable that many of the LDC's will be unable to repay the loans made to them. The losses would be staggering and could conceivably lead to the ruin of many international banks, other lending agencies, and supplying corporations. Loans made by Japanese banks and other financial institutions to countries whose ability to repay them is questionable had totalled over ¥6 trillion by mid-1983—more than a quarter of all Japan's foreign loans—and U.S. lending to the same countries was much higher than that of the Japanese.

Why were these loans made?

Following the huge increase in the price of oil charged by OPEC nations in the early and mid-1970's the other developing countries found that their exports were insufficient to pay for the expensive oil they needed. This should have resulted in a curtailment of credit, which did not take place. The reason was that the OPEC nations took in hundreds of billions of dollars from their oil sales, and since they couldn't spend it as fast as it poured in, they deposited the surplus billions in banks and other financial institutions in Europe, the U.S., and Japan. Their coffers brimming with OPEC oil money, many members of the international financial community lent these funds to the LDC's to use in buying oil as well as the machinery, equipment, and services offered by Europe, Japan, and the U.S.

Apparently many U.S. bankers thought that even if the chances of repayment were uncertain, the American government would surely come to their rescue if the loans went sour.

Even more worrisome to the LDC's than the cost of imported oil is the irresponsibility of their own people in the matter of birth control. Most of them are so overpopulated that they cannot even now produce enough food to feed themselves, but in spite of this they persist in producing large families. Population experts forecast that the labor force in Latin America and Black Africa will double in the next twenty years. Since unemployment and underemployment in those regions are already exceedingly high, ranging from 20% to more than 50% of the work force, the prospects for amelioration are dim indeed.

With this background, it is difficult for the LDC governments to adopt sound fiscal programs that would enable them to pay off their international debts, for to do so would require stringent reductions in assistance to the poor. This they dare not do, for it might well result in revolution and internecine strife.

Japanese, American, European, and LDC thinkers have been aware of the problem for ten years or more; yet in the same period bankers, bureaucrats, politicians, and businessmen have loaned money to these countries freely, evidently without giving serious thought to the demographic and political problems that would make repayment difficult.

Now that these nations face default, they are being forced to reduce their imports. Under Secretary of Commerce Lionel H. Olmer reported on September 14, 1983: "Since mid-1982 the nations of Latin America have seen their credit-worthiness and their access to international capital markets evaporate. Some, notably Brazil and Mexico, have had to renegotiate the terms of their debts or have had to suspend payments temporarily . . . the adverse effects on world trade of LDC debt problems have been quietly multiplying. . . .'' (*Business America*, Sept. 19, 1983) For Mexico, which is using money borrowed from a total of 510 foreign banks, imports in the first half of 1983 dropped 60% below 1982 levels, and almost 70% below 1981.

In considering corporate and international finance, the following ethical questions arise:

1.   Since inheritance tax laws in the United States are among the principal reasons why owners feel they must sell their family-owned companies and farms to conglomerates, would it not be wise to rewrite these laws?

2.   Forced take-overs in the United States, particularly when the raiders have as their objective looting the firm of its liquid assets, serve no worthwhile objective. Legislation against this has already been enacted in some states. Perhaps Federal laws will have to be passed to control them.

3.   The merger-acquisition mania in America leads to a diversion of scarce capital from productive purposes. Perhaps the Federal Reserve Banks should be granted the power to give window guidance, as is offered by the Bank of Japan.

4.   When a company is targeted for a take-over in the U.S., the officers often protect themselves with ''golden parachutes'' to use when dismissed or demoted. One prominent CEO exercised this ''golden parachute'' provision of his contract and resigned within a year after his company had been acquired by another corporation. Because of this lucrative arrangement, he will receive more than $2.8 million over the next four years and when his retirement benefits begin in 1991, he will receive $450,000 a year

for the rest of his life. Should not something be done to control these excesses as well as to provide some "protection," on a modified scale, for lower echelons?

5.   By raising the price of oil to high levels in the 1970's OPEC members caused economic hardship world-wide, particularly in the non-oil producing developing countries. Collapse was averted in many instances because the banks and financial institutions of America, Europe, and Japan loaned the LDC's enough funds to pay for the oil. The funds lent were actually money that the OPEC countries had deposited in the U.S., Europe, and Japan. Now the banks in the industrialized countries are faced with grave problems in trying to get the LDC's to repay the money lent them. The OPEC powers are no doubt slyly chuckling to themselves over the dilemma their shrewdness has created. They were too smart to lend directly to the LDC's enough money to pay their oil bills.

6.   It seems obvious that officers of the international banks and other financial institutions were naive and short-sighted in these transactions and were not sufficiently informed about the political, economic, population, and social problems of the developing countries to whom they lent hundreds of billions of dollars. To forestall such future errors, perhaps bank loan officers should be required to take courses in foreign affairs before being authorized to make loans. Since barbers and beauticians must pass examinations before certification, why not bankers?

7.   The U.S. international bankers who have been foolish enough to lend vast sums to the LDC's now seem confident that the government of the United States will bring them succor and rescue them from their plight but have they given any thought to the fact that it is the tax-payers who will ultimately pay for their folly? Or do they really care, as long as their own stock option benefits and golden parachutes are not touched?

Did these bankers, whom Columnist Patrick J. Buchanan has called "these amoral international money lenders," care that at a time when interest rates for mortgages on homes for young families were rising from 8 to 16 percent, they were lending hundreds of billions of dollars to some of the most odious and risky regimes in the world?

This amounts to what William Quirk has called "economic treason" in his forthcoming book, *How the West Gave Its Wealth Away*. Quirk goes on to say that these bankers "have detached themselves from the political and moral principles of their home countries" and have financed communists and dictators alike, as well as the Soviet military buildup.

8. In large part, the U.S. deficit is caused by interest paid to finance the shortfall in the federal budget, in which a leading item is defense. One would expect defense contractors to be sufficiently patriotic (and ethical) to keep costs in line, but evidently all do not, judging from some of the exorbitant charges made for items not subject to competitive bidding. Claw hammers that retail at $17 are billed to the Pentagon at $435. Plastic stool caps selling at retail for 22¢ are billed to the Department of Defense at $1,118.26. Plain round nuts which sell in stores for 13¢ are bought by other nuts in the bureaucracy for $2,043. The Navy pays $2,228 for wrenches it could buy in stores for a mere eight dollars.

Corporate policies: decision making

So much has been written about the *ringi-seido*, Japan's process of consensus seeking, that a summary will do for our purposes here. Rather than have the chief executive officer or the board draft and issue corporative directives, the Japanese prefer that a proposal be drawn up at a lower level and sent here and there in the company for comments and for approval or disapproval. Sometimes even the chief executive may plant one of his proposals in the lower echelons using the name of one of his subordinates. The originator of the proposal can enhance its chances of success through a process known as *nemawashi* or "working around the roots," in which he tries to enlist the support of some of his key co-workers over a cup of *sake* after work. Since unanimity is desirable in the *ringi-seido*, those who neither strongly support nor oppose the proposal have ways to indicate their neutral feelings.

The Japanese like the *ringi-seido* because it fosters the spirit of corporate unity and, in the event of failure, it divides the burden of responsibility. Its defect is that it is time-consuming, but an advantage is that everyone who read and signed off on the proposal already knows its details and can put the plan into action quickly when a favorable decision is finally announced.

Corporate policies: competition

The competitive spirit of Japanese corporations as well as of the people themselves has been something of a conundrum to the Western world. On one hand we hear the Japanese called "fierce competitors," while on the other we hear stories such as the one about the American sales manager who had just taken up his post at a U.S.-Japan marketing company in Tokyo. To build up sales, one of the American's first steps was to hold a contest and award a large amount of money to the top salesman of the year. When the year had ended, the sales manager assembled his sales staff in an auditorium and, with appropriate fanfare, announced the name of the winner and handed him the bundle of cash. Then he left the room. Before the American could leave the building, however, he remembered that he had left his notebook on the speaker's rostrum and so returned to retrieve it.

Upon re-entering the auditorium, he found the winner of the contest distributing the cash award equally among all his co-workers.

Whether apocryphal or not, the story makes its point well: the Japanese are not very competitive with one another in the same organization.

In Tokugawa Japan (1615–1868) we are told there was no word for "competition," and it seems it was Yukichi Fukuzawa who coined the word *kyōsō* after the advent of Western commercialism, following the Meiji Restoration. Although obviously some of the Tokugawa Era trading houses must have been trying to sell the same products to the same people as other trading houses, the emphasis on competition was so slight that there was not even a word to describe it. Instead, they talked of the system of *Wa*, which is more of a competitive cooperative relationship, if one can imagine such a thing.

Even today, while Japanese corporations may compete fiercely with each other in price wars, they endeavor to avoid forcing a domestic competitor out of business, especially if he has operated with *magokoro* (sincerity) within that particular industrial group. (If they do not, the Ministry of International Trade and Industry will probably enter the picture, with some 'administrative guidance.') And whereas the presidents of some competitive U.S. corporations dare not be seen having a drink with each other, their Japanese counterparts often assemble in industry associations, of which there are a god's plenty, to determine how they may cooperate in getting the government to give subsidies for research and development and to work out with MITI and other government officials how they should go about raising non-tariff barriers to keep out competing foreign products.

When Japanese corporations "advance" into foreign markets, however, they often remove their velvet gloves and go at their opponents tooth and nail, nor should this be surprising in view of what we know about the *"Tabi wa haji no kakizute"* or "One needs feel no shame away from home" syndrome.

Corporate personnel policies: lifetime employment (*shūshin koyō*) and pensions

The ideal of secure employment has had its tribulations in Japan. During the feudal Tokugawa Era trading houses, which were smaller and functioned under vastly different conditions, strove to offer their people long-term employment, but the industries that sprang up in the early Meiji Era, with the subsidies of the government and often with the guidance of Western advisors, followed the lead of the sweaty textile mills in Birmingham and paid their workers pittances while offering them little if any security. After World War I some labor laws protective of women and children were passed, but it was not until the industrialsts realized they could make more money by treating a worker decently to keep him at his loom or lathe than by paying him a pittance and losing him, then hiring and training a replacement. Even then it was only the large and profitable *zaibatsu* corporations that did so.

Today most of Japan's large corporations (those with more than 1,000 employees) offer lifetime employment. Some American companies also follow this practice, but the percentage is much smaller than in Japan, where about 20% of all workers enjoy its benefits in an aura of mutual responsibility between worker and employer.

In order for this practice of lifetime employment to function, manufacturers must keep their level of production fairly steady. No company in any country can do this without taking drastic measures when business declines. One of the measures taken in Japan is to aggressively sell in foreign markets when domestic orders fall off. Companies offer their products overseas at a loss if necessary to keep production lines running steadily and workers on the job. In its July 9, 1983 issue the *Economist* told of pricing the same Japanese product, a Nikon camera, on the same day in three markets. The price in Tokyo, *without* taxes, was equivalent to $253, but in New York and London, the prices were $247 and $255 *with* taxes. Considering that the cameras had been shipped half way around the world and had customs duties and taxes levied on them, it is obvious that the Japanese were doing something "clever" to price them so low abroad. By selling at such a comparatively low price—possibly at a loss or at least at no profit—overseas, Nikon's action again raises the question of ethical trade practices.

In the Fifties and well into the Sixties most corporate employees in Japan retired at the mandatory age of 55 and were given a lump-sum payment that was usually inadequate to sustain them for the remainder of their lives much above the poverty level. In fact, because many, perhaps most of the retirees had lived in company housing or in *danchi* (low-rent government subsidized apartment complexes), they used their lump-sum retirement pay to buy homes in the country districts, away from the soaring real estate costs of the large cities.

Because these retirement benefits were so low, more than a few of the retirees took employment with lower pay and fewer benefits in companies, such as sub-contractors, with whom their ex-employers had a close relationship or they sought to eke out their living by serving as advisors and consultants in fields where their "social capital" might have some clout.

Gradually the situation improved, and today Japanese corporations provide one of three kinds of retirement programs: the old style in which the retiree receives one lump-sum payment (often one month's salary for each year worked), a second which replicates the American system, and a third which is a combination of the above two: a smaller initial lump-sum followed by monthly remittances.

On the whole Japanese retirement benefits are more generous and reasonable these days, although many are still expected to retire at 55 or 60, the latter being applicable to government employees. The mandatory age varies (in 1981, 38% of corporations had a retirement age of 55 while 40% had one of 60) but has moved upward while the top executives who are directors can stay at their desks even longer.

The question of interest here, however, is whether or not such early retirement ages are ethical, especially in consideration of improving national health and growing longevity. (U.S. government employees, for instance, have no mandatory retirement age, while most American companies expect their personnel to lay down their burdens at 65. Since one form of Japanese retirement benefits calls for a lump-sum based on the number of months employed, it is more to the employer's benefit than the employee's to arrange an early retirement.)

Also deserving of mention in the context of ethics is the Japanese tendency toward "first-hired, first-fired," even in the large corporations. Unless of outstanding ability, older employees begin to get squeezed out in late middle-age, with the result that there is very little unemployment among the young but with the highest unemployment rates being among males over the age of 45. Further, according to Thomas J. Nevins, managing director of Technics in Management Transfer Inc., a Tokyo-based, labor consulting company, 18% of white-collar and 47% of blue-collar personnel are non-regular employees on contract.

These non-regular employees are seldom union members or of management rank, and they work for lower wages and with less job security after their usually brief contracts expire. It is to these non-regular employees (called *shokutaku*) that the elite regulars, with life-time jobs in the larger corporations, owe their privileged position, since the *shokutaku* are among the first to be fired in times of economic distress and without payment of any form of retirement benefits, although unions are now trying to change this.

Corporate personnel policies: the boss as a S.O.B.

Japanese corporations devote much attention to personnel matters, and this is particularly true of large corporations where life-time employment is the custom. If a man works for a company and expects to stay with it until retirement, it is highly desirable that he work in a reasonably harmonious atmosphere, since he is constrained from quitting to find a job elsewhere. The writer (HVZ) asked the director of personnel of a large Japanese manufacturing company what percentage of supervisors were considered to be *fuyukai na hito*, that is, persons unpleasant, unfair, and disagreeable to work for. After studying the matter for several months, he answered: "one in four." Foreigners who read of the importance attached to personnel relations in Japan seem incredulous at this figure. They should not be, however, for in the 1960's and 1970's stories circulated widely about Japanese companies that had installed life-size models of the supervisors—stuffed with straw or cotton—in their factories and had supplied clubs for workers to use in beating the models to relieve some of their tension and exasperation. The presence of these *fuyukai na hito* may well account, at least in part, for the fact that one in every 25 Japanese wage-earners is treated annually at a mental hospital for a tension-related illness, a figure that has almost doubled since Japan's economy began its climb in 1960.

The writer (HVZ), over a period of twenty years, has

queried people in many countries about what percentage of their bosses had been truly unpleasant to work for. The answers were the same—about 25%—in such large cities as Warsaw, New York, London, Paris, and Hamburg, but in smaller cities in the American Mid-west and South the figure dropped to approximately 15%.

Corporate personnel policies: dismissals and layoffs

The writer (HVZ) once worked for a manufacturing company in Chicago, where every summer the Executive Vice President for Finance sent orders down the line to lay off a certain percentage of the workers. Usually the figure was 10% or less. (The sales department was excluded as the company needed the orders turned in by the sales department managers.) The following January the company always increased its work force when it found that the layoffs, plus resignations of those worried about their future, had left many departments shorthanded. There were both advantages and disadvantages to these layoff policies. One advantage was that when ordered to cut its staff each department had to scurry around to find people to fire and naturally they released the least desirable ones. Those dismissed kept face by telling their friends and relatives they were released as a part of a general reduction in force. Other benefits of the layoffs were that everyone intensified his efforts to reduce waste to a minimum and endeavored mightily to be more productive.

A negative result of the layoffs was that the discharged employees were furious when they learned that the money saved was used to pay executive bonuses in December. Many felt this was not ethical and that everyone should have been kept on the payroll and the bonuses cancelled.

Corporate personnel policies: executive compensation

"Ah well, another day, another $201,000," Frederick W.

Smith, chairman of the Federal Express Co., might well have said to himself as he left his office at the end of any working day in 1982, for his total compensation package for that year came to an eye-popping $51,544,000, his daily earnings being as much as most farm workers could make in twenty years.

In the same year, the four top managers of the Toys 'R' Us Co. drew down a combined total compensation of some $75,000,000, these gains coming, like the Smith package above, almost entirely from exercising so-called ISOs (Incentive Stock Options). (Smith's salary plus bonus was $414,000, while that of the president of the toy dealer came to $1,413,000.)

During the worst recession since World War II executive salaries might well have been expected to have been cut back or at least held at the same level but in reality they grew on the average of 5.5%. The rise in stock prices that followed the recession, however, more than compensated for these relatively meager salary and bonus increases, resulting in many truly munificent examples of corporate largesse for the fortunate managers.

For the year ending May 31, 1983, the above Mr. Smith's company earned $78.4 million on sales of $803.9 million, so that his own windfall came close to equalling his company's entire profit figure. Even if profits plunge, some companies persist in giving magnanimous increases in pay to their executives, as did Union Carbide whose profits fell 52% but who increased the short-term compensation (salary and bonus) of their chairman by 21%. Mobil's profits dropped 43%. but their chairman was consoled with a raise of 36%.

Perhaps such executive self-interest and excessive compensation should raise no eyebrows in an award-prone nation that honors the 7,000 military personnel who took part in the minuscule (though commendable) invasion of

Grenada with no less than 8,612 medals, where multi-million dollar contracts are given to TV mummers and men who are adept at throwing or hitting or catching balls, and where the top two percent of the wealth-holders own half of all privately-held stock and 39% of the bonds, but there is serious concern now that the managerial class has gone too far in rewarding itself for its own efforts. Once most executive compensation took the form of straight salary and occasional bonuses, but high income taxes, ranging up to 91%, inspired the managers and their accountants to devise other forms of payment to escape such tax burdens. Even as far back as the early 1960's the after-tax income of corporate chief executives officers derived from ownership—capital gains, dividends, and other stock-based remuneration—averaged being 6.5 times more than the sum of their salary, bonus, and other compensation deriving from their management of the company.

Despite the celebrated theory of the separation of ownership and management of corporations, in 1950 the U.S. Congress amended the tax code to give more favorable tax treatment to executives (and employees) who had been given shares in the companies for which they worked, the aim of the Congress being to give the recipients a stake and more direct interest in the business. This granting of stock options is a privilege given mostly to executives; it allows them to purchase a certain amount of the stock in their company at some future date, at a price specified on the date the stock option is given: for example, $50.00 a share. If the shares rise to $100, the executive can buy the stock one morning for $50 and sell that afternoon for $100. Whereas outside shareholders buy shares at a risk, never knowing whether the stock will rise or fall, the executive with a stock option takes no risk whatsoever, for he can even decline to exercise his stock-option right if the stock does not increase in value, to his satisfaction.

Then, if he has held the stock for a certain length of time, as required by the IRS, the earnings he eventually realizes from their sale will qualify for the long-term capital gains tax rate of only 25%.

Sixty-six percent of large corporations offer Incentive Stock Option programs, with the list growing every day.

Paying such executives more money than they or their families could possibly spend while millions of their fellow countrymen exist at below the poverty level raises very serious ethical considerations. Says W. Donald Gough of the consulting firm of Sibson and Co., "The concern is that the public will perceive that executives are realizing excessive amounts of compensation relative to their contribution to the welfare of the stockholder." It is interesting to note that Mr. Gough makes no mention at all of the welfare of the employee.

Some of the executives themselves appear not to have been completely blinded by the greed of their fellows: Clarence B. Randall, former chief executive officer of Inland Steel, has said, "The senior officers in a corporation have a range of ethical questions which are peculiarly their own. The number-one man confronts a very special moral equation, for example, when it comes to fixing salaries for himself and the other executives. True, his board of directors must give *pro forma* approval to his recommendations, but it almost never challenges them." Boards of directors and compensation committees are usually rubber stamps when it comes to executive compensation recommendations.

Another business executive, Joseph E. Muckley, writing in an issue of the *Harvard Business Review* in early 1984, studied the proxy statements of 200 major publicly-held corporations and concluded that, "Those persons fortunate enough to achieve high status in our corporate society should think more of their responsibilities and less of their perquisites." Among several companies whose abuses he condemned in particular was one whose chief executive officer served as director of seven other companies that in 1982 held 119 meetings he was eligible to attend. This CEO received $196,550 for his directorships in addition to his regular compensation of $435,000, plus various perquisites.

But in that same year this CEO's company suspended the payment of dividends, lost $207 million, cut its work force drastically, and reported that its corporate pension fund assets were not sufficient to meet obligations.

It is not inconceivable that if this executive had tended to the affairs of his own company more closely, it might have ended the year in better financial condition.

Although it may offer the largest monetary rewards, the incentive stock options are by no means the only means of filling to the brim executive coffers, there being such others as executive loan programs for financing the purchase of stock bought on option and for buying homes, life insurance policies, college tuition for children, pensions, and such esoteric devices as stock appreciation rights (SARs) and "phantom stock awards." Regarding Du-Pont's system of phantom stock awards, one management consultant exclaimed, "DuPont has found a simply fantastic way to bury executive compensation," "to bury" meaning to conceal it from the eyes of the stockholders and general public.

Even when ousted for poor performance or during takeovers, executives often have contractual provisions that help soften the blow, as outlined earlier. When Archie McCardell was eased out of International Harvester, he received $600,000 as heart balm, and Frank A. LaPage, an executive vice-president at Firestone Tire and Rubber, was given $450,000 in consolation when he retired.

The conventional wisdom is that such exceedingly high

levels of compensation are essential to hold good men and to motivate them to perform their jobs with the utmost dedication. Yet there are many large, complex organizations—among them government agencies, the public utilities, large educational institutions, and the military—where the top managers seem to live quite well while turning in adequate or even highly commendable performances for much, much less pay.

Nor are all of these lavish corporations of the kind considered vital to the national security or public welfare. The Numbers Two, Three, Four, and Five on the list of 1982's highest paid executives were officers of Toys 'R' Us, a toy dealer, while tobacco company officers were also high on the list.

Nor can all of the executives be absolutely essential and irreplaceable, for the Rand Corporation once interviewed the top managers in 37 of the country's largest companies to learn if their organizations could continue to function in the event nuclear war obliterated their main offices. Most of those interviewed replied that while operations might be difficult for a while, their companies *could* continue production without the services of their top executives.

Some managers are, it seems, not only selfish but also often unaccountable for their actions. Unless there is one individual or a like-minded group with majority control of the stock who are sufficiently provoked, the managers are not easy to fire, and if the shareholders yell too loudly at them at the annual meetings, they merely arrange to meet the next time in Brisbane or Bombay or Khartoum. Committed to protecting their flanks and perquisites instead of making decisions that would benefit the shareholders *and* the employees, they put their own personal advancement ahead of that of the corporation and view themselves as an elite class pitted against the grubbing outside world.

Should the shareholders sue them for mismanagement, they merely initiate a counter-suit, using corporate lawyers and their shareholders' money.

There is no magic wand that can be waved to persuade those members of the managerial class who over-compensate themselves to be more ethical, but perhaps they could be convinced that being less selfish would be in their self-interest in the long run, which brings us to the dilemma of capitalism itself: how can the self-interest on which the system is founded be harnessed more efficiently, for broader purposes?

In contrast, Japanese executives live well and generally turn in adequate job performances while receiving more modest compensation packages, the average annual income of the presidents of companies listed on the Tokyo Stock Exchange being about $180,000. The March, 1984 edition of *Fortune* magazine reported that the salaries of "Japanese chairmen and presidents . . . are well below comparable American salaries."

In 1982 (the latest year for which figures are available), Japan's automobile manufacturers awarded their corporate presidents total compensation packages (salary, bonuses, options, and perquisites) as follows:

Toyota	$1,300,000
Nissan	510,000
Isuzu	250,000
Honda	240,000

In contrast, for 1983, America's car makers gave these total compensation amounts:

Ford	$7,313,000
Chrysler	1,858,000
General Motors	1,511,000

In Japan bonuses are normally paid twice annually and are distributed to everyone, from the president of the company to the lowliest clerk. This bonus system has certain advantages. Although the equivalent of two months' salary twice a year is probably the most common award these days, the amount is flexible so that corporations can lower it in bad times, then raise it when profits begin to accumulate. Also it acts as a kind of semi-enforced savings program because the recipients do not raise their standard of living as they would if their monthly pay were increased but instead tend to either put these biannual inflows of cash into savings accounts or buy big ticket merchandise with them. And because these goods are usually paid for in one lump sum in cash, the growth of consumer credit has been largely retarded with the result that the average Japanese family, instead of laboring under the equivalent of thousands of dollars of debt as in the U.S., has considerable savings and little if any indebtedness. (A U.S. government economist once told the *Christian Science Monitor*, "If everybody in this country started to save, America would go broke.")

Even in those American corporations that do grant bonuses, it is not common for them to be given to everyone and instead they are usually based on performance and limited to executives and sales personnel. The same is true of the granting of stock options, but there are weaknesses to the U.S. bonus and stock option policies, as delineated above. The writer (HVZ) had a friend who was president of a division of a U.S. conglomerate. The division was a profit center, and each year for five consecutive years the friend received a large bonus and generous stock options because of the profits generated. It so happened that several years before the president had come to head up the division, his predecessor had invested many millions of dollars of the division's capital in land adjacent to the factory. The reason was sound: when the division grew, it would need more land for expansion. Real estate in that area appreciated substantially in value, and when the friend needed to show a good profit in his books, he found he could do so by selling off some of the land. This he did for three of the five years. When asked if his superior in the conglomerate knew what he was doing, the friend answered Yes, because his superior too was granted bonuses and stock options on the basis of what the divisions under him were able to contribute in profits to the corporation. After working as division president for two more years, the friend found another job. In this, he had no difficulty because the executive recruiting firm he employed was able to cite his splendid profit record. Earnings can also be manipulated in other ways such as liquidating inventories and reducing R & D budgets. While not illegal, the ethics of all this should be questioned.

Corporate personnel policies: treatment of unproductive workers

Obviously, both U.S. and Japanese corporations have employees who are not productive. In the United States the longer an employee is on the payroll, the more difficult it is to fire him, but he may eventually be dismissed if he is unproductive and if extensive efforts to straighten him out by means of training or lectures have failed. In Japanese corporations and government offices, however, it is even more difficult to discharge such people because of the lifetime employment practice. Those who supervise the unproductive ones try to persuade other departments to accept them or have them transferred to subsidiaries or affiliates. Often they are sent to joint ventures with foreign companies, leading the foreign partners to wonder why the executives sent from the Japanese side are so incompetent. If Japanese companies cannot find such places for their unproductive people, they traditionally assign them desks by the window where they may sit and read newspapers and magazines or watch the street scene below all day.

These are called the *madogiwa-zoku,* or "window ledge tribesmen." Included in this group are some of the *fuyukai* (S.O.B.) bosses who have been removed from positions where they might injure the morale of people under them. In an Associated Press dispatch from Tokyo, published March 18, 1979 in the *Dallas Times Herald*, the public relations manager of Mitsui and Company stated that about 700 of his company's 11,000 employees belonged to this *madogiwa-zoku.*

Corporate personnel relations: treatment of female employees and minorities

In recent years virtually all occupations in America have been thrown open to women, and corporations have made much progress in increasing their pay and raising them to higher positions. Even so, their compensation rate remains below that of men. On October 31, 1983 the U.S. Bureau of Labor Statistics released a report, based on findings for the third quarter of 1983 of the Census Bureau's Current Population Survey. The average weekly earnings of men who worked full time was $388, as compared to $251 for women. White men averaged $399 per week as compared to $254 for white women. Black men average $300 per week and black women $234. Hispanic men drew $278 and Hispanic women $212.

It should be kept in mind that because of higher birth rates a larger percentage of blacks and Hispanics are young compared with the whites. This age factor would account for some of the differences in pay, as young people start at lower salaries and their pay increases only as they develop skills and experience and gain seniority.

Japanese women too are paid less than their men. Regular women workers receive on the average only 60% of what men are paid. In the case of part-time workers, the difference is even greater, women receiving only 45%

of what men get. According to a survey made by the Prime Minister's Office on "Female Participation in Decision-making," only 0.12% of the decision-makers in Japan's listed corporations was female, and nearly 90% of corporations had no female managers at all.

Women suffer from discrimination in other ways as well. The life-time employment practice covers full-time regular employees only. Part-timers or temporary help may be fired without hesitation. A survey conducted by the Prime Minister's Office in 1981 revealed that 22.2% of the so-called part-time female workers actually worked the same hours and days as regular employees, and of the remainder, 50% worked for more than 35 hours per week or nearly as long as full-time workers. The evidence of discrimination is undeniable.

This problem should come to the boiling point, however, when the Ministry of Labor presents to the Diet an equal opportunity bill that would ban discriminatory practices due to sex. Standing firm against such legislation is the powerful *Nikkeiren* (Japan Federation of Employers' Associations) that is making an issue of the costs such a bill would place on Japanese industry.

In reference to *Nikkeiren's* opposition, Ryoko Akamatsu, director of the Women and Juvenile Bureau of the Ministry of Labor has stated, "Already foreign countries are attributing Japan's competitive edge in the international marketplace to its discriminatory employment practices toward women." She has urged *Nikkeiren* not to persist in its opposition, which would only intensify this foreign perception.

As many as 70% of large Japanese corporations will not employ female university graduates even today, and it is at such practices as this that the Labor Ministry's bill is aimed.

Japan has its minorities just as other countries, but in

Japan, except for some Koreans, they are natives of the country, including about 3 million *burakumin*, or *shinheimin*, who have traditionally worked with leather, hides, and in butchering. These people, like others doing the same kind of work on the mainland of Asia, have been discriminated against for over 1,300 years. In India they would be called "Untouchables." There are other groups as well who are treated as inferior castes, including the *hinin*, *kitsune mochi no ie.*, etc., totalling more than 1,000,000 people. At a meeting of Japanese executives in Tokyo the writer (HVZ) was told that there wasn't even one *burakumin* in the employ of any bank in the country.

"Probably no . . . organization is more sexist or racist than the Japanese corporation," writes Professor William Ouchi, author of *Theory Z*. "Their organizations simply operate as culturally homogeneous social systems . . . that can withstand no internal cultural diversity."

Also subject to discrimination in Japan are offspring of Japanese women who married aliens, many of them being children born to Japanese women married to Koreans brought to the country when Korea was a part of the Japanese Empire, i.e. before 1945. Many of these offspring are over 50 years of age now; yet they still cannot obtain Japanese citizenship and are not entitled to a free education. They cannot obtain passports. They are not permitted to claim welfare benefits, and it is hard for them to find jobs. A few are the offspring of unions between Japanese women and members of the Allied Occupation Forces from India, Australia, Britain, Canada, and, especially, the United States. Particularly hard to find employment for are the children of Japanese women and men of color.

While most would readily concede that steps should be taken to combat discrimination wherever it is found, the foreign visitor to the U.S. might stare in wonder and dismay at some of the measures we have taken to achieve this goal. For example, in job interviews, it is now considered discriminatory to ask the applicant questions such as the following:

Religious affiliation.
Draft classification.
Dates and conditions of military discharge.
Mother tongue.
Marital status and number of dependents.
Physical handicaps.
Number and kind of arrests.

In fact, things have come to such a pass that, as one of the writers (JS) learned recently to his infinite sorrow, one cannot even place a Help Wanted ad in a newspaper for a "pretty, young woman as secretary," since the word "young" would violate the Anti-Age Discrimination Act of 1976 and the word "woman" would be regarded as sexist, an adjective which seems these days to carry a pejorative quality. In the case of the executive who is intent on gracing his office and gladdening his eye with a lovely young secretary, it is to be doubted that such measures would thwart him for long, for he would probably do just what JS did: reword the ad—then screen out all male as well as the older and non-pretty female applicants. All that the "anti-discrimination" measure accomplished was to make JS go to the bother of reviewing more applications and to needlessly raise the hopes of a lot of applicants, who had no chance to begin with.

Corporate personnel policies: employment of foreigners
Japanese, like other Asians, have strong loyalties to their own kind. They feel an ardent sense of obligation to see to it that members of their family are employed. Once this is done, they want to be sure that people in their company

or group have work. They have a sense of responsibility to the whole race and do not like to see any Japanese unemployed.

Americans, unless they are members of a minority that is notably ethnocentric, do not have so much of this loyalty, and its absence puzzles Asians, many of them believing it to be evidence of questionable ethics. A professor from India known to one of the writers is now working on a book on the subject of "American lack of loyalty to their kind," and it promises to be most enlightening.

In Japanese companies the second sense of obligation mentioned above—to be sure that people in their company continue to have jobs—does not extend as strongly to foreign employees as to Japanese. Even so, Japanese companies operating overseas do endeavor to avoid layoffs of any and all employees.

To say that Japanese have different feelings about foreigners than about their own people is only to state the obvious. Their feelings are well expressed in an article by Hideo Matsuoka writing for the *Sunday Mainichi* in September, 1981. The translation which appeared in the *Mainchi Daily News* on September 22, 1981 reads:

"For Japanese managers, depriving fellow Japanese of employment goes against their sense of mission. . . . There are many reasons behind the reluctance of big Japanese companies, including automakers, to build plants in foreign countries. One of these reasons is undoubtedly the guilt feeling the top managers have in providing jobs for foreign workers instead of to the Japanese. They feel guilty because they think that they are not living up to their self-imposed mission of securing work for the Japanese. . . . One of the major reasons sustaining the phenomenal growth of the Japanese economy is the business managers' sense of mission that they must work to increase the job opportunities for the Japanese."

In general, because of the feelings expressed above by Matsuoka, Japanese companies operating in foreign countries try to fill managerial positions with Japanese, using natives for the lower level jobs. A JETRO survey conducted in 1982 involving 150 Japanese manufacturing firms operating in the U.S. revealed that 73.6% of the managers were Japanese. It should be noted, however, that nearly 100% of the *top* executive positions were filled by them. The non-Japanese managers were—with very few exceptions—relegated to the lowest level of executive ranks. One of the few exceptions was the case of a Japanese trading company in Texas that several years ago hired an American for one of its top positions. A year or so later, it was reported in the press that under that American's guidance the branch office had chalked up a rate of sales growth exceeding that of any other of the branches in the U.S. Nothing else was reported in the press to the authors' knowledge, but it would be instructive to know how the American eventually fared in that trading company.

At about the same time, other Japanese trading companies in Texas were being sued by a group of their American employees who had learned that their Japanese co-workers were being paid bonuses for deposit back home in Japan (and not being reported for tax purposes in the U.S.) while the American employees were not given such bonuses. The Americans were furious at such arrant discrimination, while the Japanese managers were furious at such perfidious disloyalty to employer and such litigiousness on the part of the Americans. Doubtless this case, whatever its merits, did much to reinforce the convictions of the Japanese management of all companies in the U.S. that they could trust the Americans only so far and certainly not in managerial positions.

Admittedly such discrimination in wages is a thorny question. One of the writers (JS) well remembers the day some 25 years ago when one of his Japanese employees braced him in his office and asked for a salary closer in amount to the one an American co-worker was receiving. (The latter was about five times that of the former.) On the surface, his request was not unreasonable, but JS knew if he gave this man a considerable increase in pay, the other Japanese employees would rightly expect similar treatment and because their number was significant, the whole operation could become unprofitable—or nearly so. At last he had to take refuge in the explanation that the company paid standard Japanese wage scales to Japanese and standard American wage scales to Americans, although the Japanese and Americans concerned were both working in Japan. (If the salaries of the Americans had been lowered to the level of those of the Japanese, most of them would surely have quit and returned to the U.S., for even in those days their rents, which were determined by Japanese landlords, were unethically high and entirely out of the reach of anyone working for Japanese-level wages.) These days it seems the shoe is on the other foot, however, for there are more than a few Japanese in U.S.-Japan joint-venture companies in Japan who make more money than their American supervisors.

One of the writers (HVZ) mentioned to the president of a large Tokyo manufacturer that it would be wise to look into the staffing of their U.S. operation with the above personnel imbalance in mind. A short time later the president visited the United States and met all 102 employees of his Los Angeles office and told the writer that every one was Japanese.

Presidents of Japanese companies with subsidiaries in America have for years been answering complaints about such executive personnel policies by stating that they would replace some of their expatriates as soon as they could train Americans to take over, but very few such replacements have materialized. The writer (HVZ) met with a delegation of Japanese visitors from the general affairs divisions of several major Japanese firms and asked about the replacement of expatriates. (The General Affairs Division in a Japanese company is responsible for personnel matters.) They answered frankly that they had *no intention* of sending Japanese back home and filling their jobs with Americans. In Japan company presidents make what are called *tatemae* statements; that is, they say what seems fitting at the time, considering the audience, (which is surely an unethical practice itself.) The General Affairs Division people, however, are under no such obligations to make *tatemae* declarations and usually tell it as it is; that is, they make *honne*—or honest—explanations.

The Japanese policy of giving the well-paid jobs to their own kind has sometimes got them into trouble, especially in Southeast Asia. Many articles have appeared in the local press criticizing such corporate employment practices. In some Latin American countries, the governments require that their own citizens fill a certain percentage of the managerial positions in foreign companies. Japanese companies in Brazil have, in some instances, satisfied the government by hiring Brazilian citizens of Japanese ancestry with names like Tanaka, Yamada, and Suzuki, although it is difficult to say to what extent the characteristics of these people are Brazilian and to what extent Japanese.

U.S. companies in Japan frequently appoint natives to the top positions; in fact, most American companies there have no Americans at all in residence. In an article published in *PHP* in March, 1983, it was reported that the *Reader's Digest* had twenty overseas operations, and of those, only two were managed by Americans. (One of the two was Japan, but the *Reader's Digest* there had had a Japanese as president until a short time before.)

In studying the successes and failures of Japanese companies in the U.S. and of American firms in Japan, it appears the Japanese are doing much better than the Americans. Japanese companies have been far more successful in selling their products in the U.S. market than American companies have in Japan, but it has not always been so. Commencing early in the 1970's U.S. companies began to withdraw their expatriates from Japan and to replace them with Japanese. Each year since the trade imbalance has grown in Japan's favor, although this is not meant to imply that the Japanese managers have been disloyal to their American employers. It is a complicated matter, but in general it may be fairly said that U.S. expatriates, being more familiar with their own products and their home office people, may be more likely to aggressively push the sale of American goods and services, while the Japanese managers are conscious of their difficult position in trying to sell foreign goods to their compatriots in competition with local goods.

Another result of withdrawing American expatriates has been a decline in the knowledge of Japan at the headquarters of U.S. firms. Formerly an American executive would stay in Japan from three to ten years, then be repatriated to the home office after being replaced in Japan by another American. Thus communication between the home office and the Japan branch would be facilitated because at both ends were people who knew the problems of the other.

This again brings up the question of whether Japanese ethics apply to foreigners or is it a case of "Transgressions against outsiders not being considered transgressions at all." Some years ago, after a Japanese airliner had crashed, it was learned that the airline planned to pay solatiums to the families of the Japanese passengers who had died in the crash but not to the families of the foreign dead. When queried about this, the airline's initial response was that the "Japanese and the foreigners were different and, anyway, the foreigners were doubtless richer than the Japanese."

A Westerner visiting Japan for the first time will be impressed by the apparent friendliness and courtesy of most of the people he meets and may infer from this that the Japanese genuinely like foreigners and want to get to know more of them better. A 1980 Japanese government survey, however, learned that 64% asserted they did not want to associate with foreigners and had not the slightest intention of ever doing so.

Whether this denotes a positive dislike of foreigners or a feeling of superiority to them is a moot question, as is how such an attitude might be linked to the suggested exclusion of foreigners from Japanese ethical obligations. Although the Japanese fondness for foreign foods, clothing, movies, music, whiskey, sports equipment, and books is immediately apparent to the foreign visitor, most of the Japanese realize there is a danger in going too far in partaking of Western cultures. A young man from Tokyo might attend an excellent preparatory school in England, then take a B.A. at Yale and a M.B.A. at Harvard, only to find upon return to his native Japan that all that foreign schooling availed him little. Unless he goes back to obtain a B.A. from a Japanese university, he will have little chance of getting a decent job with a large corporation and then moving ahead at the pace of those with whom he attended primary and secondary schools. Generally speaking, a thin layer of Western ways is all right, but one is well advised not to carry it too far and thereby diminish from his essential Japanese character and outlook.

Corporations: paternalism

One of the writers (JS) and his Japanese wife recently watched President Reagan speak in the Diet in Japan by satellite TV. Nancy Reagan was at the President's side, but Premier Nakasone, Reagan's Japanese counterpart, sat listening to the American leader's speech without any sign of a female in attendance. Turning to JS, the writer's wife commented, "You know, I don't even know if Nakasone is married. I've never seen or read anything about him having a wife. Yet Reagan takes his with him everywhere, even to the Diet."

It is difficult to say if Mrs. Seward was expressing approval or disapproval of this shining example of American togetherness, but it is certain that more than a few of the Diet members looked at it askance, for wives do not play much of a role in the public lives of their politician-husbands in Japan. And here is another of those ambivalent areas in Japanese society that puzzle Westerners. It is assumed that any man of middle age or older is or has been married and, had a politician of that age never entered into matrimony, he would be regarded as odd indeed, although direct questions and open curiosity about his marital status would not really be good form.

At the same time Japanese corporate managers can display a degree of interest in the private lives of their subordinates that would be regarded as unethical and deeply resented in America. And most Japanese employees, according to the results of several polls, would prefer to work for a manager who takes a deep interest in their personal lives than one who adopts a "hands-off" attitude. The writer (JS) has one Japanese friend who is the president of a large Osaka corporation and who attends more than 300 weddings and funerals of his employees and important customers every year. In fact, he spends more than half his time in these activities on the behalf of his company.

In the U.S. marriage has long been regarded as a stabilizing force in the lives of men, in that husbands tend to go home early to the arms of their wives instead of carousing in pubs and chasing after women, but in Japan marriage seldom deters a man from spending many of his evenings in his *yukitsuke no bā* (favorite bar) with some of his saloon cronies. Because of this stabilizing effect, American corporations have traditionally preferred married men as managers, but this is apparently changing, for in a recent poll 34% of the chief executive officers queried replied that they thought that their managers being married was "not in the least important" to their companies while another 17 percent thought the marital state was "somewhat *un*important."

Corporate personnel policies: ethical aspects

1. The practice of offering lifetime employment, made famous by large corporations in Japan as well as by some in the U.S., seems ethically sound. Certainly it gives workers a sense of confidence and develops strong loyalties.

2. Keeping the level of production steady in Japan by aggressively seeking foreign orders when domestic sales fall off appears to be an acceptable business stratagem. When foreign orders are taken at prices that are below cost, however, leading to disruption of markets and layoffs in the distant countries, then the ethics of this policy are in doubt.

3. In both Japan and the United States about 25% of supervisors are thought of as being disagreeable, unfair, and unkind, e.g., S.O.B.'s. It would seem unethical and poor management for corporations to allow such people to continue to hold supervisory positions once their

behavior has been discovered. Retraining should be tried, and if it is unsuccessful, these people should be transferred to jobs where they supervise no one.

4. On the whole, Japan's bonus policies seem more ethical than American. Often bonus and stock option policies in U.S. corporations cause injury to employee morale, because the great majority of workers receive neither and yet they feel that they too contribute importantly to the success of the enterprise. Sometimes executives in striving to qualify for bonuses or options make short-term decisions that may be injurious when viewed from a long-term standpoint.

5. What to do with unproductive employees is a problem everywhere. Keeping the *madogiwa-zoku* on the payroll in Japan and giving them the same bonuses as highly productive workers seems unfair.

6. Discrimination against female employees has been much reduced in the U.S. in recent years, but in Japan the record is not as good, there still being many occupations and positions not open to women. Also various devices are used to keep their salaries low and deny them the benefits enjoyed by males.

7. Minorities in the U.S. are protected against discrimination by countless federal, state, and local laws. Some minorities, for instance, the Jews, Chinese, and Japanese, have much higher average incomes than do Americans as a whole. Some blacks and many Hispanics bear far more children than do most people in other groups, and this apparently has lead to less parental training and, on the average, poorer school attendance and performance records. This has made it difficult for many of them to earn as much money as others or to be as steadily employed. Some minorities have problems because many of their members do not speak English well, if at all. Japan has no problems of these kinds, but still has minorities,

although they are determined more by occupation rather than race. Overt discrimination against the *burakumin* continues and by any standards seems unethical, as is discrimination against offspring of Japanese women and aliens.

Chapter Nine

Governments: The Ethics of Their Elected and Non-elected Officials

For many years in the U.S. the word bureaucrat, for non-elected government official, has been used as a term of derision. One dictionary definition even describes bureaucracy as a "system of administration marked by red tape, proliferation, and officialism and characterized by office-holders who follow a narrow, rigid, and formal routine with great authority within their own departments."

Shooting arrows of barbed criticism at our "bumbling bureaucracy" in its capital city Foggy Bottom has long been an avocation with many Americans, whose forefathers fled Europe to escape oppressive governments and then rebelled later against what they perceived as oppression by the administration of the mother country, England.

After the frontier experience, dormant doubts and suspicions were again fanned into life as governmental regulations began to spread their tentacles westward over vast territories where for decades the law—if it existed at all—had taken the loose form of posses, vigilante committees, town marshalls, and a few, usually distant army forts: summary "Frontier Justice" as dispensed by Judge Roy Bean and his "Law West of the Pecos" of Texas and Hanging Judge Isaac C. Parker of Fort Smith, Arkansas.

Thereafter, the mills of governmental regulations ground and spread slow, but spread they did, inch by inch, mile by mile, given impetus from time to time by such spurs as Franklin Roosevelt's New Deal, the exigencies of WW II, Lyndon Johnson's Great Society, and its own built-in propensity for organizational aggrandizement and obesity. Candidates for political office learned anew that "promise, large promise" of aid and benefits offered a more certain road to election, so the number of federal hands needed to dispense this tax money for redistribution grew apace.

The Puritan ethic of government spending—"Balance the budget, stay out of debt, live within your means"— was going down in defeat before the onslaught. In 1983, of every tax dollar, 43¢ went to direct benefits payments to individuals, with another 11¢ going to states and localities, part of which was used in their welfare programs.

Willing to accept largesse from the government with one hand while beating it about the head with the other, American voters watched with dismay as the watch-dogs of the press, led by the *Washington Post*, uncovered the Watergate scandal and promoted its prosecution to its conclusion, surely a triumph for political ethics in this country and a demonstration to the world of American principles. One now wishes, however, that the liberal press would show the same zeal in exposing the on-going cocaine scandal in our Congress. Perhaps they would do so if only there weren't so many liberal members' names on the list of cocaine users.

The present-day American sees our bureaucrats as being indifferent to the use of his precious tax dollars, lethargic, wasteful, clock-watching, over-paid, and almost impossible to fire, but how many of these alleged demerits spring from within the bureaucratic corpus and how many arise from ineptness on the part of the politicians who manage the bureaucracy is a moot question.

The average time in office of these "politician-managers" is only 18 months. Typically they occupy the top four levels of government management and during the relatively short time they are in office, they adopt an "us against them" stance vis-a-vis the three million bureaucrats beneath them whom they strive to control instead of motivating and developing, since their tenure is usually too brief for them to reap the benefits of such farsighted personnel guidance policies.

But whatever else they are, our bureaucrats are not much criticized for unethical behavior, other than the lack of a strong sense of work-place obligation. To be sure, there are occasional exposures of some who make off with large quantities of government property or award unjustifiably favorable contracts and purchase orders to companies who may return these favors with post-retirement sinecures and free vacations in Jamaica. On balance, however, they are otherwise probably no more or no less ethical in their performance of their jobs than the average American.

While the U.S. bureaucracy is weaker than the U.S. executive, in Japan the opposite is the case. While Japan has no Pentagon, the U.S. has no Ministry of International Trade and Industry. Where Washington—a city devoted to politics—concerns itself more with defense and strategic issues and assigns matters concerning Japan a low priority (except for the current trade imbalance issue), Tokyo—a cultural, economic, *and* political center—concentrates on economic policy. And the office of the U.S. president wields more power than that of the prime minister in Japan.

Given these differences in our bureaucracies together with a general unawareness of them, problems in communication continually arise between the two governments, and these are exacerbated by linguistic and cultural barriers and by the fact that in the U.S. specialists in some region or country (such as Japan) are often passed over in favor of generalists in the upper levels of our bureaucratic hierarchy.

By contrast, the Japanese bureaucracy was born of the ideal of selfless service and loyalty fostered by the Confucian ethic of the feudal era. Ranking beneath only the court nobles in the vertical feudal power structure of the time, the samurai held absolute sway over the remaining three classes of society—the farmers, artisans, and merchants, any of whom might be abruptly shortened by a head by a flashing sword if he incurred the lordly displeasure of a samurai.

When the Tokugawa Shogunate ended and was replaced by the newly restored emperor Meiji and his imperial faction in 1868, it fell to the lot of the samurai to form the administrative backbone of the new government in Tokyo because as a class they were better qualified for this task and because the abolition of the fiefs and the dethronement of their lords had deprived the warrior class of employment as well as their two swords and *chonmage* (topknots). With a mighty effort the new administration's planners focussed the loyalty of the samurai—and those below them—on the nation and its emperor through the promotion of a bureaucratic ethic of personal sacrifice for the public good and selfless endeavor, among other means.

Yet today in a country marked until 1945 by its relative absence, public corruption is more prevalent than it has been at any time since the beginning in 1868 of Japan's modern age. True, today Japan's bureaucracy—and especially such ministries as MITI—is a elite group carefully selected from among the best students graduating from the University of Tokyo and a few other top universities and its numerical ratio to the total working population is smaller than in the U.S., France, West Germany, or Great Britain. Even so it is showing signs of separation at the seams, with worse to come if the Japanese people do not develop an ethic of responsibility as citizens. Even the Lockheed scandal might never have gone beyond the first magazine report of Tanaka's financial irregularities had it not been for inquisitive foreign journalists who persisted in raising the subject at press conferences in Japan.

What has happened, according to some Japanese scholars, in the years since the close of the Pacific War is that the group ethic based on self-sacrifice for the public weal is gradually being replaced by egoism, the philosophy of being primarily concerned with one's welfare and future. Even though many bureaucrats are becoming less group-oriented, at least comparatively, and more individualistic, the people are still held largely in thrall by a tendency to view bureaucrats as their masters, not their servants, and to seldom question official acts, words, or prerogatives.

The old phrase *Kanson Mimpi* (Respect the officials; despise the common folk) is still laden with relevancy in Japan.

As bureaucratic ethics begin to falter, Japan's bureaucratic-industrial complex evinces an even closer degree of cooperation among its triangular foundation of politicians, officials, and private business leaders. In many instances, this cooperation has become collusion, the adhesive element of which is the easy transferral of the officials from government into private industry.

In 1977, for example, 27 percent of the members of the House of Representatives in Japan and 35 percent of the House of Councilors were ex-bureaucrats, figures that probably are higher today. While still in office, bureaucrats may use their authority and budgets to build support and earn the good will of the electorate and obligations for themselves in private industry.

Many officials, however, remain at their posts until well into or even past middle age, then resign or retire to accept positions in a segment of private industry that would benefit from their presence and their close ties with their former co-workers. This transfer is called *ama-kudari* or descending from heaven, with the word 'heaven' saying much about the Japanese attitude toward officials and their place in the scheme of things.

Some bureaucrats even move back and forth, as in the notable case of one man who retired at age 61 from MITI, joined a computer company as its vice-chairman, and then after two years there moved over to become president of JETRO, a quasi-governmental organization.

A Japanese company considering an action that is legally equivocal would go first not to a lawyer but to the responsible government agency and working, if feasible, through a proper introduction would meet the official with jurisdiction to request his explanation of the law or regulation.

Even then the supplicant Japanese company must contend with the concept of *tatemae* and *honne*, the former being what one is expected to say officially for public consumption and the latter being his true feelings or in this case just how he would interpret the law. Needless to say, one can hardly expect the official to make a *honne* statement on the spot, unless the letter of introduction and recommendation is from a former *sempai* (senior) or benefactor. What usually happens is that a cornucopia of dinners and drinks will follow, during which the supplicant will strive to establish a close emotional rapport with the bureaucrat to create an atmosphere conducive to the *honne* revelation. The dual facade of the bureaucrat in this instance is also called the *omote-ura* syndrome, the *omote* (front) being the strict, official countenance seen by the public and the *ura* (back) being the informal, relaxed, evening-hours face that is easier to deal with. Therefore, the purpose of almost all such contacts is to create an atmosphere in which *ishin-denshin* or heart-to-heart communication becomes possible and where the bureaucrat will "open his belly" (*hara wo waru*) and express his *honne*, which the supplicant can only hope will be favorable to his cause.

This often-required interpretation of the law is why the so-called administrative guidance (*gyōsei shidō* or *kankoku*) of Japan's government agencies can even be taken by private industry as legally binding. Any looseness in the wording of a law leaves ample room for bureaucratic interpretation, which then has the force of law.

For several years the question of just how powerful MITI is has been debated by observers of Japan's economic actions, with some holding that this agency is a monolithic, omnipotent bureaucracy before which all men tremble and pray and others saying instead that while possessed of much power, MITI is nonetheless often ignored or at least confronted and opposed and circumvented by more than a few in private industry. Those who support the former position—the creators of and contributors to the Japan Inc. theory—often hold further that such a degree of collusion between government and private industry is unethical and antithetical to the principles on which the free nations of the world should conduct their economic affairs.

To be sure, there are telling arguments on both sides. Some go as far as to say the U.S. should develop its own version of MITI to better compete with Japan. If we try to do this, however, we may also have to try to alter some of our fundamental attitudes, for we Americans generally view our government's role as regulatory in essence while the Japanese accept theirs as plan-rational and developmental. They expect MITI to support Japan's worldwide marketing strategy, allocate scarce resources, set goals, phase out industries of lower productivity and lesser need, and guide and support R & D.

We would have to change, if possible, our view of bureaucrats as over-paid, time-serving meddlers who police and harass, often unwarrantedly, our legitimate commercial activities and begin to see them instead as officials who are ready and even eager to help us find new technologies and pioneer new markets.

Such a change in our perception could not be mandated nor could it take place overnight. Our bureaucrats themselves would have to make some very fundamental changes in their attitudes and actions, to say nothing of the changes that would have to be made in many of our very specific anti-business laws. Whether or not this is feasible or even conceivable is a moot question, but without these changes it would be practically impossible to realize the almost instinctive cooperation that exists between the bureaucracy and private business in Japan.

With the world perceiving Japan to be a rich nation, the question of Japanese magnanimity, both as a nation and as a people, is being raised more often these days, with the central query being, is it ethical to be so affluent and yet do so comparatively little for others?

Indeed, this question of *daikokumin no kindo* (the generosity of a great people) has long troubled observers, and one recalls the early post-war years in which many crippled war veterans dressed in white hospital gowns and military caps staggered on crutches and artificial legs up and down the aisles of Japan's trains bowing and begging, often to the tune of heroic military marches played on harmonicas. To be sure, Japan was poor indeed in those times, but there was the gnawing suspicion that public indifference and even hostility ("They lost the war for us, didn't they?'') was as much to blame for the financial plight of those pitiable men as was the generalized poverty of the people and the country.

Even today part of Japan's alleged niggardliness can be traced to the Japanese view of themselves as a poor people, and there is more than a little justification for the saying that "the figures prosper, while the people suffer.''

Every year in Japan a leading bank compiles international statistics to announce what it calls a happiness index, based on research into such matters as the social infrastructure as well as climate, income, purchasing power, job satisfaction, *inter alia*, with the result that the Japanese always rank very low in this rating. Or for a more personal view, ask any Japanese businessman or his wife who has recently spent several years in the U.S. how he feels about living conditions in Japan. To be sure, he or she may be pleased to be back with friends and relatives and all that is culturally familiar but when asked about comparative living conveniences, they—if you can persuade them to be perfectly candid—will express disappointment.

Seeing themselves in this light as they do, the people of Japan are not, relatively speaking, much moved to be generous to others. For example, in 1982 the average American contribution to the Community Chest was the equivalent of ¥1,700 (about $7.20), that of the Australian was ¥960, the Canadian was ¥800, and that of the Japanese was a mere ¥168. Nor do their religious beliefs encourage generosity to outsiders and strangers, as is the case with Christianity. Further, among the business community, the concept of community service is limited mostly to one's own company or at the most to his industry.

In the field of government instead of individual activity, however, Japan must be given higher grades, for their ODA (Official Development Assistance)—although declining for the past two years—still totalled $3 billion in 1982, ranking it fourth in the world after the U.S., France, and West Germany.

However, financial grants from non-governmental or private voluntary organizations tell another story. In 1981 Japanese contributions to developing nations from such groups amounted to only $27.3 million in comparison to the $1,108 million given by the U.S. and the $371.1 million contributed by West Germany. Even little Holland gave more than three times as much as Japan. Again this is partially attributable to the concern of Shintoism and Buddhism with their own domestic realms at the expense of foreign peoples.

A government's taxation of its own corporations, the tax scale, and the methods of collection are not only a strictly internal matter but also one into which questions of ethics should not intrude, although, of course, compliance with tax regulations is another matter. (Japan has what might be called a highly creative system of taxation of both corporations and individuals, as described elsewhere herein, in that the system must be given much of the credit for creating Japan's economic success.)

Statistics that compare the ethics of individuals and corporations in both countries in complying with their tax obligation are not available, but one can assume that the lower average tax rates in Japan encourage a higher level of compliance, as they would elsewhere. One notable aspect of Japanese corporation taxes is that an element of negotiability often enters into the picture, with tax officials and corporate accountants sitting down together, perhaps after arriving at the *honne* stage in their relationship, and reaching an agreement on how much is owed and how much will be paid and when.

And this is still another situation in which the *amakudari* custom is useful, since many corporations try to employ, as long-term consultants, tax officials shortly after retirement, especially those who have worked in the tax office having jurisdiction over that company.

Knowing this, the *Kokuzei-chō* (National Tax Administration Agency) transfers its tax assessors to other branches quite frequently.

One government tax on corporations that is muddying relations between Japan and the U.S. at the time of this writing is the unitary tax.

In 1967 a Multi-State Tax Commission (MTC) was set up to audit U.S. companies that operate in several states because it had been found that some companies engaged in what they euphemistically called "advantageous intra-company bookkeeping" to take advantage of lower-tax jurisdictions. A company with offices and plants in both, say, California and Delaware and production and assembly work divided between the two might find it to its advantage to under-invoice what it made in California and shipped to Delaware and then to show more profits in Delaware, where the tax on corporations is less than in California.

As the MTC rolled up its sleeves and got to work, they found that such was indeed the case so they decided to take a target company's nationwide profits and then calculate each profit center's tax bite on that state's proportional share of those profits.

A hefty increase in revenues resulted.

Later it was decided to extend this method—another instance of creative taxation but in a different sense—to multinational corporations as well, for it seemed quite within the realms of possibility that a, say, British multinational with a Hong Kong subsidiary that made fasteners and shipped those fasteners to the U.S. for use in the final assembly of a certain piece of equipment might well over-invoice the fasteners to take advantage of Hong Kong's low corporate tax rate and show higher costs and lesser profits in the U.S. operation.

As of this writing, 12 states are applying worldwide

unitary taxation while several others seem to be on the point of adopting it. *Forbes* magazine of January 30, 1984 quoted a Florida legislator as saying, "It was like finding money in the streets."

With their expanding organizational growth in the U.S., Japanese multi-nationals are now protesting with increasing vehemence the application of this unitary tax to their American assembly operations, pointing out—no doubt correctly—that while it may increase tax revenues somewhat, it will discourage them and their fellows from the consideration of future expansion in the U.S.

The authors are reminded of one method of calculation used by the Japanese tax offices in calculating the income tax of resident foreigners when they last lived there. (It may well still be in use today.)

Foreigners in Japan paid income tax on what they earned in Japan for the first five years of their residence and after that on their world-wide income. Since the tax officials suspected that some foreigners paid taxes only on that portion of their income remitted to Japan while depositing part or even most of it, including what was due them for their work in Japan, in banks in their country of origin, the Japanese devised a formula that endeavored to calculate the foreigner's total income on the basis of the size of his rented quarters.

If the foreigner rented a dwelling larger than forty-four *tsubo* (about 1,600 square feet) in size, the tax office made the presumption that his total income, in Japan and abroad, had to exceed a certain level, no matter how little income he actually reported and no matter how much or how little rent he said he paid, because there might be collusion between the resident foreigner and the Japanese landlord.

In a slightly different guise, it was an early Japanese version of the unitary tax.

Chapter Ten

The Ethics of Legal Action

Criticism is mounting in the United States against the practice of settling disputes in court rather than through negotiation, arbitration, or mediation. Our national litigiousness has nourished a legal establishment that has grown from one lawyer for every 1,879 people in 1958 to one for every 375 in 1983.

At the beginning of 1984 an estimated 625,000 attorneys were practicing law in the U.S., while in Japan at the same time, they numbered a mere 15,000, with only 12,500 of them in private practice, making the American ratio 21 times more per capita. Nor do Europeans require nearly as many lawyers as do Americans, although even they nourish far more than do the Japanese, there being about seven times more per capita in Britain than in Japan and nearly four times more in West Germany.

American courts lag far behind in handling cases, with judges at all levels complaining of the overloads. The Supreme Court is struggling to find ways to reduce the volume of cases appealed, suggesting that lower appellate courts might well be the places of last resort for many of the cases that now go to Washington D.C., where 30,000 lawyers work. Chief Justice Warren Berger has charged in public speeches that the litigiousness of the American people has reached an unreasonable stage.

Legal fees charged by private law firms in the U.S. are estimated to exceed $30 billion a year, but these charges are only a part of the cost. The expense to U.S. companies, government agencies, and various other organizations of maintaining in-house legal staffs runs into many billions of additional dollars.

Every year 150,000 new laws are passed by our local and national legislatures. As Goethe said, "Laws and rights multiply like an evil disease." We are faced with a situation in which an excess of law has weakened the rule of law itself. At least ten million cases are carried on our court dockets at any given instant, whereas in Japan only about half a million civil actions are brought in an entire year.

So dedicated have we as a people become to a fiat of Ferdinand I (1503–1564), "Let justice be done, though the world perish," that we are not shocked into corrective action when we hear of a company of lawyers fighting the ruling of a government agency for twelve years in the courts, with transcripts and other documents totalling one hundred thousand pages. The issue at litigation? The wording on the labels of peanut butter jars.

Our federal system leaves us with a different body of law for each state and territory, which makes precious little sense. The jury system lets ordinary citizens who may know next to nothing of the law try to apply legal knowledge and doctrines to the court process of discovering the truth and establishing legal facts. And our criminal law enforcement system is clearly failing miserably at its task of insuring for the weak and the aged among us the safety to work and live in our cities.

Perhaps as many as a quarter of our people are involved in legal action every year, with the head of one of our government agencies reporting not long ago that he was at that moment the target of 225 pending suits. This massive legal action has been likened to the junction of two mighty rivers in flood, with antagonistic currents, counter-currents, and cross currents all striving

strenuously to dominate others. Its cost—about one percent of our Gross National Product—drives up the prices
of our exports, worsens the trade imbalance, and
increases unemployment by using up funds better spent
on plant, R & D, and penetration of foreign markets.

In February, 1984, Chief Justice Warren Burger
delivered a stinging critique of the legal profession before
the American Bar Association in Las Vegas, in which he
clearly indicated that he believed there was a causal link
between the "sharp decline in public confidence" in
attorneys-at-law and the doubling of the number of lawyers
in the past ten years. Blaming an excessive desire to
generate income for too much protracted legal maneuvering, the Chief Justice recommended a "few carefully considered $5,000 or $10,000 penalties for such actions." En-
dorsing more out-of-court settlements, he said lawyers
"tend to forget that we ought to be healers of conflicts."

Historical background
Since Colonial times, Americans have been quick to refer
their disputes to judges for decisions, although apparently never at the high rates experienced in the 1970's and
1980's.

Reading the court records of the Dutch settlements in
New York in the 1600's leaves the impression that anyone
annoyed by another person immediately referred the matter to a magistrate for a ruling. The submission itself,
however, of disputes to the courts at least demonstrated
a certain standard of ethical behavior on the part of the
colonists, for in many other parts of the world at that time
disputes were still being settled by the parties concerned,
in many instances with knives, clubs, or guns. One of the
characteristics of Colonial America was a comparatively
low level of crime, a principal reason being the religious
principles of the immigrants, many of whom came here

in order to practice their religion without government interference. Also, judges and magistrates had reputations for fairness that made the settlers willing to entrust their problems to them for resolution.

Visitors from Europe even in those early days noted with surprise the large number of lawyers and law suits. In Britain it had been difficult to become a solicitor or barrister, but in the Colonies the opposite was true. The Frenchman, de Tocqueville, writing in the early nineteenth century, observed that American lawyers were regarded as our equivalent to nobility and that the widely accepted way to redress wrongs in this country was to pass a law or file a suit.

Even so, this evidence of a litigious spirit worried our ancestors, and in reference to this concern U.S. Attorney-General William French Smith, in a speech in May, 1983, reminded his audience of certain words of Abraham Lincoln, who, it will be recalled, was a lawyer before becoming a politician: "Discourage litigation. Persuade your neighbors to compromise whenever you can. Point out to them how the nominal winner is often the real loser—in fees, expense, and waste of time."

History of law in Japan

Until the end of the feudal age the Japanese had no understanding of the concept of law, in the Western sense. That they as individuals might have rights, under the protection of the law, was not realized. If disputants were of the same class, their quarrels were generally resolved by conciliation and compromise, but if one's social class was superior to that of his opponent in the dispute, then the force of the superior's position and power alone usually carried the day. The few codes that were in force enunciated ethical guidelines or protected the privileges of class but contained few specific legal procedures for redress of wrongs. In 1892, for example, all the codes that had been written down during the preceding 1,200 years were compiled, but these did not exceed one thousand pages: only two volumes.

Like the Chinese, the Japanese of those times—as well as many today—believed that egocentric arbitrary religious and moral precepts, such as those the Western world would bring them at a later date, were an indication of the absence, not of the presence, of religious and moral wisdom and of a comprehension of the entire thrust of human experience.

During the Tokugawa Era the task of escorting disputants to the magisterial courts fell to men called *kujishi*: innkeepers who, in time, came to advise on proper legal procedures and the completion of documents.

Those persons having civil problems in their own communities tended to settle them between themselves, often prodded by thinly-veiled coercion from village headmen. Judicial and administrative functions were not organized separately, being in that respect somewhat like the methods followed in certain Communist and rightist dictatorships of the twentieth century. Torture was used as a means to gather "facts," whether in criminal or civil proceedings. No appeal was allowed to a decision made by the authorities. As in China at that time groups or their leaders were often liable for the conduct of individual members. Without approval of the village leadership and their overlords, suits could not be brought in the Shogunate courts. When efforts were made to do so, the punishment of the petitioner was often harsh, in some cases even death through torture. Personal and social relationships were usually structured according to Confucianist teaching, and individuals had little opportunity for recourse if abused by superiors.

After it was opened to the West in 1859, Japan was exposed to the cultures of many countries. Foreigners who came to live in Yokohama, Kobe, Nagasaki, Tokyo, and other Treaty Ports feared to entrust their lives and property to the Japanese courts and to the uncertainties of a nation without a sound, long-established legal system harmonious with Western standards. A consequence was that for the first forty years, that is, until mid-1899, expatriates were usually tried in their own Consular Courts. Actually, however, Japanese interests did not suffer from the extraterritoriality protection given foreigners, for often enough it would seem the Consuls treated their own nationals more severely than the Japanese would have. The Japanese, a step at a time, changed their own system by adopting European code law, so that from 1899 on foreigners were tried in Japanese courts, where the record for impartiality proved to be commendable.

Current practice in resolving disputes

Vestiges of some feudal practices continue even today in Japan. A 1942 law recommends that disputes be solved on the basis of "sound morals and with a warm heart," words that would bring an American lawyer to the brink of despair. Conciliation, for instance, takes place far more often than in the U.S., partly because the Japanese simply do not feel comfortable in the atmosphere of hostile confrontation that characterizes courts of law, which the Japanese regard as an embarrassing experience that violates their privacy and to which they will appeal only as a desperate last resort. Then too, as pointed out by Takenori Kawashima, a famous sociologist and jurist, the Japanese do not readily accept the idea of universal concepts of justice that exist and function independent of the wills of the persons at dispute and do not like to assess good and evil in others. Even judges will urge antagonists to seek conciliation and will often suggest compromises.

Most of their nation's lawyers work in the large cities where there are district courts: particularly Tokyo and Osaka. With few exceptions, their offices are small and each lawyer will average having only one or two clerks to assist him. Being few in number, Japan's lawyers are generally so busy that they will not undertake cases with issues that will not justify large fees.

Japanese prefer conciliation over court trials for a reason deriving from Oriental custom. If a dispute goes to trial and a judge hands down a verdict, the defeated party loses face publicly in addition to whatever other losses he may incur. While both the accuser and the defendant will believe right is on his side, they are encouraged to restrain their assertiveness in the interest of achieving compromise. If the accuser persists in proclaiming the correctness of his position and demanding that legal action be taken, he runs the risk of being ostracized for his obtuse refusal to consider conciliation through compromise and, if he wins in court, for bringing embarrassing loss of face to the other litigant.

Other barriers to litigiousness in Japan are the non-refundable filing fees, which must be paid in advance and equal a percentage of the amount sued for, and the lawyer's fee, which must be paid in any event, since contingency fees are considered unethical.

Nor is the law much used as a ladder to political prominence or affluence. Not one of the 16 postwar Prime Ministers has been a lawyer, and only 51 of the 763 Diet members are members of the legal profession.

Further, only about 20% of all Japanese lawyers enjoy an annual income of over $43,000.

Japanese contracts usually end with a clause stating that in the event of disagreement, both parties agree to discuss the matter in good faith and try to work out their differences.

One anomalous aspect of conciliation as it is practiced in Japan deserves some comment as a postscript to the above. Despite this undeniable devotion to the principle of conciliation on the part of the Japanese in general, it seems to be accorded much less attention in the area of informal male-female relationships, especially by the distaff side. Whereas in the U.S. quarrels between mates and lovers are often settled in a denouement that features a "let's kiss and make up" scene in which both parties confess to being partly or wholly to blame, this happens much less often in Japan, where the Japanese female seldom gives an inch, admits to no fault on her part even in the interest of conciliation, and wards off all incursions against what she rigidly regards as the basic correctness of her stance.

To be sure, this is a subjective judgment on the part of one of the coauthors (JS) based on his own experiences and of those of a number of his foreign acquaintances long resident in Japan. Even so, it may well have a wide validity and if so, one conceivable explanation is that traditional male dominance has so suppressed Japanese women that they can ill afford to show any leniency or forgiveness at all. With their backs already to the wall, they have no fallback positions, no room left in which to display magnanimity.

Language and the law in Japan

In Japan, because of the ambiguous meanings of many words, it may often be difficult to determine exactly what a law means. Although some words have core meanings that may be determined from study of their Chinese characters, their peripheral meanings are often vague and difficult to define precisely. A reason for this problem can be traced back to the Japanese decision to superimpose an alien (Chinese) system of writing on their spoken language. Often one of the new characters borrowed from China would retain vestiges of the original Chinese meaning while serving to express the perhaps somewhat different meaning of the spoken Japanese word as well.

But whatever the reason, the feeling in Japan is that the meaning of a provision of the law should not be limited to what the legislators wrote in the statute books, but should be sensibly interpreted to mean what responsible citizens feel it ought to have provided. Mr. Masaaki Imai, in the June 27, 1978 issue of the *Japan Economic Journal*, pointed out that some Japanese laws are not precise, as noted in another chapter, and their interpretations are often left to officials of the concerned government agency. He added that this created a problem for foreigners, who, on reading the law, still do not know how it would be applied in a particular instance. To add to the confusion, interpretations of the law might change when circumstances change. Sometimes even answers to the same question differ, depending upon the position and role of the speaker. The formal answer is what would be expected considering his position, while a completely candid answer may be reserved for an informal meeting and, more likely than not, would be vouchsafed by a lower-level person. On occasions, it may not be given at all, unless rapport exists, and sometimes it will be given by a third person who has the confidence of both.

Because of cultural differences, foreigners who are unaware of their ways of wording their thoughts may believe Japanese officials and businessmen to be unethical, but if they learn something of the language and customs and get to know a number of Japanese personally, they should be able to obtain honest answers to their questions.

Whether the statutes are unclear or not, Japanese bureaucrats may at times seem imperious when they hand down their interpretations, reflecting a historical arrogance on the part of the bureaucracy and the fearful respect they were widely accorded. During the Allied Occupation, American advisors encouraged Japan's government functionaries to be respectful and considerate of the public. Some improvement was made, but even in 1984, Japanese complaints about the cold hauteur of their bureaucrats are still heard.

Political pressures often influence decisions in Japan, as in any other country. If special interests exert enough force, bureaucrats at times interpret the law, or rather, bend the law to accommodate those interests. Where the interpretations are clearly wrong and injure foreigners, then other outside pressures may be called for. Appeals to the courts can be made, but in view of the crowded dockets, much time may elapse before redress is obtained. If fair-minded government officials take an interest in the case, they can sometimes find a way to overcome the obstacles. Representations by foreign governments are, of course, useful.

In summary, recourse to the courts may be necessary to obtain redress, but political pressures are more likely to get results in a reasonably short length of time—without the dangers inherent in making the adversary lose face in a court confrontation.

Despite the weaknesses of their own system, Japanese corporations operating in foreign countries are sometimes more critical of the foreign legal system than their own. Mr. Akio Morita, one of Sony's founders, expressed such views in a speech given at the Kennedy School of Business recently. Among the points he made, as reported in an article entitled "Do Companies Need Lawyers?" in *Japan Quarterly*, January-March, 1983, were:

1. If Sony paid much attention to the advice of lawyers (in foreign countries), some of which is conflicting, it would be unable to do business at all.

2. Attorneys-at-law in America sometimes create

business for themselves by encouraging clients to sue over trifling matters.

3.   Japan has nothing quite like the U.S. contingency fee arrangement, which seems to encourage recourse to law.

Legal aid for the poor

In Western countries, various organizations provide free legal aid for those under the poverty level, and in America these legal aid assignments are sometimes sought by fee-hungry men of the law as sources of additional income.

In contrast, Japan expends the equivalent of only $2,500,000 per year on such no-cost legal aid, while the British government spends about thirty times as much, with a population less than half that of Japan.

Fees charged by lawyers

The cost of providing legal aid for the poor in America is high and is ultimately charged to the public in the form of taxes, with the fees, whether billed to a government agency or private organization, running from about $50 to $250 per hour.

At times legal fees in general challenge credulity. Three Washington, D.C. lawyers, for instance, recently charged $10,600,000 to represent several Sioux Indian tribes in a mineral dispute, and, in another instance, a fee of $160,000 was paid to lawyers for representing Labor Department employees who won an award of only $30,000.

Although some lawyers earn $250,000 a year or more, most receive far less. After deducting substantial office expenses, the average lawyer probably takes in about $40,000 a year, according to an article by Richard Greene, "Lawyers versus the Marketplace," in *Forbes*, January 16, 1984. Competition for business is forcing some men of the law to accept less money nowadays than they would have five years ago. Starting salaries for newly-graduated lawyers in the ten largest law firms in Dallas, Texas, range from $33,000 to $35,000, for example.

Lawyers also find accidents and disasters to be profitable fields to plow. In 1980 a fire at the MGM Grand Hotel in Las Vegas, Nevada, took the lives of 85 people and injured 700 others. The 250 lawyers who became involved collected at least $90,000,000 for their services.

Prospects for reform

In the American Bar Association's annual convention in July, 1983, experts warned that the number of lawyers is expected to exceed one million by the next decade, and that this would inevitably lead to more "ambulance chasing" and other fee-engendering activities. One law school professor at the convention even went so far as to propose methods of preventing non-lawyers from competing on their preserves. Since both the U.S. Congress and state legislatures are dominated by lawyer-members, some of these men, when framing laws, ascertain that the interests of the legal profession are protected and that would-be competitors are forbidden from activites the lawyers wish to monopolize.

In Japan much of the work that would be reserved for lawyers in the United States is performed by scribes or scriveners, at low cost. Divorces, for instance, can be arranged without recourse to a practicing lawyer. Wills are usually prepared by judicial scriveners, who also fill out various other forms for submission to the courts. Many scriveners are law school graduates who did not pass the examinations to take advanced training. Administrative scriveners are used for the start-up of a new business, since they know the legal requirements and have the necessary forms. They also have Japanese character typewriters and use them when preparing forms for submission to government agencies. (Most small Japanese companies have no such typewriters, which are large, unwieldy, and expensive: more like small printing presses.) Scriveners have the reputation of being both competent and reliable.

In the United States, as the number of lawyers mushrooms, Gary Huckaby, a former Chairman of the American Bar Association's Committee on Delivery of Legal Services, has observed that he is seeing a growing number of tactics designed to increase legal work and income and stated, "It used to be that (out of court) settlement of a dispute was the first road a lawyer would take. Now settlement is the last road we take."

Huckaby also noted a tendency for several lawyers representing the same client to come to court simultaneously on the same matter, boosting client bills. He stated that sometimes the sole function of the additional lawyer or lawyers was for "one to pat the other on the back after he sits down." (*Dallas Times Herald*, July 31, 1983)

Without doubt such tendencies injure the image of the legal profession. A Gallup poll, conducted for the *Wall Street Journal* and reported on Nov. 2, 1983, queried the public as to how they rated the honesty and ethical standards of various groups. Twenty-seven percent rated lawyers as "very low or low" against the twenty percent who gave low ratings to business executives and the ten percent to medical doctors.

Russel Baker, a syndicated columnist for the *New York Times*, proposed on June 11, 1983 that the "U.S. should export to Japan one lawyer for every three automobiles imported into the U.S. This would reduce America's lawyer population by about 600,000." After all, each country should sell abroad what it has too much of at home.

While the United States complains about Japan's cultural barriers to imports and points out such examples as a distribution system that is expensive and wasteful, the

Foreign Investment Review Agency of Canada, in a September, 1983 release entitled "Investment Barriers in the U.S.," protested that the American legal system was so complicated that it could be considered a "cultural barrier" itself.

Without a doubt, America's litigiousness wields an overall deleterious effect on our society. Civil suits filed in Federal courts alone now exceed 200,000 a year. State courts handle far more; in 1977, for instance, more than 12,000,000 were filed. An article in *U.S. News and World Report*, Dec. 20, 1982, expressed the view that all this litigation serves to dampen the enterprizing spirit. Because of the huge volume of pending cases, prompt judgments are impossible and four or more years will often pass from filing until the court hands down a decision, with expensive legal fees being a heavy burden in the interim.

The wheels of justice grind slow in Japan as well, with it taking about as long to try a case as it does in this country. (A Japanese lawyer is reported to have commented, "You *can* get justice in Japan—if you live long enough.") But in Japan the delays in reaching verdicts have the effect of making the public reluctant to refer disputes to the courts. The Japanese government could easily correct this problem by permitting more law school graduates to become *bengoshi or* practicing attorneys, but it fears that in time the Japanese would develop the same deleterious fondness for litigation seen in America and Europe, increasing the cost of doing businees and reducing Japan's competitive strength in world markets.

After graduation from law school in Japan, one takes an examination to enter the required two-year course at the Legal Training and Research Institute of the Supreme Court. Of the thirty thousand law school graduates who take this examination every year, 90 percent are eliminated at the first stage. The second stage, which lasts eleven days, is made up of oral and essay writing tests. Only about 450 students, or 1.5% of the original number, pass this second stage, and not all of them enter the legal profession as *bengoshi*, judges, or procurators.

In contrast, more than 50% of law school graduates taking state bar examinations in the U.S. usually pass.

Alternatives to legal action in resolving disputes

Marshall J. Breger, member of the American Bar Association's Committee on Public Interest Practice, has stated that the high cost of lawyers could be traced to their monopoly over dispute resolution. He pointed out that in America lawyers are employed for tasks that in other countries would be performed by civil servants, laymen, business consultants, or even clergy. He suggested that the use of informal dispute resolution processes not requiring precedents or formal procedures might well be considered. He argued that in such situations it might make sense to restrict or even ban the use of lawyers, while encouraging participating by law advocates, friends, clergy, or neighbors. He drew attention to the conciliation courts created in 18th century Norway to protect the citizens from dishonest lawyers who tried to incite them to quarrel over trifling matters.

In some U.S. cities efforts are being made to promote private adjudication and conciliation. Even the Federal Trade Commision encourages the use of private resolution techniques in disputes over warranties on automobiles.

A spur that might encourage such efforts at compromise and conciliation by intermediaries would be to continue to report, as the *Wall Street Journal* did recently, the rewards that may be gained. In the case of Texaco Inc.'s $9.89 billion bid to take over Getty Oil Co., Getty management and family members were barely on speaking terms with each other, and acceptance of the bid was in doubt until the First Boston Corporation, an investment banker and Texaco's advisor, was asked at the final minute to act as intermediary, to conciliate contrary views. If Texaco's bid is successful, First Boston will receive $10 million for the expenditure of 79 hours of effort. A mere $126,582.30 an hour.

Speaking before the University of Southern California law school graduation ceremony in 1983, U.S. Attorney-General William French Smith stated: "Lawyers should remember that often the best service they can provide a client is to keep him out of court." He added, "We should be modest about what lawyers do," suggesting that "non-judicial routes to justice such as arbitration, negotiation, and administrative process deserve greater employment as alternatives that can complement the judicial system."

That compliance with Smith's advice is much needed is reflected in the charge of the president of the Federal Legal Services Corp. that this country suffers from "legal pollution."

Efforts are being made to teach Americans how to settle their disputes without going to court. In Dallas, Texas, for instance, on June 9, 1983 an all-day training conference was held by the American Arbitration Association and the Dispute Mediation Service of Dallas, Inc. Adversaries are being taught in training courses such as this how to settle their differences without facing one another in court. Negotiation is the first step recommended, and if it fails, the disputants may call upon mediators to reconcile them. Mediation is particularly popular in settling labor disputes, with arbitration being another option.

Books written to guide laymen away from lawyers are popular, with the best-selling *How to Avoid Probate* being an example. Others have such titles as *How to Incorporate Your Business Without Using a Lawyer* and *How to Agree on a Divorce Settlement*.

Despite all the efforts to reduce legal fees, a counter movement that may well cause them to rise substantially instead has begun, in which labor unions, in an effort to keep their members contented, are demanding that employers agree to provide workers with prepaid legal services. Heretofore workers have, of course, paid their own legal bills, including fees for arranging divorces, settling traffic violations, writing up wills, etc. Under some newly negotiated union contracts, however, employers have agreed to bear these expenses. An estimated 25 million people in the U.S. will be covered by prepaid legal services by the end of the 1980's, providing good reason to fear that litigation will rise sharply as workers seek free legal help in a wide variety of problems that they might have somehow solved on their own before.

Increase in health costs

In the medical field, labor unions negotiated ever more generous packages covering hospitalization, surgeons, dentists, podiatrists, etc., and workers have increasingly sought these "free" services paid for by their companies, whereas previously most employees—when faced with paying their own bills—thought twice before buying professional medical help, especially about minor ailments. This has led to an enormous increase in the cost of medical services.

In 1960 the United States spent less than $26 billion on health care, but the comparable figures for 1982 exceeded $362 billion; nearly fourteen times as much. This rise in health care expenses has contributed to the decline in the competitiveness of many American products abroad. For example, included in the price of American-built automobiles is $300 per car in medical premiums, most of which is mandated by labor union agreements. A contributing reason for the massive increase in medical premiums has been the malpractice insurance physicians and hospitals carry. From 1960 on many lawyers waxed prosperous from the suits they filed against doctors and hospitals, who, to protect themselves, subscribed to ever larger and more costly malpractice insurance. By 1983, many surgeons were paying premiums in excess of $30,000 a year, with their patients paying the insurance bills, of course.

Nor do Japanese companies lag far behind in providing health care for their employees. A Health Insurance Law promulgated in 1961 established comprehensive medical care insurance for the entire population. Examination of various aspects of Japanese health care reveals many of the same problems found in the United States, and since 1961 the cost of medical care has expanded grossly much as it has here.

More than half the population of Japan is enrolled in employee health insurance plans, some managed by the state and others by private insurers supported by major corporations. Anyone who is not classified as an employee or an employee's dependent is covered by national health insurance or other insurance schemes developed for specific occupations.

The health insurance plan is a heavy drain on the national treasury, which is especially worrisome since Japan's fiscal imbalance is so precarious. As in the U.S. where medical service is regarded by many as "free", the public demands there are often unreasonable. Physicians are criticized for growing rich by writing unnecessary prescriptions, this being an area in Japan where unethical practices are frequently cited. The problem is that physicians fill their own prescriptions, buying the materials from pharmaceutical companies at one price, then selling the drugs they prescribe to their patients at considerably higher prices. Japanese doctors also are given special tax breaks, annoying wage earners whose pay envelopes are much lighter because of tax deductions.

In an article entitled "Bridging the Communication Gap: How IBM Succeeded in Japan," the publication *Jurist* compared the legal cultures of the U.S. and Japan in 1982, and the ten items compared make it appear that the Japanese should have less reason for neurotic behavior than Americans if this analysis is correct. For example, in Item 1, "Consciousness," Americans are said to characteristically assert their individual rights, while Japanese look for harmony inside the group. In Item 2, "Conflict of interest," Americans seek resolution in courts whereas Japanese dispose of conflict through negotiation. In Item 5, "Sanction to rule violators" (sic), Americans strive to recover material loss, whereas Japanese seek to recover emotional loss. And in Item 6, "Base for Conscience," Americans are concerned with universal justice whereas Japanese again try to attain harmony inside the group.

If the *Jurist* is correct in this estimate, then the report from public health sources in Japan that the percentage of middle-aged businessmen suffering from neurosis has risen sharply in recent years is puzzling. Is neurosis the price of harmony? Or is it the price of economic success?

Intellectual Property Laws in Japan

Although Japanese manufacturers are noted for the improvements in productivity and quality they have made, especially since the 1960's, a wide gap in creativity still exists between them and Western manufacturers. Japanese companies, although excellent in making improvements on foreign products, are still dependent to a considerable degree on inventions made in foreign countries. (Of the 18 major break-through inventions in semi-conductor chips that have been made in the world since 1947, one has come from West Germany and all the rest from the U.S. None came from Japan.) When the Japanese see something novel they want, they try to arrange to produce it in their own country, compensating the inventors through license agreements. Unfortunately, however, Japan's laws and patent practices often make it difficult for foreigners to have their intellectual property rights properly honored there.

To worsen matters, MITI now proposes a revision in the copyright law to make it permissable for Japanese companies to copy parts of existing computer software without the approval of the original developers. In short, they now want to legalize what they have often done illegally in the past.

David S. Guttman, an American patent attorney and Chairman of the American Chamber of Commerce in Japan Patents, Licenses and Trademarks Committee, writing in 1982 in the magazine *Patents and Licensing*, brought out a number of inequities in Japan's intellectual property registration system that resulted, in some instances, in foreign companies receiving only partial compensation for their intellectual properties, or none at all. Among the problems he mentioned were:

a. It takes much longer for U.S. companies to get patents or trademarks registered in Japan than it does for Japanese to get them registered in America.

b. Whereas the U.S. and most other industrialized nations have laws by which service marks may be registered and by which trade secrets may be protected, no equivalent protection is granted in Japan.

c. Foreign companies filing certified copies of patent applications in Japan in order to get recognition of their earlier home country applications find the Tokyo Patent Office unduly rigid and often lose priority rights because of this bureaucratic stubbornness. Bureaucratic rigidity in Tokyo has little or no effect on Japanese companies since these Patent Office rules apply only to foreign filings. As an example, if the U.S. Patent and Trademark Office should be slow in issuing the certified copy required by Tokyo or issues one that is even slightly defective, the Japanese refuse to allow an extension of the three months' period for filing. The result is a complete loss of all rights in Japan to the foreign invention.

By comparison, in the U.S. the Patent Office does not require a certified copy of a foreign application until it needs it during examination, which often takes place years later.

d. Japan's patent and trademark rules require that for an application to be finally approved, it must be published in the *Official Gazette* so that competitors will be made aware of it in the event they wish to oppose approval of the application. The language of the *Official Gazette* being Japanese, a time-consuming translation is necessary, with the result that it may be impossible to reach an informed decision as to whether or not to contest the decision in the two months' time allowed.

e. Foreigners' names are entered in the Tokyo Patent Office computers in the *katakana* syllables used in Japan. Unfortunately, this syllabary often reproduces foreign names inaccurately. For instance, Louis Villa would appear in *katakana* as Ruisu Biira. To add to the problem, foreign names are indexed by personal names rather than family names, so all "Louis's" would appear in succession, whatever their surnames. Thus, Louis Turner might be followed by Louis Goldstein.

f. Trademarks are, according to Japanese law, granted on the principle that the first to apply has priority rights. This often has an adverse effect on foreign companies, for Japanese may register foreign marks that are not their property before foreign owners can get around to doing so. If this happens, the foreign manufacturer cannot use his own trademark when selling in Japan. Although the authorities can refuse to register to a Japanese a foreign trademark that has already become well-known in Japan, it may be difficult to define legally the precise meaning of "well-known."

g. Trade secrets being valuable assets, they are generally given legal protection in industrialized countries, the United States Uniform Trade Secrets Act being an example of such protection. Japan, however, takes a different view, and one authority there has said that under criminal law, the value of a trade secret does not exceed the value of the paper on which it was written. (Report of the American Chamber of Commerce in Japan, Licenses, Patents and Trademarks Committee, Jan. 28, 1971). The above ACCJ *Journal* article by David Guttman indicates no improvement during the intervening years.

Some surmise that the theft of IBM trade secrets by Hitachi, Ltd. and Mitsubishi Electric Corp.—the subject of countless articles in the world press in 1982 and 1983—may have been regarded by the Japanese as no more than a minor offense because of their own indifference to the stealing of trade secrets. In any event, IBM settled its theft case against Hitachi Ltd. when the latter agreed to give IBM advance looks at its new data processing products for five years.

In this connection, a strange example of American legalism took place early in 1983 when our Social Security system purchased $7 million worth of computers from Hitachi. IBM was the loser in the competition because its price was slightly higher, and under the law the order had to be given to lowest bidder: in this instance, the unethical Japanese company.

Foreign companies doing business in Japan must sometimes take action to defend their designs and trademarks. Unfortunately, Japan's judges don't seem to regard unauthorized reproducers of foreign products as unprincipled as foreigners do. As a consequence, most problems have to be settled through negotiation rather than by court action, and this judicial leniency has led to a substantial increase in copying in recent years.

Although the government of Japan could and should do more to protect the intellectual property rights of foreigners, it must be remembered that certain other countries, particularly in the Far East, have much poorer reputations. Taiwan, for example, seems unwilling to enact effective legislation to offer protection to foreign copyrights, and its record of enabling foreigners to defend their patents is also open to severe rebuke.

The Japanese themselves have been victimized by foreign copying of their own trademarks and designs, with the worst offenders being Taiwan and Hong Kong.

A problem in protecting intellectual property rights is finding means of preventing employees from moving to competing companies and taking their knowledge of such trade secrets with them. President Seiro Takehara of the International Management Consultants Association of Tokyo, a recruiting firm, stated in an article in the Sept. 20, 1983 *Japan Economic Journal* that "We should scout engineers themselves instead of doing petty things like stealing information. . . . For the time being we will concentrate our efforts on scouting Japanese brains currently employed overseas."

In recent years Japan's huge trading companies have intensified their search for foreign technology. An article in the *Japan Economic Journal* of April 20, 1982 stated that "Sumitomo Corporation has assigned as many as 80 male members of its 180-man Electronics and Electric Division to the importation of high technologies in the electronics field. It is sending them to the U.S. to ferret out new and promising technologies."

Another major trading company, Nissho-Iwai Corp., according to the same *Japan Economic Journal* article, ". . . is determinedly crisscrossing the world for new technologies and technological information. . . ."

While abuse of patents, copyrights, and trade secrets may not necessarily result from these activities, Japan's record in these matters makes the observer uneasy over what might happen in those cases in which the legal owner of the desired intellectual property refuses to license or sell it.

Opposition is being heard to letting the Japanese buy any foreign technology at all. In September, 1983 the British government, for instance, asked Japan to take several steps to reduce the trade imbalance, with one request being that the Tokyo authorities advise Japanese enterprises to stop insisting on producing licensed products in Japan and instead import the foreign-made products themselves.

The United States is increasingly concerned over the illegal transfer of intellectual property rights to Communist countries. Sensitive products that would not be granted U.S. export licenses still reach these countries, but in the form of drawings, models, and photographs, with Japan and Sweden being two of the intermediary countries. Drawings and blueprints are legally exported to buyers and licensees in those countries that agree not to re-export them, but large sums of Communist money seem to have made certain buyers forgetful of their agreements.

Other ethical questions:

1. The increase in American litigation may, in part, be due to publicity given to huge settlements. When the public reads that someone has sued and then won an award of, say, $10 million, it excites the covetous imagination. Readers might remind themselves that they would have to work a lifetime to make so much money. When the op-

portunity presents itself, they may quickly look for a lawyer who will take questionable legal action on their behalf. Is the public so keen on making money by such means?

2.   Two American lawyers who have lived and worked in Japan for most of the post-Occupation period and who are, of course, familiar with both U.S. and Japanese legal practice hold the opinion that despite considerable differences the public is equally well served in both countries. They do not believe that justice is less common in Japan than in the U.S. If the two lawyers are correct in their appraisals, then it follows that the American public is being badly cheated because there are twenty-one times more practicing lawyers per capita in the U.S. than in Japan. The cost of supporting these lawyers is staggering and constitutes an unreasonable and non-essential burden on the economy. There would seem, therefore, to be sound reasons for a reform of the American system.

3.   When the Japanese indicate, as they sometimes do, to foreign corporations or individuals their preference for verbal instead of written commitments, do they truly intend to abide honorably by the verbal commitments or do they merely want the leeway to ignore the commitment when it suits them to do so?

4.   When the chemical plant of a subsidiary of the Union Carbide Co. leaked toxic fumes in 1984 in Bhopal, India, killing many people, a flock of American lawyers flew to India and invited Indians who are suffered harm or loss of relatives to sign authorizations to file damage suits against the American parent company. This ambulance-chasing tactic seemed incredible to many Japanese who said it was most unlikely that under similar circumstances involving a Japanese chemical company in India even one Japanese attorney-at-law would have tried to stir up litigation against a company from his own country.

Chapter Eleven

Negotiations, Conferences, and Contracts

When Japanese and foreign corporations enter into cooperative relationships, whether long-term or short-term and whether to buy, sell, or produce jointly, the terms of the relationship are generally set down formally in writing, in the form of a contract. Although the Japanese might, in their hearts, prefer verbal agreements, international commercial practice weighs against them. Extensive negotiating sessions pave the way to these contracts.

The Japanese have been described both as "hard-bitten, tough negotiators" and as "having no negotiating sense at all." Doubtless many Japanese will fit one description or the other and even more will stand somewhere in between. But whatever else one may say about how the Japanese negotiate, few would contest the assertion that the Japanese negotiating style seen most often by foreign businessmen is a far different style from the one they are accustomed to at home, and this extreme difference in style has occasioned frequent allegations that Japanese negotiators are ambiguous, devious, evasive, and stubbornly slow—all of which add up, in the eyes of many, to unethical business practice.

If we grant there may be some substance to both of the two extreme views of Japanese negotiators noted above, e.g., "hardbitten negotiators" and "completely without negotiating sense," then it must follow that not every foreign businessman will have the same experience when he sits down to the pre-contract bargaining table across from his Japanese counterparts. Even so, while granting that exceptional situations may be more than a few in number, certain relevant comments can be made that may be helpful to those about to embark on such negotiations as well as at least shedding light on, although perhaps not definitively answering, questions about ethics and good faith.

Basically, these brief comments on negotiating style (or styles) divide into three parts: the style itself, language used (or not used), and ritualistic aspects.

American negotiators tend to be enthusiastic promoters, advocates eager to stand out among their own team, desiring quick results, ready to argue, bargain, even indulge in a bit of play-acting at times. They often leave the impression that "the sooner we wind up here, the sooner I can get on that jet to Seoul and nail down another good contract over there."

An early adumbration of a fundamental Japanese attitude toward negotiations was given by Masahiro Abe when, in reference to pending talks with Commodore Matthew Perry, he reported to the Shogun's council, "Our policy shall be to evade any definite answer to their requests while at the same time maintaining a peaceful demeanor."

In contrast to many Americans, Japanese negotiators certainly have no wish to stand out, such visibility being anathema to most of them. They want to work as a team, move slowly, commit themselves to nothing initially—not even the date of the next conference. When pressed for commitments, they tend to take refuge in silence while becoming inwardly all the more determined not to yield, not to take firm positions until they are fully ready to take such positions. If, as some may, they do yield to pressure and give a tentative 'yes,' it should always be borne in mind that such a 'yes' obtained by face-to-face insistence or pleading is not nearly as reliable as a 'yes' offered of their own free will. Sometimes the Japanese avoidance of strong position statements at the bargaining table puts one in mind of what Thaddeus Kosciuszko, a brigadier general in the American Revolution, once wrote, "Rather than getting my way by quarreling, I would return home and plant cabbages."

It is the turtle's pace of negotiations with the Japanese that has threatened to rupture many pending business possibilities. Nissan officials, for example, negotiated for 15 months with the state of Tennessee before they settled on a site for their $660 million assembly plant there, and one of the coauthors once spent two and a half years, off and on, in negotiations between the Chicago company he represented and a Japanese maker of portable household appliances.

In estimating how long it will take to reach a corporate conclusion, rules of thumb vary from five to eight times as long as in the West, for Japanese businesses reach their decisions by an exquisitely elaborate and traditional process of group mulling and consensus seeking that seems to be intuitive. What saves such Fabian tactics from utter disaster is that by the time the contract is signed, everyone concerned in the Japanese corporation, from junior management up to the top, knows the business proposal in thorough detail, can implement it quickly, and, perhaps most important, will lend it much support because he appreciated his opinion being asked in the usual consensus-gathering process.

Robert March, a professor of international business at Aoyama Gakuin University in Tokyo, has written in an excellent article on Japanese negotiations that in this regard the American negotiator has been characterized as the nomadic hunter, the horseman, even the carnivore type: highly mobile, quick to attack and quick to retreat, tearing and tugging at the body of his game. Being nomadic and independent, he will retreat from a prepared position without any sense of having been defeated, only to re-form and attack again from a different quarter.

The Japanese, on the other hand, is like an agricultural herbivore, close to his land, protective of his domain, communally united with his own kind. Being herbivorous— and ruminative, he moves slowly in actions and words.

At the conference table, the American will likely be aggressive and ask for more than he expects to get, then retreats, perhaps makes another aggressive feint, only to retreat again until a position of possible agreement is found.

The Japanese waits for such initial moves by his foreign counterpart, who, he hopes, will thus show his hand first or make a move he can use to his advantage. He has been likened to the *sumō* wrestler who often wins his match if he can resist his foe's first mighty shove, then take advantage of that instant when the opposing behemoth is off balance to trip him or use his momentum to push him out of the ring.

If his counterpart is slow to open the dance, the Japanese, the passive realist who feels no compulsion to fill silence with words, may sip tea and wait in patient silence ("Well-timed silence hath more eloquence than speech") or idly offer a few social amenities or passing thoughts on irrelevant topics. As the silence lengthens, the Westerner may feel uneasy and awkward and so press on with premature revelations. Such extended periods of silence may crop up again and again during lengthy negotiations as the Japanese reflects or collects his thoughts. Or at times it may even be that he simply has nothing to say.

In a similar way, a long delay in answering a direct question may unnerve the Western participant, although it need not necessarily do so, since a carefully thought-out response is considered by the Japanese more respectful than a quick answer contrived in haste.

Even American negotiators who are experienced enough to approach the bargaining table in a subdued, low-key manner may be able to restrain their enthusiasm and eagerness to conclude an advantageous deal only so long and then become excited and lose their sense of caution, so that finally, although seemingly pushed back by the assertive enthusiasm and apparent logicality of the foreigners, the Japanese often emerge from the series of negotiations having made fewer concessions than the other side.

Later in the commercial relationship, after the contract has been signed and the business is well under way, the Japanese may approach the Western company with a different kind of negotiating manner for the purpose of gaining concessions not covered specifically in the contract. This is called *Naniwa-bushi*, after a 15th-century style of narrative chanting still popular in theaters and on television. A comparison could be drawn between the *Naniwa-bushi* reciters and the peripatetic troubadours of feudal Europe who rode from castle to castle singing of chivalrous deeds and romances, of dynasties and crusaders.

Told in three distinct parts, the *Naniwa-bushi* first sets the stage, next relates the portentous, often tragic events that befall the characters in the drama, and finally laments these misfortunes.

How this *Naniwa-bushi* style is used in negotiations can be illustrated by the recent experience of one of the coauthors (JS). A Japanese company had agreed to perform a certain service for him, for which it was fully paid in advance. When the service was not performed on schedule, JS began sending first letters, then telexes of inquiry. Finally, apparently realizing that here was one foreigner who would not be content to let the matter just ride for a while, the Japanese company agreed to meet him when he was next in Tokyo to "explain their situation."

At the meeting, the Japanese company expressed their warm appreciation for favors shown them during the several years of acquaintance. Next they described the depressed conditions in their line of business and the bankruptcy of two other companies that owed them money. Lastly they pleaded rather lugubriously that JS permit them to postpone the pending service for about six months, at which time they could carry it out on an even larger scale than initially agreed.

It was classic *Naniwa-bushi* style, and JS agreed to the postponement—but for reasons other than the force of the melodramatic appeal.

Whether the Japanese speak in Japanese for interpretation into English during negotiations or in English, their underlying manner of communication impresses itself on both languages with a resulting tolerance of and even fondness for ambiguity so pronounced as to raise again the question of whether or not they are negotiating in good faith.

Although the observer might not reach such a conclusion after noting the loquacity of many Japanese women and more than a few Japanese men, the Japanese nonetheless do cherish a tradition of silence, ambiguity, and indirection that colors their style of negotiation. They tend to communicate, in the words of Nobel Prize Winner Yasunari Kawabata, by means of a 'quiet understanding,' in which the truth lies in the implied rather than in the stated. Eloquence is expected more of the stage performer than of the serious man of affairs. In the cause of refinement, they believe that one should not express his thoughts to the very end but should allow them to dangle unfinished in the air, leaving the provocative aftertaste that is called *yoin* in Japanese.

Replying to a recent questionnaire, many Japanese chief executive officers gave as their favorite quotations or best-liked mottoes certain phrases that were clearly paradoxical and seemingly inconsistent. The saying liked by more of the respondents than any other was "*Shōshin ni shite daitan*," meaning something like "Acting timidly but with a bold heart."

A similar paradox was the one quoted by Minister of Finance Michio Watanabe to Prime Minister Margaret Thatcher at their 1982 meeting: "*Ku-soku-ze-shiki, Shiki-soku-zeku*," with the meaning of "Empty is full; full is empty."

Why this Japanese preference for paradox, ambiguity, indirection, and even at times silence? Among the oft-given explanations are their racial homogeneity, their long history of being, for the most part, just one race with only one language living in a very small amount of space, so closely knit that what they call *ishin-denshin* or heart-to-heart communication is often possible with little reliance on specific words. Another is the sheer necessity, arising from living in highly congested communities, of being ever conscious of the other fellow's face, of not calling a spade a spade if it risks embarrassing anyone. And the third is the influence of Zen Buddhism, which regards written and spoken words as deterrents to intuitive grasp of the essential reality of nature and man.

Preference for the non-specific comment has given rise to contretemps that might even be humorous if they did not have such serious consequences. One often-quoted instance is what ex-Premier Sato said during the textile dispute of the early Seventies when asked by President Nixon to try to persuade Japanese textile manufacturers to lower the level of their exports to the U.S. What Sato replied was interpreted as "I'll do my best," which was accurate literally, but which in Japan is usually taken to be politely negative. When Sato did nothing to reduce textile exports, Nixon felt betrayed, leading to a rupture in relations between Nixon and Sato.

A reverse example took place several years before that when the chief of Japan's Self Defense Agency asked U.S. Defense Secretary McNamara to allow former residents of the Bonin Islands to pay visits to the small archipelago where they were born but from where they had been evacuated by the Japanese government. "I'll consider it," answered McNamara, which the Japanese took to be a negative reply as it would have been so interpreted in Japan.

Several months later, to their surprise, the request was granted. McNamara had meant exactly what he said: he would consider it. Then he granted the request.

Occasionally, a Japanese businessman, remembering what he has learned about the American fondness for the direct statement, will take himself in hand and force himself, when the occasion seems to suggest it, to clearly say No to his American counterparts. Unfortunately, lack of experience in such directly-expressed negation often leads him to almost shout "NO!" in loud, ringing tones that ruffle the other side's feathers. It seems that with these persons the direct expression of a negative sentiment is such a formidable, precedent-shattering experience that they think, "In for a penny, in for a pound" and go all the way in their vehemence. When one hears of a Japanese industry spokesman or government functionary characterizing a displeasing foreign proposal or reaction to a Japanese proposal as "rubbish" or "hogwash" or "childishly unrealistic" or other statements that would have brought countries like England and France to the brink of war, it might be borne in mind that the Japanese responsible is treading ground he has seldom treaded before and may even think he is dealing with Westerners in the style in which they like to be dealt with.

On the other side, when Westerners in negotiating sessions confront the Japanese with propositions that the Japanese feel are absurd, the usual reaction of the Japanese will be to refrain from saying clearly that "your proposal is simply out of the question" and instead make a minor concession more as a gesture of goodwill than as a concrete counter-proposal. But the foreign negotiators may not recognize this underlying intent and instead think that the minor concession is so meaningless that the Japanese side is playing them for fools and is being unethical, deceitful, and uncooperative.

Expressive events such as rituals are integral parts of most cultures. They help to enhance the impact of important values.

In Japan conferences are rituals utilized to fortify the unity of a group. This does not mean they have no other utility value. Even negotiating conferences can have a dual purpose, one being ritualistic. While initial negotiations may be tense sessions with lesser utility as rituals, later conferences with the same participants may become more relaxed and friendly. Smiles are seen more often and humorous remarks may be passed back and forth. At this stage one of the purposes of the negotiating conference—after both parties are reasonably optimistic that a satisfactory agreement will be concluded—is to begin to tie the bonds of cohesion, to be supported by dinners and drinks in a social atmosphere. While the foreign participants may feel they have more important business to attend to than this seemingly idle chatter, they should not rush off to other affairs until ample time has passed for this growing sense of camaraderie to suffuse the foundations of the budding relationship. An hour or so spent in such desultory talk could save weeks of effort later.

"Foreigners negotiate contracts; Japanese form relationships."

Because Japanese laws and regulations are subject to differing interpretations by different officials, and perhaps at times even by the same official on different occasions, foreigners often doubt that such flexibility can be ethical. After all, they point out, the officials are men (or women) and are, therefore, imperfect, and their judgments can be influenced by extralegal factors both human and social.

This same flexibility operates in the area of contracts. Because change is the most certain thing in our lives, the Japanese opt for a flexibility that can be responsive to changing circumstances. Even when a tightly worded contract is in force, the Japanese will show little hesitation in asking for a revision when they believe that changed circumstances justify such a change.

Even though resigned to the contract they will likely have to sign with foreign corporations with whom they are discussing significant business, the Japanese hope to build with the foreigners a lasting relationship that will keep both parties working with each other because they *want* to go on working with each other, not because, like it or not, they are bound by a piece of paper that states certain intentions and obligations that had significance under the circumstances existing at the time it was written. They believe this 'lasting relationship' should be based on an aura of mutual trust that is more important than the printed promise. When a contract cannot be avoided, the Japanese will prefer one that is brief and generally worded to allow for maximum flexibility, except for descriptions of technology.

Japan's largest cement company, for example, states it

has never had a formal, written contract with any customer or supplier. Such companies are not at all unusual, but when disputes arise between two Japanese corporations, whether bound by contracts or not, both parties will try to avoid court action, since that would be a tacit admission of their inabilities to reach a compromise. Courts will also delay action in such cases, partly because they want to allow the litigants ample time to explore and arrive at a compromise.

What makes such conciliation and compromise not only possible but even probable between disputing Japanese corporations as well as between individuals, whether the binding agreement is written or verbal, reflects the nature of the circumambient society. Because a formal introduction probably brought the two parties together in the first place, the same agents of introduction may be used effectively to smooth over differences. Quite often the person who introduced both parties is one who is respected by both and wields influence over both. He then becomes the de facto court where under his guidance conciliation leads on to compromise and a non-legal resolution.

Even when the relationship was formed without benefit of an introducing agent, the closely-knit society around it will provide other pressures to compromise, not the least of which is public opinion.

Here it is that foreign companies—and individuals— are at a distinct disadvantage, at least those without the long years of residence in Japan needed to build up 'social capital,' that is, in this instance, adherents to one's cause and guarantors of one's bona fides. This being so, the foreign corporation newly arrived in Japan has little choice but to insist on a binding contract, although the chief foreign negotiator at the discussions leading to contract would be well advised to make comments suggesting that while he fully trusts the other party and would have preferred not to ask for a contract himself, his legal department in the home office insisted that he come back with one in hand.

One of the coauthors (JS) has had two experiences that may be instructive. In both instances, he discussed books he might write, in Japanese, with two of Japan's largest publishing houses. Both asked him to proceed with the books, which he did, spending eight months on one and twelve on the other. At the time of the original discussions, the American part of his experience urged him to insist on contracts and advance royalties, but his experience in Japan cautioned him that to do so would be contrary to Japanese practice and might even bring about a rupture. He managed to allay his concerns with the foolish assumption that the Japanese involved were gentlemen of their word. He could not believe that they would really ask someone to spend a total of twenty months of his life working full-time on projects they might reject out of hand with no consideration of compensation.

And yet that is exactly what happened, and JS was left without recourse. Had he been a Japanese, he might have found among his relatives or close friends one who knew, say, a high official of the Japan Publishers' Association or some other economic organization having wide clout. To that person he would have gone, with hat, present, and proper letter of introduction in hand, and on bended knee to plead his case and thus would have perhaps obtained redress. (One of the works, fortunately, was published elsewhere. The second has not been yet.) What was perhaps most distressing was that neither publisher had the courtesy to explain why they rejected the manuscripts.

Chapter Twelve

Ethics in Advertising

In discussing ethics in advertising, it seems advisable to begin from the premise that deceit is often present, for in marketing any product or service, the seller takes the position that his product or service is superior to others or is cheaper . . . or both. Since the word 'best' is singular as is the word 'cheapest,' they can apply to only one, and others making similar claims are, *ipso facto*, not entirely truthful. Such is the nature of the beast.

While one could wish that the superiority of products and services was self-revealing instead of declamatory, we may have little choice but to accept advertising as it is and do what we can to keep it from straying too far beyond the boundaries of ethical behavior by working for the universal adoption of an Advertising Code in which subscribers promise, among other things, that "We will not use our advertising as an instrument of aggression against our customers—nor to evoke vast materialistic instincts or sexual urges." At the same time, to be safe, we might do well to bear in mind this caution: "When a company brags of its products and a woman boasts of her virtue, shun the former and cultivate the latter."

Unethical or questionable advertising practices can be divided into several categories, the first being the most readily identifiable: false or grossly exaggerated claims made about products and services. If a supermarket announces it will sell peaches for 60¢ a pound when actually they cost 65¢ a pound, then that obviously constitutes false advertising.

The Federal Trade Commission, which was created in 1914 at the urging of advertising clubs, polices advertising claims in an effort to keep them as ethical and accurate as possible. By 1970 44 of the states had enacted Truth in Advertising legislation that support the FTC in this mission. The Better Business Bureau has a National Advertising Division that addresses itself to nation-wide advertisements, while the local Bureaus review ads to determine if they comply with the Better Business Bureau's Code of Advertising.

In Dallas, Texas, in 1982, for example, the Better Business Bureau reviewed 1,573 ads and investigated the accuracy of 386 of them by actually visiting points of sale and examining the merchandise and the prices. Surely efforts such as these do much to keep advertisers truthful, even though it must be admitted that 1,573 ads is only a small percentage of the total number that inundated the residents of the Dallas Metropolitan area during that year.

Recent "truth in lending" laws have also done much to enhance truthfulness about interest rates and lending policies. In January, 1983, when the new laws were still not so well known, a survey was made to determine the percentage of compliance with them and it was found that this ranged from 1% in Philadelphia to 35% in Miami. By mid-June, when the regulations were better known, the percentage of compliance had risen to 87% in Philadelphia and 86% in Miami. (The fact, however, that only 1% of credit advertisers in a major city like Philadelphia were presumably acting in the spirit of the ethical ideals propounded by the truth in lending laws is a disturbing comment on the fundamental proclivities of the credit advertisers in their pristine or unpoliced state.) On the highway near the home of one of the authors (JS) stands a large billboard on which a local bank proclaims, in reference to its loan policy, "Our attitude is YES," probably giving the unwary the impression that any and all loan applications brought to them will be approved. If challenged, the bank could, of course, protest, "Our attitude is Yes, we want to help you in your business, but, needless to say, we can't do so if you don't have the necessary collateral," and it might not be easy to take the bank to court, but there is little question that such advertising is unethical—and the sign still stands at the time this was written (1984).

While the very nature of false advertising lends itself to legislative control, advertising practices of the merely misleading category are more difficult to deal with, nor has much effort been made to do so. Consider a TV commercial that JS saw this week that offered diamond rings for sale at $10.00. The diamond in each ring was proclaimed to be "1/4 point" and the ring was "layered 14-carat gold." The unlettered, the unwary, and the foreign-born (with their sometimes less-than-adequate English) among us might not know that a "point" is only one percent of a carat and might confuse a point with a carat and think they will receive a quarter-carat ring for their money. Also, "layered" is a far less familiar word than "plated," and again they might think, if they think about it at all, that the solid gold of the ring is constructed layer upon layer in the fashion of Danish pastry. Voila. For only $10.00, they will be able to buy a quarter-carat diamond ring made of 14-carat solid gold. "Hurry," as the advertisers are wont to say, "Do it now! Don't wait till tomorrow. This offer is limited."

"Limited" is another of those treacherous words advertisers are so fond of using in their continuing drives to deceive the public. The viewer or reader thinks, "If this offer is limited to perhaps only one or two weeks, I'd better rush out and take advantage of it right now, before it's too late.''

But, of course, an offer can be "limited" to one year or one hundred years or a millenium.

In the promotion of diets, diet pills, and reducing parlors, "up to" is another example of one of those phrases the about-to-be-seduced should walk around with caution. "Lose up to 30 pounds in three weeks, or your money back.'' Suppose 1,000 obese persons tried diet pills for three weeks. One of the 1,000 lost 30 pounds, while the other 999 lost less than five or no pounds at all. The advertiser would still be technically correct, if unethical, in saying, "lose *up to* 30 pounds.''

"Or your money back. . . .'' is a claim that must drive the FTC inspectors up under the eaves. While some advertisers use delaying tactics and other obstacles to avoid having to return the payments to dissatisfied customers, it is probable that most will make the refunds. But the point at issue is that most customers won't go to the trouble of asking for it. Either they have lost the address or they don't recall the exact words of the advertising claim or where they saw the ad or they don't want to take the time and trouble to write the letter to justify the refund and wrap up the "unused portion" and carry it to the post office. Advertisers know this. Doubtless painstaking studies have been made that will prove that only a very small percentage of customers will ask for a refund by mail, no matter how poor the product or how false its claims. Yet it is this very expression "or your money back" that lulls the would-be customer into thinking, "Well, if they are so confident about the product as to make that claim, then it must be pretty darned good.''

Studies have been made that show that two of the most effective expressions in visual and audible advertising are "new" and "exciting." Just what constitutes a "new" product is a question that should be seriously addressed by the FTC. Many makers of consumer products—foods and cosmetics come easily to mind—will make a very minor, perhaps even insignificant change in their ingredients or in the way they mix or flavor their ingredients—and declare it to be a completely new product. They know that the audience will comprise, in addition to those who have never tried their product—say it is canned chili—only two other categories: those who have tried the chili and like it and those who have tried it but do not like it. Since like and dislike, even of the very same product, is often a seasonal matter, with the same man disliking the product the first time he tries it but liking it the next, one month later, because of his mood or physical condition or what he had eaten a short while before, the advertiser knows that to increase sales, he must persuade the man who tried the chili once but did not like it, to try it again. He cannot really change the food for if he did, he might lose those who already like the chili as it is, so what he must do is to *say* he changed it, to say that it is entirely new whereas the truth is that he may have done no more than increase the number of beans in the can of chili from 100 to 105.

In the interests of ethical advertising, it would seem the FTC should require that *substantial* changes be made before such a claim will be countenanced and that each change be filed with that agency in detail before such advertising begins.

"Excitement," like beauty, may be in the eye of the beholder, but surely it strains credulity and taste when an advertiser prates about an "exciting" recipe for mashed potatoes or travel luggage or a pair of sun-glasses. The word exciting brings to mind—or *should* bring to mind—the vision of people jumping up and down, cheering and waving their arms, their eyes alight with pleasure and anticipation. Just how a new recipe for mashed potatoes or a laundry detergent can arouse such a reaction is difficult to perceive, even though the word has been used about soaps, suitcases, recipes, and a host of other things that at best are mundane, prosaic, and singularly lacking in emotional appeal by their very nature.

When 'exciting' is used in the advertising of harmful products—the 'exciting' taste of such and such a cigarette—then ethical doubts deepen. Yet just what is clearly harmful and what is not seems to be difficult for the consuming public to determine.

Tobacco is a case in point. The Surgeon General of the U.S. has testified before a committee of the House of Representatives that "Government findings blame smoking for 340,000 deaths a year and ... call it the chief preventable cause of ... premature death in the nation."

The Tobacco Institute, however, fought tooth and nail against a subsequent proposal to place more specific labels about the dangers of smoking on tobacco packages and charged that the proposal to mandate five such specific labels was nothing more than a "thinly veiled effort further to harass and ultimately eliminate an important American industry." Even the Rockefeller Foundation apparently lent its weight to those benefiting from the tobacco price support program by identifying them as doctors and lawyers, churches and banks, mill workers, farmers, truck-drivers, and, in many cases, widows.

Presuming that the ethical, decent man or woman is one who has some concern for the welfare of his fellow Americans, it is hard indeed to imagine how he or she could engage in the raising or marketing or advertising of tobacco and still sleep easy at night.

Liquor is similar but not quite the same, for alcohol in moderation may even bring one or two minor benefits, a claim that has never been made for tobacco by a thinking American in recent history.

In any event, the Distilled Spirits Institute does stand against the following:

1. Advertising liquor on radio or T.V.
2. Advertising on billboards or in other media near any army or navy establishment.
3. Advertising in any publication bearing a Sunday dateline.
4. Liquor ads that show women drinking or holding drinks.

Although it is difficult to understand why the last prohibition should be applied only to women—a point sure to be assaulted by female activitists soon, such a code does at least indicate that the industry has a certain sense of responsibility toward the public and is to be commended for that.

Still, the advertising of other products that are apparently harmful has not yet been condemned by any codes of ethics, examples that come to mind being such foods as chocolate and homogenized milk—the latter being identified by Dr. Kurt A. Oster, chief of cardiology emeritus at Park City Hospital in Bridgeport, Connecticut as the conclusive biochemical explanation for atherosclerosis, a disease that leads to more deaths annually than cancer.

Another unsavory aspect of advertising that would not lend itself to easy control by legislation is its awesome weight. In this media-saturated age, people find themselves up to their necks in an ocean of promotional messages that tout the entire gamut of consumer products and so zealously aggrandize them that they capture public attention to a degree out of all proportion to their intrinsic worth.

Advertising on this scale is made distinct from ordinary advertising by its very intensity and becomes what P.T. Barnum called puffery but what now goes by the name of hype. Steven M.L. Aronson, in a book entitled *Hype*, defines it as the merchandising of a product in "an artificially engendered atmosphere of hysteria."

In such a raucous din, it is this very seduction of the consumer into buying something he may not need and probably did not even know he wanted that can be called into court on the charge of being unethical.

If hard sell in the form of culture-crushing inundations of hype is questionable ethically in the U.S., the situation leans in the opposite direction in Japan, where advertising relies more on the development of images and dependence on life-style associations rather than on bluntly direct ("Buy this NOW!") product sell and where consumers prefer to be romanced and courted into the purchase of a service or product with soft words and music. The fast-talking, argumentative, wordy sales pitches appearing on TV screens in America are seldom if ever seen in Japan, where viewers cannot tolerate the aural levels of advertising communication typical in the U.S.

So soft is the 'sell' in Japan that one may not even be sure what is being sold—a comment often heard from American advertising agency representatives after watching Japanese TV commercials for the first time.

It has been said that one can tell the ideals of a nation by its advertisements, and it is true that the understatement, inference, and suggestion that characterize Japanese advertising reflect their national penchant for speaking obliquely and softly or letting someone else speak for them.

One such TV commercial is a 24-second filming of a puppy running along the rain-drenched streets of Kyoto at night, with a 4-second product shot at the close of a glass and a bottle of Suntory whiskey. Just how a puppy running along the wet streets of an ancient city can be construed to be an endorsement for a brand of whiskey is difficult to apprehend, unless we unleash our imaginations a bit and suppose that the dog is hot on the trail of his master who always drops in at his favorite Suntory bar on rainy nights, but then that is stretching it a little.

Another commercial treasured in the memory of one of the authors showed two young nattily-dressed men going out for a leisurely drive in the country where at length they stop their convertible, get out, and answer a call to nature in the ditch beside the road. The product advertised? A certain brand of gasoline.

Still another is a commercial currently showing in the U.S. in a TV series called "Japan 120." One of the sponsors of the series is a package and freight delivery company by the name of Sagawa Express. While showing a couple of shots of the ancient city of Kyoto, the narrator's voice is heard saying, "Kyoto is a city many Japanese wish to visit. In the world of transportation, Sagawa Express is a leader." End of another non sequitur commercial. Is the message that even as Kyoto is beloved among cities, so is Sagawa beloved among freight forwarders? Or is it that since many Japanese wish to visit Kyoto, Sagawa Express trucks would get them there faster and cheaper? Or is the message the medium?

On the surface Japan might seem like a wonderland to foreign advertisers. It has a single language, a literacy rate of about 99%, and a TV household penetration of 97%. There is only one ethnic sensibility to deal with. (Foreigners are usually depicted as boorish nerds if not outright criminals, to which no one protests. Or if they do, they are ignored.) And the country has four newspapers and 50 magazines that are circulated nationally to a broad-based readership. But its advertising landscape is studded with pitfalls that even the experienced and knowledgeable may not always detect in time. For example, some years ago the Coca-Cola Company in Japan decided to adver-tize with the slogan it was then using in the U.S. and in other countries: "It's the real thing."

Before long, however, the Fair Trade Commission cracked down in an unusual show of strength and forbade the slogan's use. "Why? What's wrong with saying that?" Coca-Cola asked. "Well, there are lots of 'real things,' " the FTC answered. "Your slogan makes it seem that yours is the only genuine soft drink."

Vagueness and indirection, however puzzling to the Westerner, are not really ethical questions, but what is or very well should be a subject of ethical inquiry is the matter of taste, or lack of it, in Japanese advertisements. One prize-winning soap commercial featured a small child breaking wind in a public bath, while Yamaha advertisements make use of the Crucifixion to sell stereo equipment. A perfume ad claims that their scent will "change anyone into a woman in two hours, even a nun."

But the commercial that should win any Tastelessness Contest hands down was one that opened with a full-body shot of an elephant, then zoomed in on the elephant's erotic equipment. The mammoth creature began to pass water, with the camera following this action to the ground, where it steamingly flooded about ten square yards. At the close the announcer said, "No matter how heavy the demands you put on it, a genuine Emoto Septic Tank will never let them flood you out."

This kind of advertising strikes an odd note in a country known for the sensitivity and delicacy of its art, but it must be remembered that we men in the West refrain from such crudities often more to protect the sensitivities of our womenfolk than our own, while in Japan the men do not often concern themselves with female reactions to their style of communication, whether vulgar or refined.

And for all their vaunted indirection, Japanese advertisements can sometimes be very direct, indeed. For instance, whiskey is widely promoted on TV with commercials as often as not showing young women, who may appear to be only 17 or so to Western eyes but who may actually be 18 or 19, quaffing a tumbler half-full of straight whiskey with high good humor and a smile of delight, then refilling the glass in preparation for an early replay of the scene. That so much liquor poured straight down a young woman's gullet might knock her flat on her back does not seem to be a matter of pressing interest to the advertisers.

Whereas alcoholic beverages are produced and sold by private corporations in Japan, cigarettes are the products of the Japan Tobacco and Salt Corporation, which is a government-owned monopoly under the jurisdiction of the Ministry of Finance. In 1982, 300 billion cigarettes were sold in Japan, bringing in the equivalent of $11 billion in gross revenues.

Although cigarette packages do carry a warning to smokers "to be cautious about smoking too much" for their health's sake, the Ministry of Health and Welfare, while realizing that cigarettes can cause lung cancer, is under pressure from the Ministry of Finance not to campaign strongly against smoking, making Japan the only country in the world that permits cigarette advertising on television.

As a consequence, the air in rooms throughout Japan is blue with tobacco smoke and the incidence of lung cancer is rising swiftly, although the Japan Tobacco and Salt Corporation continues to stoutly maintain that cigarette smoking is not a health hazard and that its benefits outweigh any possible dangers.

Even Prime Minister Nakasone hesitates to take a firm position on the smoking of cigarettes, saying only that they should hurt no one if the smoker follows the printed instructions "to be cautious about smoking too much."

Chapter Thirteen

Corruption, Bribery, Scandals
and
Sex Tours

"Donshū no uo wo morasu."
(Laws catch flies but let hornets go free.)

Comparing degrees of corruption in Japan and in the U.S. would be a challenging task indeed. For one thing, definitions differ; for another, the best corrupters, like the best spies, are never exposed, so their successes cannot be decried.

Still, for those interested in the other's culture and business climate, certain observations can be made that may illumine some of the dark corners.

Two scandals—Watergate in America and Lockheed in Japan—have served to sensitize both countries to issues revolving around *fuhai* or *haidoku*, as the Japanese name such matters, with results that may enhance levels of ethical concurrence, or at least so one would like to think.

But the fundamental nature of *homo sapiens* cannot be easily changed until the world advances to the stage of the successful manipulation of genes, buttressed perhaps by cradle teaching. So the question remains: have Lockheed and Watergate changed our basic attitudes—or are the guilty just more careful not be found out?

One usable definition of corruption is the inducement to do wrong by bribery or gifts or entertainment, and by using this definition as a jumping-off place for these comments, we can begin to identify several of the areas in which there are marked distinctions between the Japanese and the American ethical points of view.

The custom of gift-giving, for example, pervades most facets of the Japanese culture. One should always bring a gift with him when visiting another's home, no matter what the occasion. If you spend a weekend in a resort an hour or so away from your town of residence, you customarily return with small remembrances for members of your family, close friends, and often even your neighbors. If your mother enters a hospital, you should give her doctor a present to insure his special attention to her treatment, nor should you forget your mother's nurses. When one of your children faces school entrance examinations, you would be well advised to make offerings to his teachers and the school principal, even in the case of kindergartens. When that child has completed the education process and enters a company for life-long employment, you should remind him of the importance of *tsuketodoke*, the summer season and year-end gifts to his superiors and benefactors. When that child marries, all the wedding guests will bring presents and will themselves receive remembrances upon leaving. When your wife borrows a half-dozen eggs from a neighbor, they should be with returned with some small item: a *kimochi no shirushi* or evidence of one's appreciation. When a business executive goes to Paris, he would do well to buy souvenirs for those close to him in his office back home.

The wife of one of the authors (JS) sells cosmetics at the Neiman-Marcus Department Store in Houston, where it is not unusual for her to sell one or even two dozen bottles of perfume to Japanese businessmen who say they will distribute them to their female staff upon return. And at the mid-summer and year-end seasons, Japanese corporations are wont to send out large baskets of liquors and provisions (*tsumi-awase*) to many of their customers.

Per unit of sale, Japanese corporatrions spend *nine* times as much money on gifts and entertainment as do U.S. companies.

As bothersome and time-consuming as all this never-ending attention to the custom of gifts is, the Japanese regard it as a vital lubricant in their social and commercial relations. The presentation of a souvenir costing only a few dollars would seem to be harmless enough, but at what value does a gift become a bribe? The custom is so deeply-rooted in Japanese society that few if any gift-givers would feel any guilt over the offering of even quite expensive items, but no one would deny, if he could be completely candid, that the purpose of the gift, large or small, is to influence the receiver to do something that he would not ordinarily be expected to do and perhaps even should not do. Even the time-honored verbal formulae that accompany the New Year's gifts express this in just so many words: "You did much for me last year, and I hope you will oblige me again this year with your special favors."

Against a background of this almost constant offering of gifts for favors, it is not difficult to understand how small gifts become large gifts and how little favors become big ones.

According to one source, a member of the Japanese Diet may have to spend as much as $25,000 *a month* in sponsoring cultural shows and buying gifts for his supporters, in addition to what he spent to get elected. (In the case of a leading candidate this can be as much as $1.5 million.) Since his annual salary as a Diet member is less than $100,000, it is obvious that he must use his own funds, if he is independently wealthy, to make up the difference—

or sell political favors for cash or accept donations from businesses, with the knowledge that the favors will have to be repaid somehow, sometime.

The 'black mist' of corruption has plagued Japan's politics ever since the end of World War II, featuring such well-known scandals as *Shōwa Denkō* in 1948, the nationalization of the coal mining industry in that same year, shipbuilding in 1954, prostitution in 1957, the Bushū Railways in 1961, the Kuzuryū River dam in 1965, Lockheed beginning in 1972, and Grumman about the same time. If these are the principal scandals that have been exposed to the scrutiny of the public, how many more lie undetected in safes or memories?

The Lockheed scandal is too well-known to justify a detailed recounting here, but its essence was that in order to insure the sale of their widebodied TriStar passenger planes to All Nippon Airways, Lockheed's agent in Japan, a trading company, asked the aircraft manufacturer to pay ¥500 million to be used as a bribe, with Kakuei Tanaka, the prime minister at that time, being one of the presumed recipients.

The matter might never have been brought to light had it not been for the enterprising efforts of one freelance reporter who was given the assignment to look into the financial activities of Tanaka by a magazine.

Tanaka's trial for accepting a $2.2 million bribe began in 1977 and ended in October, 1983. A verdict of guilty was handed down, which Tanaka—the vigorous head of the largest political faction in the Diet—immediately appealed. In December of 1983, a general election was held, in which Tanaka's constituency returned him to his seat in the Diet in a landslide victory, while his Liberal Democratic Party (LDP) won only 250 seats nationwide: six shy of a majority.

Two traditional factors at work here have contributed

to this drama in political ethics. One is that the Japanese still tend toward an unquestioning submission and deference to those in power, as expressed in the proverb, *"Nagai mono ni makarero"* or "Kings have long, strong arms." This reflects the psychology of the Japanese by which they meekly submit to injustices done by men of greater power than themselves.

In 1976, the *Yomiuri* and the *Asahi* newspapers ran public opinion polls that found that 41% of those questioned were not at all shocked by the Lockheed scandal. Perhaps they felt as Justice Minister Hatano did when, in 1983, he commented on the ethical scene in his country, "Politicians' ethics, personal ethics, and society's ethics are all different. Seeking a morality of cleanliness and honesty as in traditional ethics from a politician is like asking for fish at a vegetable shop."

The second operative tradition is that Japanese society has always accorded private loyalty priority over public loyalty. Supposedly Tanaka passed along all or much of the $2.2 million bribe to the members of his faction and to his constituents. He was, in other words, more loyal to his immediate group than to the nation at large, which is a quite acceptable order of things to many Japanese.

But not to all. Not any longer. In the recent general election, the opposition parties used the fact of Tanaka's conviction to attack the LDP establishment and its big business supporters and while they did not "sweep the rascals out of office" as one opposition leader had demanded, they did arouse enough public disfavor to hand the LDP a resounding slap in the face.

There were two other unusual aspects of the Lockheed case. One was that Tanaka, in a totally untypical reaction to his court conviction, did not apologize to everyone and retire as gracefully as he could manage to his rural retreat. The other was the completely open and direct manner in which A. Carl Kotchian, the president of Lockheed in 1972, was approached for the payment of the bribe ... so direct that Kotchian called it "Japanese-style extortion." According to Kotchian, Toshiharu Okubo, an official of the trading company intermediary, told him in no uncertain terms: "If you wish to be successful in selling (your) aircraft, you would do well to pledge five hundred million yen." Five hundred million yen amounted to $2.2 million.

Such direct broaching of so delicate a matter is not at all typically Japanese. Even when both parties are fully aware that the money changing hands is a bribe, seldom would the briber says to the bribee, "Here is one hundred thousand yen (or dollars or francs). Count it. I am giving it to you, and in return you must agree to give me the secrets of the design of your new widgit." That is decidedly not the Japanese way.

Rather, the supplicant asks a favor, bows, and leaves. Perhaps that evening or the next, he has cash in an envelope (or a new set of golf clubs or a case of Scotch) delivered by messenger to the home of the person approached by the supplicant. How does he know how much to send? He doesn't. Not exactly. But doubtless precedents exist. Perhaps he knows one who bribed an official for a similar favor two years before. He takes the official's lifestyle and probable needs into consideration. He knows if he offers too little, the official may drag his feet. If he sends too much, he suffers an unnecessary loss. After giving the question careful consideration, he comes up with what he thinks is about the right amount and sends it along.

Why Mr. Okubo of Marubeni was so direct in his demand to Kotchian is a puzzle, unless it was because he was dealing with a foreigner who had no experience in "Japanese-style extortion." He may have felt this was no time for subtleties. Better to lay it right down on the table in plain sight.

Despite all this, one should not jump ahead to the conclusion that all Japanese officials are corruptible. Certainly not. Most are as reasonably honest as officials in the U.S. or England or Germany.

In fact, in all probabilities, the average American businessman working in Japan has never had the experience of actually bribing a Japanese official. One never slips a Customs inspector or policeman a few bills in the hope that his transgression will be winked at. Corruption exists, when it exists at all, at much higher levels—levels into which very few foreigners have entré.

Another aspect of Japanese ethics that militates against such corruption is the concept of group honor. In a large American corporation, a top executive might be exposed for corrupt practices, be fired or tried and punished, and that would be the end of it. While the company might regret the momentary bad publicity, it would look upon the misdeed as the act of an individual, an act for which the company does not bear responsibility. But not so in Japan, where the misdeed of any one member causes loss of face to the entire group.

When admission irregularities at Keio University in Tokyo were exposed in the press recently, shop-keepers along the street facing the school told newspapermen that both the faculty and the students appeared to slink about, hunched over with their eyes cast down as if ashamed to straighten up and look anyone in the eye.

When one of the authors (JS) worked for a Japanese camera manufacturer in the Fifties, there came a day when the employees heard the news that the company was being sued by the German maker of Rolleiflex and Rolleicord cameras for alleged imitation. The employees all left their desks and gathered in the corridors to mill about, ashen faced. Eventually JS was able to partially allay their consternation by pointing out that many large American and

European corporations were in an almost continual process of litigation, of suits and counter-suits. Before that it looked for a while as if they might all bolt from the building.

When the news of the Lockheed scandal began making headlines in Japan, Japanese reporters in the United States rushed to Lockheed's headquarters to see what news they could elicit there, and many of them filed stories about their surprise at finding that the employees of Lockheed were going about their daily rounds in an apparently unconcerned and carefree way. Because of the Japanese concept of collective honor, these reporters had fully expected to find the employees pale and shaken and anxious to hide their faces. They reported back to Japan that the Lockheed workers "had no sense of shame."

When JS went to work for the Japanese camera manufacturer mentioned above, he was pleasantly surprised at his employer's generosity in expense account matters. For instance, whenever a member of the staff made a business trip abroad, the company gave him a considerable amount of *shitaku-kin* or 'preparation money,' which, in practice, he could use any way he wanted but which was intended to outfit him in new apparel so that he would not be an embarrassment to the company (and to Japan) when he was in foreign parts. For those who made frequent foreign trips, as JS did, this became a respectable windfall.

Once he and the president of the company attended a photographic exhibition in Cologne and when this had ended, JS left for Switzerland and the company president, a Mr. U. . . ., said, "While you're in Zurich, you'd better buy yourself a really good Omega watch." JS had noticed Mr. U. . . . casting disapproving glances at his inexpensive Seiko time-piece several times but protested, "I'm afraid I can't afford an Omega."

"Oh, don't worry about the money," Mr. U. . . . replied, "Just charge it up to the company."

JS was also given expense account privileges that almost equalled his salary. This was the amount of money he could use for "social expenses" without any question or required justification or prior approval, and in those days most of these expenses were pre-tax write-offs.

Nowadays the tax officials have altered the rules somewhat so that a company capitalized at ¥10 million or less is permitted to expend up to four million yen (about U.S. $23,500 at today's exchange rate) free of tax yearly, but larger corporations may be allowed only half that amount—two million yen—in tax-free social expenditures.

Even so, Japanese enthusiasm for and devotion to this social lubricant appears little diminished. For instance, the national taxation bureau announced that entertainment of clients by Japanese corporations set a record of the equivalent of $15 billion dollars or about $40 million every day . . . in 1983, although more than half of the companies reported losses for the year.

In fact, according to the giant *Asahi* newspaper, "The Japanese style of entertaining customers is done on a scale unmatched anywhere else in the world." Nor do the above figures include the stupendous sums spent by the employees themselves—and so not a matter of record—when they entertain each other with their own money, which, for many, is several nights a week and for some, almost every night.

Alcoholic beverages form the core of all this entertainment, and the Japanese spent nearly twice as much on liquor in 1982 as they did on defense. Indeed, their corporate social expenses even exceeded their entire social welfare budget.

With all this devotion to whiskey, sake, and beer, it should surprise no one that Japan has often been called a "drunkard's paradise," and this is still applicable except for the stringency in recent years of the gendarmes in dealing with those who drive automobiles while intoxicated . . . which is very stringent indeed. Still, what saves Japan's night life from complete collapse in the face of this draconian attitude on the part of the police is the fact that most of Japan's businessmen go home after their favorite bar closes by train, tram, or taxi, and for this reason, the station master of *Shinjuku-eki*, Japan's busiest terminal, reports that as many as forty men vomit on his platforms nightly from excessive indulgence.

The U.S.-made products that have done especially well in Japan's market are those sold directly to the consumer—such as Coca-Cola, McDonald's hamburgers, Kentucky Fried Chicken, paper diapers, Parker pens, photographic film, et al—with price, quality, and advertising being more important than who knows whom and how many drinks or dinners they have had together. The less successful products and services are often those offered directly by the American businessman to the Japanese businessman, which are usually better promoted in atmospheres away from the office or factory.

Those who support sizable entertainment expenditures point out that this permits both sides in a business arrangement to really get to know each other, lays the groundwork for negotiating and smoothing over possible future misunderstandings, and obviates much of the need for contracts and expensive legal advice.

The opposing viewpoint is that such socializing in bars and nightclubs has just two purposes, neither of which is ethical or commendable: One, to provide pleasure in the form of food, wine and female companionship for those who sign the vouchers, and two, to influence the judgment of those being feted, to cause them to place lesser emphasis on price and quality and dependability but instead give more thought to how many dinners and drinks one has been provided with.

In the U.S., the accounting of entertainment expenses is much stricter than in Japan, with the result that, relatively speaking, much less money is expended for such purposes. Another difference between American and Japanese practices is that generally speaking the Japanese feel it important to do much of their entertaining of prospective clients before the business proposal is consummated or even broached, while Americans tend toward the opposite arrangement of getting to know the other fellows as the matter at hand progresses, although obviously there are a great many exceptions to this.

Westerners in Japan are often shocked by the expenditure of money on entertainment. Articles appear in the press from time to time telling of bars that charge the equivalent of $20 for a can of beer and $50 for a shot of whisky. There are also published reports to the effect that many of the bills run up at bars and nightclubs are shams, that nothing was consumed, and no entertainment offered. The bar and nightclub operators apparently bill companies for supposed entertainment and drinks, then split the sums collected with the employees of the companies. Lastly, public revelations have been made that much of the so-called business entertainment isn't to please customers or clients, but for the personal enjoyment of the employees of the companies, and in some instances to treat friends and fellow employees.

Shenanigans such as these are seldom permitted in U.S. companies in Japan, and as a consequence American businessmen there spend far less money on entertainment and business gifts than their Japanese counterparts. Nor are the U.S. corporations necessarily handicapped in their dealings with Japanese because of the reduced sums available for entertainment and gifts. Americans succeed in part because the Japanese themselves are really not pleased about the heavy entertainment and gift expenses they have to incur and do not expect foreigners to participate in. Also, because they are more careful about spending money, Americans tend to select gifts and entertainment that, though less expensive, are especially fitting and give a good impression to the Japanese. The writer (HVZ) found that the secret in selecting a gift for a Japanese businessman was not in the costliness of the article purchased but how well it suited his interests and tastes. When advancing the interests of a company in Texas, he would take a collection of Indian arrowheads nicely mounted in a frame. When selling equipment manufactured in Massachusetts, he would often take along an illustrated book showing the settlement of the Pilgrims in Plymouth. The Japanese were delighted with gifts like these, and often they found a place for them in the company reception room. Entertainment was designed to appeal to the level of sophistication of the Japanese. It was recognized that it would be foolish to try to equal or outdo the Japanese at their geisha parties and night clubs. What the Japanese appreciated most was exposure to foreign food and entertainment. The writer found that some of his Japanese customers liked French food, so he took them to lunch or dinner at the fine French restaurants in Tokyo. Others had never seen the inside of a Western-style home and how foreigners lived. For them the appropriate thing to do was to have them come over to dinner at home and serve American-style food.

The expatriate American's reticence to throw himself wholeheartedly into a program of entertainment and gift-giving has been strengthened by our Foreign Corrupt Practices Act of 1977, which has created an atmosphere where each American expatriate businessman must give consideration not only to the benefits to his employer of the favor he may bestow on a foreign businessman but also to its ethical aspects.

One study conducted at the University of Southern California concluded that a general backing off from "corrupt practices" has not hurt our foreign commercial operations, but some disagree with both the methodology and the conclusions of this study, saying that most probably clever businessmen have simply found other, less obvious ways to accomplish their goals, for—no matter what the crusaders and missionaries among us may think—our adherence, no matter how strict, to our own ethical standards will not expunge corruption in those many foreign countries where baksheesh has been a way of life for centuries.

In the view of most foreigners as well as many Japanese wives, the packaged sex tours, disguised as sightseeing trips, that are so popular with Japanese men these days are both flagrantly unethical and downright immoral. Sponsored by corporations for their employees and clients and by professional associations for their members, they escort yearly nearly one million pruriently eager Japanese men to such cities as Manila, Seoul, Taipei, and Bangkok, where accommodations with a broad spectrum of sexual frills and thrills await them, often in 'Japanese-only' bistros and brothels.

The authors know of no instances in which invitations to participate in these tours have been extended to foreign businessmen, but in the early postwar period, sex was often an integral part of an invitation to go out for dinner in the evening.

But all this has changed. Prostitution became a crime in 1958, although it did not die out. Japanese hosts have become niggardly and more indifferent to the goodwill and less eager to win the favor of the foreigner, be he a resident or a visitor. The number of *daruma-geisha*—those who will adopt the prone posture for anyone over twelve—has decreased to a point approaching zero, and the price of a night club hostess has continued to climb astronomically. And, perhaps most important, the Japanese now do not want their country to be regarded as a free-sex paradise. For that sort of thing, they say, one goes to Korea or Thailand or Taiwan or the Philippines. Not to Japan.

But none of these have altered the plain fact that the business of providing sexual frolic still flouishes unabated in Japan, although under somewhat different guises from the old *karyūkai* (the flower and willow world) where the *baishumpu* (the sellers of spring) plied their trade in caste-ridden cities that "knew no night." Tokyo's Yoshiwara district was closed down by the Anti-Prostitution Law of 1958 and kept closed by the national desire to present a moral front to the foreign visitors who thronged into Japan at the time of the 1964 Olympics. Youth hostels, tea shops, and boy scout facilities attempted to fill the vacant space in the Yoshiwara for a time but little by little Japan's solons (about whom the cynical say that it's never a question whether or not a Japanese politician keeps a mistress, only how many) did just what they vowed they would do when forced by the postwar power of the female voters to shut down the good-time houses; they would not enforce the anti-prostitution law with harsh judgments or severe fines but would let those who desired to buy or sell sexual services reconstruct the industry inch by inch.

Now the visitor to the Yoshiwara can find, among other establishments, the "Nun's Palace," with the massive bronze temple lanterns that adorn its lobby, where the ladies wear the habits of Buddhist nuns and cater to assorted sexual whimseys that evoke the delicate joys of blasphemy for about $125 for an hour and a half.

Those jaded with such sacrilege can move on down to the town of Kawasaki between Tokyo and Yokohama, where customers of the "Penthouse" are met at the station by chauffeurs in livery who escort them in Mercedes-Benz limousines to what looks like an Arabian Nights palace. And when the gamut of Penthouse pleasures has been run, they can push on to the shores of Lake Biwa and become members of the "English House" (*Eikokuya*) for annual dues of about two thousand dollars, which do not, however, relieve them of the necessity of paying some $145 for an hour and a half of Turkish bathing with various intriguing accoutrements. What then do their annual dues buy them?

Their own personal towel with their name embroidered on it and a pair of Pierre Cardin slippers.

Elsewhere hotels shaped like passenger liners—one is named "Queen Elizabeth"—are tied up to docks and draw the blasè through their portals with such magnets as rotating elevator beds and musical waterbeds.

Last year in Tokyo an enterprising man named Yamada concluded that there were so many Japanese businessmen who wanted to travel without the encumbrances of legal love that he might make money providing female partners, mostly coeds, O.L. (office ladies) free on weekends, widows, and divorcees—for the trips. After the first ad, he was deluged by applications from both sexes, and his *Ryokō-Kurabu* (Travel Club) became as a great success.

Another entrepreneur set up what he called a "Mistress Bank" and invited interested parties to apply. He charged men some $825 and women $200 to join. Again a flood of applications poured in. Each member specified his or her desires in the matter and quickly enough they were matched with a suitable partner in sinful cohabitation.

A typical case of a happily matched mistress is that of a Tokyo university coed: an economics major who was long on academic ambition but short on cash. Shortly after signing on, she was introduced to a 48-year-old filling station owner who pays erotic devoirs to her every two weeks, and in return for these twice-a-month sessions in the Old Four-Poster, she is enriched by a monthly stipend of $330.

According to the weekly magazine *Shūkan Yomiuri*, the classiest of these "lovers' banks" has signed up 132 steady patrons, of which the most numerous group is that of members of the Diet.

The millions of American men together with a lesser number of women who were exposed to the sexual mores of foreign cultures during WW II helped release America from the pall of Victorian morality and doubtless contributed to the Sexual Revolution of the Sixties. This has resulted in a distinct dichotomy in American sexual attitudes: an older generation who still cling to the belief that a woman should go to her marriage bed in a unsullied condition in contrast to a younger generation who seemingly attach less value to virginity.

What is certain is that many younger Americans have become promiscuous or, if you prefer, liberated, but to what extent this has contributed to their fundamental happiness or unhappiness is more difficult to assess. Are one hundred casual sexual encounters with partners one tolerates but does not love superior to ten or even one encounter with a person who drains one's well of affection? Are casually conceived offspring born into illegitimacy worth the all too brief emissions into dank tunnels? The view varies perhaps with the age of the beholder.

Japan too is troubled by a dichotomy in sexual values or ethics. In an atmosphere where sexuality is pervasive, open, and even applauded, it is disconcerting to come up against cold statistics that show that only 12 percent of

Japanese women from 16 to 23 in age have had sexual relations. And the figure for men of the same ages is only 18 percent. (Comparable figures in the U.S. would be 35 and 46 percent.)—One wonders just how such figures were arrived at and if they are accurate.

To understand the ethics of sexual behavior in Japan, it is essential to understand first that the Japanese regard sexual activity merely as a function of the body, like eating and voiding: one that does not involve absolute judgments of morality. To be sure, other social strictures come into play that keep many Japanese women chaste, but these, for the most part, center on concepts of face and shame.

These attitudes hark back to Buddhist teachings in Japan. While Buddhism as it was known in India and China called for the believer to smother all emotions, both pleasant and unpleasant, the Japanese version of imported Buddhism did not rigorously enforce precepts against sexual activity, and sexual and emotional love were viewed as being not inconsistent with religious devotion.

Ethically speaking, sex in Japan is an entirely different ball game.

Afterword

Even as the last chapter of this book was being written, U.S. Treasury Secretary Donald Regan was giving vent in Tokyo to his "extreme disappointment" at the lack of progress in solving the problem of the trade imbalance between Japan and the U.S.

According to the *Japan Times* of March 25, 1984, Regan stated that for the past three and a half years he had heard many Japanese saying they would promote market liberalization but he had seen no real action. Reflecting his frustration, the Secretary then "gestured and pounded on the podium to make his points."

Many other Americans feel just as Donald Regan did. As long as U.S.-Japan trade continues to be as massively advantageous to one side only as it now is, doubts about ethical economic behaviour will spread—and these in turn will raise questions about the sincerity of the good will and friendship that has been building between our two peoples in the post-1945 era. Other ethical perceptions, if favorable, will diminish or, if pejorative, will intensify. Unethical economic behavior will transmute itself into unethical political and social and even individual behavior, or so the men on the streets in Kansas City and Nagoya will be tempted to conclude.

The trade imbalance *must* be addressed seriously and with a sense of urgency, no matter what its cost in temporary economic disadvantages. If not, it will magnify and then corrode the entire relationship. If the U.S. builds protectionist walls that interdict much of its trade with Japan, it will turn more to other trading partners, including the awakening Chinese giant, thus bypassing and partially isolating Japan, whose markets and sources of supply will become more distant and probably more unstable and difficult. Nor will those markets and sources be as easy to mesmerize into unjustified expectations by promises of corrective action and pleas for understanding. The European and South American nations are learning their lessons about the Japanese, too, while those in Asia learned theirs earlier.

As suggested elsewhere herein, four effective measures that could be quickly taken would be the "Naked Japan" proposal (for the complete elimination of tariffs and trade barriers) of Rokusuke Tanaka of the Liberal Democratic Party, the surcharge on Japanese imports, the complete liberalization of the Japanese money market, and the adoption in the U.S. of further quotas on imports from Japan with the proviso that American industries so protected take effective measures to reduce costs and improve productivity.

In addition to the above four measures, the United States should establish a number of export trading companies along the lines of those recently permitted by legislation. They would have departments specifically devoted to business with Japan and would be staffed with Americans who had a good knowledge of Japanese customs, business practices, negotiating methods, commerce, history, and language. These people would scour medium and small businesses in the United States and locate products and services needed in Japan and then thoroughly explore the Japanese market, giving every assistance desirable to both U.S. and Japanese companies in an effort to consummate profitable business. If necessary to make the trading companies financially strong enough to succeed, they would be granted tax relief.

U.S. companies in Japan should require their American employees to have adequate knowledge about the language and culture of the country where they make their living, in addition to the requisite technical skills. Even as Japanese corporations operating in the U.S. are often staffed with three or four times as many Japanese managers at they really need (U.S. postings are often a form of reward), so we should dispatch to Japan a great many enthusiastic and energetic American men and women who are well-trained and who seek opportunities for sales of U.S.-made goods anywhere and everywhere.

In summation, what is really needed is a thorough overhaul of several of our national attitudes so that—

1. We greatly increase our consciousness of the importance of exports.
2. We understand that in order to solve the trade imbalance, drastic political and commercial measures must be taken.
3. We insure that Americans whose assignments encompass business dealings with the Japanese are given all the training necessary for them to become competent experts on Japan.

Americans *can* do these things. During World War II, we proved beyond any doubt our ability to learn—and to use what we learned—about foreign countries. We could do it again, if we would only put to good use those Americans who pursue and acquire such knowledge.

Yet sadly we do not make use of them. We live in the Age of the Generalist, not of the Specialist (except in the scientific and technical fields). Neither our government agencies nor our private corporations nor our communications media utilize, to any appreciable extent, Japan (or China or Korea) area-and-language specialists.

Indeed, such specialists are not only usually ignored but also are often suspected and rejected because of the erroneous assumption that only native Japanese can understand the culture of Japan and because truly extensive knowledge of any foreign culture, and especially an Asian culture, is fallaciously interpreted to mean preference for that culture over one's own. Additionally, our executive personnel departments in home offices are seemingly unaware of the need for such people or, if aware, do not know where or how to find them.

These are the attitudes we Americans must change—while making strong representations to the Japanese that they too must change some of theirs. Somewhere deep in the collective consciousness of the Japanese is an *amae*-type belief that the U.S. is obliged to tolerate the trade deficit because of its 'elder brother' role in our trans-Pacific relationship—that the U.S. is so rich and so powerful and so generous that how can tiny Japan and its exports really cause the American giant to flicker an eyelash?

Yet stern anti-Japan measures on our part lie waiting in the immediate offing and will surely materialize if both of our two peoples do not act quickly and decisively while there is still enough popular good will on both sides of the Pacific to remedy the crisis.

Once the U.S.-Japan trade is in approximate balance, our two countries could achieve a bilateral relationship that would be long-lasting and vastly beneficial to both sides: one that could be the foundation of a new Age of the Pacific.

INDEX

Accountants' Code of Ethics, 80, 81
American policies in staffing operations overseas, 202, 203
Anti-foreign bias in Japan, 38, 39
Apologies in Japan, 19
Automobile imports into Japan, 143, 144, 145

Bank songs and principles in Japan, 62, 63
Better Business Bureau, 81, 260
Bureaucratic interpretations of the law in Japan, 229, 230

Calvinist work ethic, 103, 104
Chrysler, 129
Compensation of executives, 188–194
Confucianism-five relationships, 29
Counter measures to reduce Japan's trade surplus, 156, 157, 158, 159, 162
Crime in Japan, 36

Dallas, T.V. prime-time soap opera, 72, 73, 74
Detroit crime rates, 145
Discrimination in Japan against burakumin and others, 197, 208
Discrimination in Japan against female workers, 195, 196

Entertainment practices in Japan, 279, 280, 281, 282, 283

Federal Trade Commission, 260, 262, 263
Ford, 129

General Motors, 129
Golden parachutes, 174, 177
Guttman, David, S., 240, 241, 242

Hagakure, 101
Hirata, Atsutane-Japanese virtues, 27

Ishida, Baigan, 88, 89, 102

Japan's aircraft manufacturing policies, 136–141
Japanese attitude toward bureaucracy, 212–216
Japanese loyalties to their families, groups and nation, 198, 199, 200
Japan's military procurement policies, 135, 136, 137
Japanese policies toward foreign employees, 200, 201, 202

Kyocera Company cemetery, 86
Kyowa Hakko Kogyo Co.-prayers, 85

Luther, Martin, 104

Madogiwa-zoku (Window ledge tribe), 194, 195
Michelman, James H., 76, 77
Mitsuyo Manufacturing Co.-services for the dead, 84, 85

"Naked Japan" Policy of Rokusuke Tanaka, 162

Obligations in Japan, 55
Organization for Economic Development rules of behavior, 81, 82
Otsu factory, 113, 114

Passin, Herbert, 51, 78
Perry, Commodore-public baths, 15
Pioneer Electronics Corp., 114
Protestant Work Ethic (Puritan ethic), 47, 210

Quality control circles in Japan, 118

Rescript on Education-Japan, 30, 31
Rikkyo University Study of Japanese and American workers, 111
Rohlen, Thomas P.-book, 62, 63
Rotary Club code of ethics, 79, 80

Sarakin, 67–71
S.C.A.P. directives regarding moral teachings in school, 35, 36
Seward, Jack-biography, Cover 3

Books by Lotus Press Ltd.

NON-FICTION

THE JAPANESE	J. Seward
MORE ABOUT THE JAPANESE	J. Seward
AMERICA AND JAPAN	
—The Twain Meet—	J. Seward
THE EMPEROR'S ISLANDS	
—The Story of Japan—	G. Matsumura
NINJUTSU	
—The Art of Invisibility—	D. Draeger
READING YOUR WAY AROUND JAPAN	B. DeMente
JAPAN: The Coming Economic Crisis	J. Woronoff
JAPAN'S WASTED WORKERS	J. Woronoff
PIONEER AMERICAN MERCHANTS IN JAPAN	H. F. Van Zandt
IMAGES OF JAPAN	A. Tsuchiya
—A Photographic Souvenir—	& B. DeMente
INSIDE JAPAN, INC.	J. Woronoff
WORLD TRADE WAR	J. Woronoff
SHOPPING YOUR WAY AROUND JAPAN	B. DeMente
IAI	
—The Art of Drawing The Sword—	D. Craig
JAPAN'S COMMERCIAL EMPIRE	J. Woronoff
THE SHOGUN'S RELUCTANT AMBASSADORS	K. Plummer
THE JAPAN SYNDROME	J. Woronoff
JAPAN: THE HUNGRY GUEST	J. Seward & H. Van Zandt

Shibusawa, Eiichi, 102
Showa Boeki Co. hymn, 66
S.O.B. bosses, 185, 186
Sokaiya, 167, 168, 172
Suzuki, Shosan, 89, 90, 91, 92, 101, 102

Tanaka, Kakuei, 57
Taxes, 219, 220
Ten Commandments, 45

Unfair Japanese trade practices 141–152
United States-forecasts for possible future stoppage of food exports, 153, 154, 155
United States Foreign Corrupt Practices Act, 82
United States immigration policies, 154, 155

Van Zandt, Howard F.-biography, Cover 2

Watsuji, Tetsuro-book on ethics, 21

In World War II co-author *Jack Seward* went through the most intensive Japanese area-and-language course ever offered in the U.S., graduating second in his class. Shortly after the close of the war, Seward was sent to Japan for duty with one of Douglas MacArthur's staff sections, the first of the jobs that were to keep him there for a total of 25 years.

He has taught courses in the history of Japanese culture and the Japanese language at two universities in Texas and has been the president of a publishing company, a newspaper columnist, and a frequent contributor to a variety of magazines.

Seward is the author of 27 books on Japan, including *Japanese in Action*, a perennial best-seller on how to study the Japanese language and how to understand its native speakers, and *The Japanese*, the most widely read book on the Japanese people ever published.

He has also written two books in the Japanese language, one of which—*Tekisasu no Koinobori*—achieved best-seller status in Japan.

He now lives with his Japanese wife and two sons in Houston, Texas where he contemplates relations between his own country and the one where he spent almost half his life.

The Editors
Lotus Press